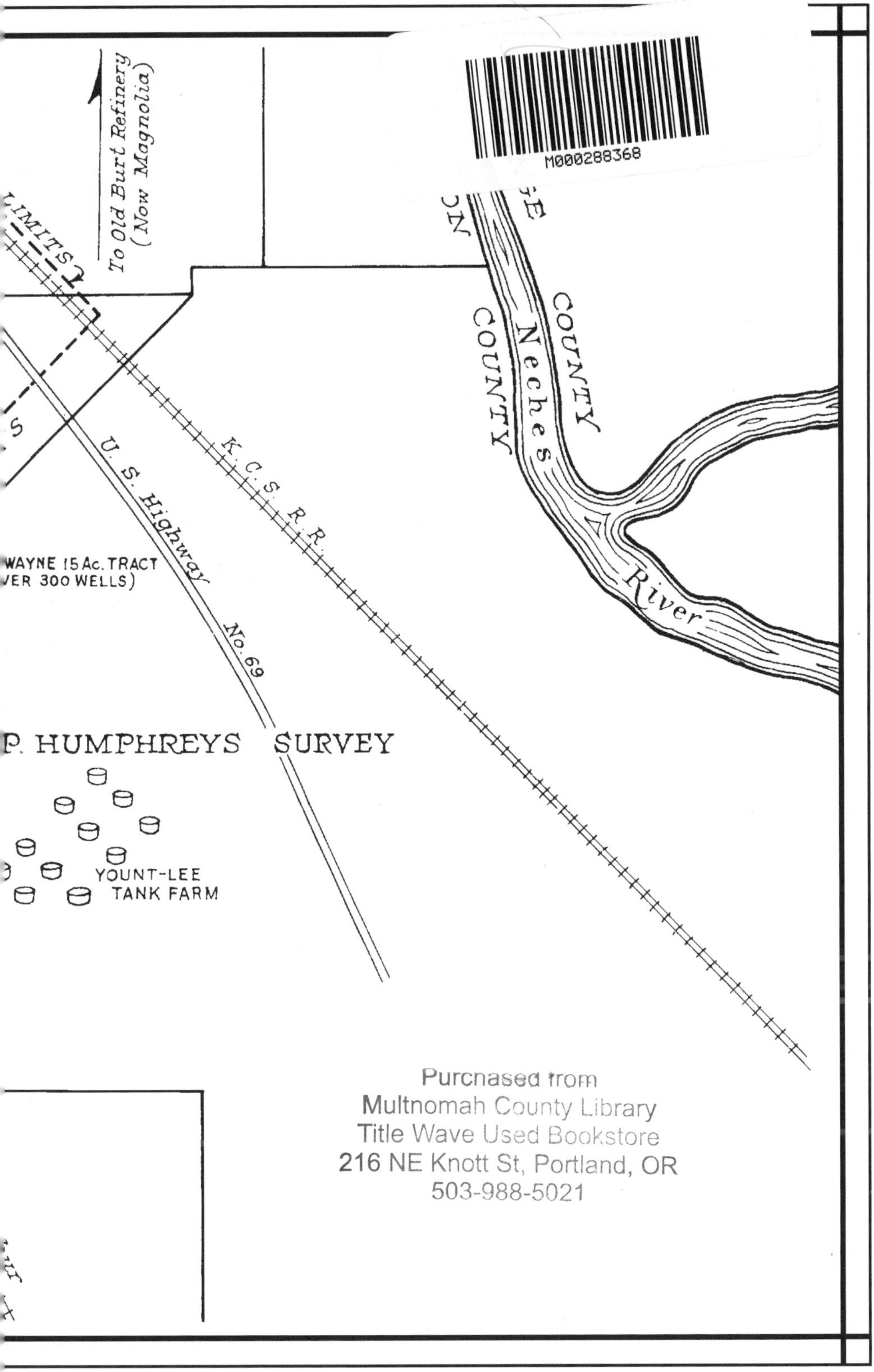
To Old Burt Refinery
(Now Magnolia)
LIMITS
K. C. S. R. R.
U. S. Highway No. 69
WAYNE 15 Ac. TRACT
VER 300 WELLS)
P. HUMPHREYS SURVEY
YOUNT-LEE
TANK FARM
COUNTY
Neches River
COUNTY

SPINDLETOP

SPINDLETOP

SPECIAL
1901
CENTENNIAL
2001
EDITION

James A. Clark
Michel T. Halbouty

Gulf Publishing Company
Houston, Texas

SPINDLETOP
Special Centennial Edition

Gulf Publishing Company
Book Division
P.O. Box 2608 □ Houston, Texas 77252-2608

10 9 8 7 6 5 4 3 2 1

Library of Congress Cataloging-in-Publication Data

Clark, James Anthony, 1907–
Spindletop / James A. Clark, Michel T. Halbouty.—Special Centennial Edition
p. cm.
Includes index.
ISBN 0-88415-813-6 (alk. paper)
1. Petroleum industry and trade—Texas—History.
I. Halbouty, Michel Thomas, 1909– . II. Title.
TN872.T4 C55 2000
338.2′7282′09764145—dc21 99-013006

Printed in the United States of America.

Printed on acid-free paper (∞).

This book is respectfully dedicated to

Pattillo Higgins

the hero of Spindletop,
and the army of wildcatters and optimists
whose unswerving faith in themselves
and dogged determination to climb higher up
the ladder of success has led all mankind
to a fuller and better world.

Contents

Illustrations/Photos

Acknowledgments

The authors are deeply grateful to the hundreds of friends whose help and advice has made this book possible. While it would be impractical to include the entire list of those who have helped, it is desired to give credit to the sources of information without which it would have been impossible to write the book.

Pattillo Higgins, Al Hamill, Marion Brock, Everett Brashear, Charles Carroll, Johnny Callaghan, Lon D. Cartwright, Tom C. Driscoll, Howard Lee, Donnie Lee, William Gilbert, Boyce House, Will E. Orgain, Beaman Strong, A. D. Moore, W. D. Gordon, Marrs McLean, Tom Galey, Ted Galey, Ed Prather, T. T. Hunt, W. W. Ward, Merita Mills, Burt Hull, Phil Justice, L. W. Kemp, Mrs. J. Frank Keith, Mrs. Olga Wiess, Mrs. John Thomas, Ed Kilman, J. W. Kinnear, Anthony Fitzgerald Lucas, Matt McAlister, Mike McKissick, M. W. McClendon, John W. Mecom, Scott Myers, Wright Morrow, Chilton O'Brien, J. H. Phelan, B. E. Quinn, Hardy Roberts, Paul Weaver, Steve Wilhelm, Hop Wright, Wallace Davis, Howard Hicks, Spencer Robinson, Dr. Carl Coke Rister, and others contributed materially.

The files and assistance of the Spindletop Fiftieth Anniversary Commission, the *Beaumont Enterprise* and the *Beaumont Journal*, the *Houston Post*, the *Galveston News*, the *Houston Chronicle*, the *Houston Press*, the *Port Arthur News*, the *Lake Charles American*, the *Austin American-Statesman*, the *New Orleans Times-Picayune*, the citizen newspapers of Houston and the volumes of files contained in the library of the Lamar College of Technology at Beaumont and the Texas State Museum in Austin. Credit is also given for assistance by the Tyrrell Public Library in Beaumont, the Gates Memorial Library in Port Arthur, the Houston Public Library, the Library of Congress, the Rice Institute Library and the libraries of radio stations KXYZ, Houston, and KFDM, Beaumont. The Gladys City Oil, Gas and Manufacturing Company's files were most valuable.

The public-relations departments of the Sun Oil Company, the Gulf Oil Corporation, the Texas Company, the Humble Oil and Refining Company, the Magnolia Petroleum Company, the Stanolind Oil and Gas Company, the Texas Gulf Sulphur Company, and C. A. Warner of the Houston Oil Company were most cooperative.

In addition to the above, the authors wish to acknowledge with deepest thanks the untiring efforts and patient advice of Estelle Clark, who typed the manuscript and spent endless hours in research and conferences to aid in the successful completion of *Spindletop.*

Preface to the Centennial Edition

In recognition of the centennial anniversary of Spindletop, the awesome giant that heralded the liquid fuel age, it is appropriate to reissue the volume, *SPINDLETOP,* which relates the exciting discovery on a little hill just three miles south of the town of Beaumont, Texas.

The word Spindletop brings back memories of the efforts of those few men who believed in what they were doing and stuck with their convictions until they brought in the gusher that flowed oil at a rate of 100,000 barrels a day. The book's dedication to Patillo Higgins says it all.

It was indeed one of the highlights of my career to have been able to call Higgins a friend and to have had the privilege to interview him many times for the original book, which was published in 1952. There is nothing new to the story in this centennial volume. There was no need to add anything because the epic, as written by the late James A. Clark and me, describes the events and the significance of the impact of the discovery not only on Texas and the nation, but also on all the world.

Spindletop became a symbol that marked the eventual scientific and technological progress of the fledging industrial revolution and the oil industry to which it gave birth. It was the beginning of the liquid fuel age that inaugurated the rise of America to dominant world power and its people to an abundant life.

The discovery at Spindletop led to the creation of companies such as Texaco, Cities Service, Gulf Oil, Sun Oil, Magnolia Oil, Humble Oil, and others. Many of these companies started from the humblest of beginnings and were created by men and their ideas that were molded at Spindletop.

The "Gusher," as it was called, caused a steady increase in the use of oil—in locomotives, sugar mills, factory furnaces, residential stoves and heaters, ships, smelting plants, and power plants to generate electricity. Uses multiplied each day.

Spindletop proved that large quantities of oil existed and could be brought to the surface, and this realization inaugurated industrial and domestic uses never before possible.

Spindletop is the very symbol of the American "can-do" spirit and proof that a single event can unequivocally change every facet of a civilization.

This centennial volume is dedicated to those pioneer petroleum explorers whose fortitude and courage led to the discovery that provided a fuller and better world.

Michel T. Halbouty
Houston, Texas
November, 1999

Preface

Spindletop is a little knob of land rising out of a swampy prairie in the southeast corner of Texas, a few miles north of the Gulf of Mexico. There, on January 10, 1901, a new age of human progress was born when the first great oil gusher roared in. There and then America was blessed with the supply of energy and the incentive to move up from a secondary position in world affairs to that of undisputed leadership.

Before Spindletop, oil was used for lamps and lubrication. The famous Lucas gusher changed that. It started the liquid fuel age, which brought forth the automobile, the airplane, the network of highways, improved railroad and marine transportation, the era of mass production and untold comforts and conveniences. It revived and gave growing impetus to competition in all fields, but particularly in oil. It was a crushing blow to all forms of monopoly, and opened a thousand new frontiers, awakening the dormant pioneer spirit of the country.

The great gusher heralded a new industry, born amidst the most magnificent boom ever experienced, that is as native to America as the waters of the Mississippi. There were no precedents for coping with the fabulous financial boom, the geological phenomenon, the unheard of technological problems, the scientific challenges and the tests of human endurance and resourcefulness. Without individual freedom of thought and action, these accomplishments would have been impossible.

Spindletop not only gave birth to an industry and a new age, it also developed the men to man it and armed them with the ingenuity and resourcefulness necessary to progress. So well did it imbue its sons with the spirit of their industry that even today men of no other nation can compete with Americans in the field of petroleum. And therein lies the difference between western progress and the old world across the seas. Even in most foreign lands oil is produced by American men, methods, and means.

Scientific and technical development have come out of the chaos of Spindletop. Waste and fraud have been eliminated. The wildcatter's risk is greater, and the rewards are smaller. But as long as individuals can venture with a hope of success, America will thrive on the blessings of the hill south of Beaumont.

Spindletop stands as a fountainhead of American progress and prosperity and as the symbol of an industry. We hope its story can help Americans to better appreciate the debt they owe to Spindletop's pioneers and the great fraternity of men who have guided the development of the industry it started.

James A. Clark
Michel T. Halbouty
Houston, Texas
April, 1952

SPINDLETOP

CHAPTER ONE

The Prophet

As Pattillo Higgins rode toward Beaumont on the afternoon of January 10, 1901, he was met on the outskirts of town by Jim Collier. "Hey, Bud," Collier yelled, "the well blew in on the hill this morning and the people in town are saying you are the wisest man on earth."

Higgins lifted himself in his saddle and looked in the direction of the hill. He could see a cloud of dark mist out toward Gladys City.

That morning at 10:30 the Lucas gusher had roared in like a shot from a heavy cannon and had spouted oil a hundred feet over the top of the derrick out on the hummock that the world would soon know as Spindletop.

Beaumont had been blasted out of its normal tranquillity. Four miles to the south of the little Texas town was one of the greatest natural phenomena man had ever seen. News tickers were flashing the story to the four corners of the earth. Excited men were already pouring into Beaumont. And this was only the beginning.

Captain Anthony F. Lucas, yesterday's wildcatter, was today's man of the hour. Newsmen, oil men and financial and industrial leaders were quoting and requoting his words around the nation.

Pattillo Higgins, his fellow citizens knew now, was the real prophet of this great event, whatever it was to mean. It was ironic that it should happen while he was out of town. That day Higgins had been in the woods looking over timber lands. Jim Collier's greeting was the first he knew of the discovery.

"Hell, Bud, ain't you surprised?" Collier inquired.

"Not exactly, Jim," Higgins said with a smile. "Don't you remember that I've been telling everyone for more than ten years this would happen?"

II

It all started years before. In fact, it started when Pattillo Higgins first gave up his logging job on the upper reaches of the Neches to return to his home town and enter business. A former Peck's bad boy, Higgins had surprised the populace by coming home, joining the Baptist Church, and getting himself started in real estate.

That was back in the middle eighties. He still had some five or six years to go before he got interested in finding oil and building industry. He was a loose-jointed, tall, blue-eyed, one-armed young man who had a reputation for being better in a scrap with his one arm than most Texans were with two. The son of the town's only gunsmith, he was an expert draftsman, a fine mechanic, and a self-educated man with complete self-assurance, who did well in anything he undertook.

Spindletop Springs, south of town, on the banks of the Neches River, was an ideal spot for outings. One afternoon

Higgins, who now taught in the Baptist Sunday school, took his class there on a picnic. When the picnic was over he and the children drove to the round mound a mile or so west. Up on the hill, which rose some fifteen feet above the surrounding prairie, be punched a cane into the ground and then lit a flame as the gas escaped. It was fun for the children and it intrigued Higgins. He made a mental note to come back and find out more about it.

During the next few years Higgins' real-estate dealings brought him a good living and he acquired some land of his own. He became a recognized specialist in timber lands. Since he was his own boss, he had time to engage in his hobbies. A consuming interest in education caused him to spend hours in study. Not only did he master the Bible, but he studied economics, history, chemistry and even philosophy. An aptitude for mechanics and designing inherited from his father was always useful. His years in the woods and on the river taught him to recognize nature's signs. In those years he also learned to deal with men.

Pattillo Higgins held two important views. One was that for a man to be a success in any field he must know mechanics and be able to build and invent. The other was that anything another man could master, he could master, too.

His curiosity frequently lured him back to Big Hill, as the natives called the low prairie mound. One of the attractions there was the sour wells resort. It consisted of a half-dozen square boxes fashioned out of cypress boards, containing blue, green and yellow waters, with a range of palatability and odor from that of lemon phosphate to kerosene and the revolting flavor of rotten eggs. Some waters were to bathe in. Others were to drink. The range of its effects was equal to that of its colors and odors. The water would either bind its partakers tighter than the head of an Indian war drum, or send them scampering to the tall timbers with a case of what was quaintly referred to as the flying axe handles.

The superstitious steered clear of the mound at night. They reported a ghost which came from the hill on nocturnal visits to Spindletop Springs down by the river. Others would see the wraithlike figures of St. Elmo's lights dancing wildly about the mound at night.

The hill wasn't an ordinary place. There was a scientific answer to its peculiarities that Pattillo Higgins would find somewhere.

III

In the course of his business, Higgins had acquired several hundred acres of land east of the Neches in Orange County. He looked on it as good farm land. Riding across the tract one day on horseback after a heavy rain, he noticed an unusual reddish outcropping on the ground. Dismounting, he examined further and found a moist and plastic clay. Looking about he could see there were acres of it. He took a sample to town and tested it chemically. It was an unusually high grade of brick clay.

Already convinced that his part of the country had many natural advantages for industrial development, he considered the possibility of a brick business. At that time it was necessary to bring brick in from the East when it was needed. Houston, ninety miles west, had started building multistory brick buildings; soon Beaumont would do the same. So Higgins resolved to sell the idea of starting a brick factory to local capital.

It didn't take too much selling. Several men of means encouraged Higgins and agreed that he should take a trip east to look at operating brickyards. Within a week he was on his way. He visited brick plants in Pennsylvania, Indiana, Ohio, and New York, to learn the cost of equipment, methods of operation and types of skills necessary. The most interesting thing he noticed was that oil and gas were being used for fuel. Plant managers explained that these fuels were easier to install, more efficient to operate, and that they burned with a constant temperature. That was something neither wood nor coal would do. As a matter of fact, they explained, without such fuels it might not be wise to consider going into the brick business.

While he was in the East, Higgins took the time to visit several oil fields to learn more about the source of fuel for brickyards. He inquired about methods used in determining the existence of oil or gas and was convinced that such methods were fairly simple. Pattillo Higgins looked around for nature's signboards and found them. What he found were the same signs he had seen on Big Hill, such as the odors of the escaping gas, the texture of the earth and the taste of the water.

If oil and gas could be found in Pennsylvania, there was no reason it couldn't be found in Texas, Higgins reasoned. With this fuel, industrial possibilities would be unlimited.

The oil men he talked with spoke of geology as it applied to recognizing surface indications of oil. They were certain that oil would never be found anywhere except in the East.

Higgins decided he would have to know more about geology. That was one subject he had not included in his studies. The success of his new venture might depend on finding oil and gas. Before he left the East, he wrote a letter to the director of the United States Geological Survey requesting available information on petroleum geology, particularly as it pertained to the Gulf Coast.

The brick business didn't develop. When Higgins returned home he found that Beaumont's venture capital had gone into a new furniture factory. This was a disappointment, but he was consoled by the fact that he had found an entirely new interest in life in the oil fields of Pennsylvania and Ohio.

For weeks he read the government's book on geology. From it he gleaned information that completely fascinated him.

The scientific facts it explained were devoured and digested. But when it came to conclusions, he parted company with the government's geologists. The booklet stated that oil-bearing rock probably did not exist along the Gulf Coast. Out on the mound at Big Hill he had seen things the geologists hadn't written about. Why did sulphureted hydrogen gas come oozing out of the copperas springs, causing bubbles to play on the water like minute raindrops?

The authors of the booklet were smart men, but they were wrong. There was oil and gas at Big Hill. Plenty of it. That was Higgins' conclusion. But to be certain, he rode back to the hill and explored every possibility. He dug post holes six to ten feet deep and found everything he needed to convince himself.

From the crest of the hill he looked around the countryside. There was the railroad to Sabine Pass on the west. It wasn't more than a mile east to the river where packets and barges plied their trade. It was less than fifteen miles south to Sabine Lake. The land was a flat prairie all around the hill in every direction except to the east, where a vast marshland started on the Orange County side of the river. Four miles to the north was Beaumont. With the fuel he could produce from the hill this could be the greatest industrial center in the South. Nature had not only painted her signboards here, she had endowed this country with every advantage and resource.

On the north edge of the hill Higgins saw a little sign which read: "This 1077 acres for sale—cheap," and gave the name of the agent. The tract was in the James A. Veatch survey. Higgins went directly to the agent in Beaumont and found that it could be bought for $6 an acre. As a matter of fact, $1000 would buy an option on the entire tract for several months.

IV

At home that evening Higgins didn't sleep. He spent most of the night working on figures and studying the county map. He noted the bayous, the lakes and the wooded sections. His plan in its entirety encompassed an area extending fifteen miles from the hill to Sabine Lake, and covering a swath five miles wide.

The next morning Pattillo Higgins was out early. He took his plan to the town's leading men. As the hours, then days, went by, he realized he was not getting anywhere. When he spoke of oil he spoke of wells producing thousands of barrels. When he spoke of returns for stockholders in his industrial city, he spoke of millions of dollars. He had been given the light to see, but he hadn't been given the power to convey his foresight to others. Frustration met him at every side. It seemed that men who had previously respected him were now avoiding him.

Was there no one who would help? It was this question that brought back to his mind an offer made nine years before. He thought of George W. Carroll, now the president and general manager of the Beaumont Lumber Company, and one of the most prosperous citizens in town. Why hadn't he thought of Carroll before? Why didn't he think of him first as the man to share this potential wealth? Tomorrow he would certainly see Mr. Carroll.

On the night that Higgins had come out of the tall pines along the river to accept conversion, he had been met by George Washington Carroll after the services. Impressed by Higgins' decision to join the church, Carroll had stopped the younger man to offer him help should he ever need it. Carroll was the head of the lumber company for which Higgins had worked, and he had been a neighbor of the Higgins family in Beaumont for years. The town's leading Baptist, he was proud of Higgins and had been largely responsible for his acceptance by the rest of the citizens.

A man of tremendous energy and drive, an able executive, George Carroll was to become Beaumont's most prosperous and prominent citizen. He was to run for governor of Texas and vice-president of the United States on the Prohibition ticket. He would become as rich as Croesus because of Pattillo Higgins. Then he would die humbly in a single room in the Y.M.C.A., and be buried simply from a church, both of which had been built with his dollars. Here was a Baptist that even the irreverent Mr. Mencken could accept.

Higgins met the young lumber executive next morning in Carroll's home. He spread his plan out on the floor so that he could explain in detail the great potential wealth lying beneath the hummock a mile west of Spindletop Springs. Geological indications had been correlated with a homemade chemical analysis of the soil and waters from the hill. The terrain's adaptability to industrialization was indicated on a dog-eared county map. After looking over the plans, they drove out to the hill.

The odor of the sour wells permeated the air. It was perfume to Higgins, though, because it revealed much of his story. The horse was hitched to a coffeeberry shrub and Carroll followed Higgins from one oil and gas indication to another. Then Higgins showed Carroll the tract of land which took in the west edge of the hill.

Carroll considered the matter on the way to town, and decided to invest $1000 in the option if Higgins would arrange for a joint loan to cover the remainder of the purchase price. Higgins was certain Frank Alvey, cashier of the bank, would make a loan if Carroll would sign the note. The deal was made on that basis.

Now Higgins wanted the remainder of the survey, which, when completely assembled, would take in two-thirds of the hill. He made an extensive investigation of the ownership, and found that the survey consisted of some 2750 acres. Captain George W. O'Brien held 1350 acres, J. F. Lanier had 273 acres, and about fifty acres were in the name of the Cleveland Heirs, with titles in an almost inextricable confusion.

Higgins and Carroll agreed that their company should have the entire survey, if possible, and Higgins was authorized to negotiate for the other land. Being a man who believed the most difficult task should be tackled first, he went to the law offices of Captain George Washington O'Brien.

Tall and handsome, with a disarming Irish twinkle in his eyes, O'Brien was a fine lawyer and a conservative man in his middle fifties. An eminent citizen, he was the first resident attorney in Beaumont, the founder of the town's Methodist Church, and grand master of the Masonic lodge.

Captain O'Brien listened attentively to Higgins' offer to purchase his land. He asked what the land would be used for and who would assist Higgins in financing the purchase. Higgins said that he believed it had industrial possibilities, maybe oil, and that Carroll was his only associate. Trying to temper his enthusiasm, so as not to run up the price, he explained the surface indications and his reasons for believing there might be oil under the hill. The Captain said he would like to think about the matter for a few days and invited Higgins to return.

In those two or three days O'Brien recollected three incidents of his earlier life which had always intrigued him. He recalled how, during the Civil War days, he and his men, while camped on the hill, had been annoyed by the odor of gas seepage. Then, there was a letter which he had received from one of his fellow officers after the war, predicting great oil discoveries in this part of the country. And finally he remembered a man who, years ago, claimed to have traced a tremendous oil vein from the Rocky Mountains right down to this section.

And so when Pattillo Higgins returned at the appointed time, O'Brien informed him that while he was not interested in selling his property, he would, however, be willing to put his acreage into a company that might be formed by all of the landowners in the survey.

V

A few days later four men met in O'Brien's office to form a company that was to have a tremendous part in bringing about a new world and a new concept of abundance. Besides Higgins, Carroll and O'Brien, the fourth man was J. F. Lanier, who owned the only other tract of significant size in the Veatch survey. He was coming in under exactly the same terms as O'Brien.

"Gentlemen," said Pattillo Higgins, "if you will support my plan you will all become millionaires. Further than that, if other citizens of Beaumont will help finance this scheme, they will all become millionaires too."

Then he produced a sketch he had drawn the night before. It depicted eight or ten sections lined or shaded to indicate different subsurface strata. An uplift in the lines was explained as the condition that existed on the hill. Geologists, he explained, called the fold of these uplifted strata an anticline. It was caused by some unusual subsurface condition. Then he explained what he had learned of gravity, pressures and subterranean water levels. In a few minutes he demonstrated that he was no dreamer, but a practical geologist who had devoted much thought to his subject.

When Higgins finished his discussion, George Carroll, who had been elected president earlier in the meeting, asked if anyone had given thought to a letterhead for the company.

Higgins had his suggestion ready. He brought forth a rough design that he had worked up. Across the top in bold, shaded letters were the words, "Gladys City Oil, Gas and Manufacturing Company." In smaller letters, centered beneath the company's title, was its location, "Gladys City,

Texas." The capital stock of $200,000, the names of the officers, and location of the main office in Beaumont were shown in a box on the left under the heading. Prominently displayed was a photograph of little Gladys Bingham, a member of his Sunday school class, for whom he proposed to name his city. Then in a long, narrow sketch across two-thirds of the top of the page was a drawing of Higgins' idea of the city's future appearance. In the foreground were about twenty-five oil-storage tanks of varying sizes. Behind the tanks were the smokestacks of a dozen plants, and several brick buildings.

The other stockholders questioned the advisability of having a letterhead depicting a non-existent scene. Higgins replied that if this picture could prod the imagination of others, it would be helpful in selling stock in the company to finance the oil operations.

Higgins then presented an outline of a plat of Gladys City. It covered almost twice as much land as the company held, including all of the hill. It was his idea that soon others would want to get into the Gladys City company. Industrial and residential lots surrounded the hill. The Gladys City industrial lots, he explained, were in the center because they were the only two lots on which he expected to bore for oil and gas. Mineral rights would not be sold to others. There were churches of all denominations, a hospital, parks, schools, a college, a large hotel covering two entire squares, a fire station and a glass plant specifically provided for. Railroads were shown as crossing each other at right angles in the very center of the platted area.

It was an ambitious plan on paper and the other stockholders seemed pleased with it. There was some doubt on the part of everyone except Higgins, but he was authorized to engage L. E. Daniell, a civil engineer, to survey the area.

Higgins' enthusiasm was refreshing, but his associates saw that they were in for a little more and a little faster action than they had bargained for. These were conservative men who were aware of pitfalls and wanted to take every step only after a thorough examination of the ground ahead. They all had faith in Higgins, but they could foresee trouble in adjusting their tempo to that of a prophet.

The first meeting of the Gladys City Oil, Gas and Manufacturing Company closed. The minutes were dated, August 10, 1892.

CHAPTER TWO

Three Holes in the Hill

Six months later George Carroll and Captain O'Brien were harassed and beaten men. Day after day they had been hounded and annoyed by Pattillo Higgins. They sat together in the French Café pondering their problem.

Their trouble, as Higgins had told them, was that they couldn't make up their minds. From the day the Gladys City company's charter had been received, Pattillo Higgins had been ready to start work. The other directors had postponed things until they could be certain it was wise to borrow and spend the money necessary for drilling operations.

Higgins had just left them after delivering a good-natured but hard-hitting appraisal of their action. He had told them the story of the captain of a schooner who would run his vessel into a port to unload. When he had unloaded his cargo and found that the wind was fair for sailing he would wait to see if it would hold out. Then, Higgins told them, the wind would change and the captain would wait again for more favorable weather.

"Gentlemen, he kept that up and never got out of port," Higgins said. "Let his stupidity be a lesson to us."

Higgins had tried to get his associates to buy more land around the dome. He had also told them of two other oil prospects where land was available for the Gladys City company. When they declined to expand their holdings, Higgins had gone out individually and bought options on the land for himself. In doing this, Higgins had far overextended his credit and now he was afraid his directors were going to leave him with unpaid notes.

Before they left their coffee, Carroll and O'Brien decided that they would engage the services of M. B. Loonie of Dallas, a sewage contractor who had been recommended by Higgins for boring the first hole on the hill. Loonie had explained that he would sub-contract the job to W. B. Sharp, a young but experienced well man.

Later in the week the directors met and approved the contract. The date was February 17, 1893.

II

Pattillo Higgins and Walter Sharp saw eye to eye on most things. Sharp probably didn't believe that he was going to bring in a well that would produce thousands of barrels of oil daily, but he didn't debate the point with Higgins, the general manager of the Gladys City company.

He was interested in Higgins' story of his tribulations as they rode out to the hill. He was also interested in how Higgins had acquired the fine quarter horse and the gig they were riding in. Mr. Caswell, the druggist, had tried to sell them to him, but Higgins had proposed a trade for land in Gladys City. Caswell had declined, saying he needed the cash, $325. Higgins convinced George Carroll he needed the transportation, so a block of land had been given to Higgins who had, in turn, borrowed the money from the bank using the land as collateral.

"Some day," Higgins chuckled, "I will have a laugh on old Doc Caswell. That land will be worth tens of thousands of dollars. I think it is the best horse trade a man ever made."

Sharp would live to see the day when Higgins would sell that block of land for $85,000.

Out on the hill Higgins staked location for the hole. He drove his gig directly to a point near the copperas pond and told Sharp to start digging right there.

It was less than a week later when Loonie called Carroll and reported that Higgins had ordered him not to start the well. In fact, Higgins had told Loonie to load his equipment and take it back to Dallas. Carroll was amazed. He called O'Brien, who hadn't heard of the order. A directors' meeting was called and Higgins explained his arbitrary action. He had looked at the light rotary equipment and he knew that it would not get down to the oil. There was no use wasting the Gladys City's time as well as that of Loonie and Sharp. Loonie had been told that good heavy equipment was necessary to go 1000 feet, and the contract had been signed for 1500 feet, unless oil was encountered before that depth. Oil, Higgins said, would be found at around 1000 feet, but that depth would never be bored with a machine only slightly bigger than a coffee grinder.

Loonie turned to Sharp, who said he felt that he could do the job. He had drilled wells deeper than that with the same equipment in other places. Higgins said he had never drilled a well in the kind of formations he would encounter here and that he would never get down 500 feet deep.

O'Brien explained to Higgins that if the contractors were not permitted to proceed that the company would have to pay them $5500 anyway. They had been given a contract to drill the first 1000 feet for $3.50 a foot and the next 500 feet for $4 a foot. Higgins still insisted that it might be better to compromise and pay them off, but he yielded to Carroll and O'Brien, who knew that Sharp was probably the best man in his field in the state.

Pattillo Higgins' pride suffered somewhat when the directors ordered that there would be no further interference with Sharp. It was stated in a resolution of the board that Higgins' authority as manager of the company did not include directing the operations of the contractor, and that in stopping the work when he did, he acted without authority.

This was the first rift between Higgins and the members of the board. It was not considered serious, as Higgins admitted his error openly and privately resolved to do everything possible to assist Sharp in boring the hole.

Sharp, however, hadn't gone more than sixty feet when he realized he was confronted with a serious problem. There he ran into a quicksand that gave him several days' delay. After that he ran into strange formations every thirty or forty feet. He had six months to get down 1500 feet or hit oil. Now he was averaging about fifty feet a month. When the six months had elapsed, he had made a little more than 300 feet.

Higgins agreed to a two-month extension of the contractor's time. He knew Sharp couldn't get down to the oil in that time, but he wanted him to have a chance. Furthermore, he was getting information from their cuttings. His only consolation had been that the hole was bearing out his theories as far as it went.

In the next two months Sharp was not able to improve his rate of progress and decided not to seek another extension. Loonie's bondsmen were sued by the Gladys City company for non-performance of the contract, and most of the money invested by the company was recovered.

The time lost had been disastrous to Higgins. The money he had invested in land had been lost. He was deeply in debt. His creditors even refused to accept the land he had in the Gladys City block or the thirty-three acres he had purchased outside the block on the hill. They wanted cash, and so Higgins had to sell some of his older holdings, such as the land in Orange County, where the clay was located, to pay off part of his indebtedness.

In spite of this disaster, Higgins still believed in the hill. He had a serious encounter with the local newspaper which reported that the Sharp hole was dry. A reporter had obtained the information from one of Sharp's employees and had printed it. Higgins insisted that the newspaper explain that the hole was not dry—that it was incomplete. He pointed out that the contractor was obligated to go 1500 feet and had gone only 418 feet, even with an extension of time. Again, he insisted, oil would not be reached until a hole was bored at least 1000 feet. There, he said, the greatest oil wells in the world would be found.

Higgins was still manager of the Gladys City company, but he was receiving no salary. The company had little money. He was being paid, with his consent, in land. His faith in the hill was as great as it ever was, and the land he owned would make him rich, he reasoned, when oil was found.

Beaumonters were not surprised at the results of the first hole. They had begun to believe Higgins was overenthusiastic, and that he should devote his time to something more productive, like the timber, cattle or rice. His associates were discouraged, and Lanier had sold his stock to Carroll.

Carroll, the only man who had actually put cash into the venture, retained his faith in Higgins, but he had been drained. O'Brien had not lost confidence completely, but he had grown lukewarm. He still believed Higgins was right about oil, but he felt that the dream city was something they could forget

III

Out of a clear sky one day, the Gladys City company received a proposal to lease its land for mineral development. The offer came from the Savage brothers, who described themselves as oil-well borers from West Virginia. They were willing to pay a fair bonus and give a 10 percent royalty, but they wanted all of the Gladys City land.

Pattillo Higgins was against it. It meant that the Gladys City company would wind up without control of the oil and gas production. This meant that his hopes for a great inland port and industrial city would vanish, or, at least, that others would be in the driver's seat. His argument was that this would eliminate everything he had planned for Beaumont, Gladys City and Jefferson County. As seriously as the company needed the money, it must not succumb to this easy way out.

Carroll and O'Brien knew that what he said was right, but they also knew their limitations. The panic of 1894 was in full swing. The lumber business had been dealt a severe blow. As lumber went, so went Beaumont. It was impossible even to consider paying another contractor to bore for oil. The first experience had resulted in most contractors shying off the hill. The price would be much greater than before, and no bondsmen would be found to stand behind the contractors.

The vote came and Higgins was adamant to the last, but he lost. The lease was made with the Savage brothers. Higgins had absolutely no authority in this case, but he could still talk. And talk he did when he saw the equipment the Savage brothers were unloading on the hill that late spring morning in 1895. Higgins said it was not as good as that Sharp had. He was right. The Savage brothers were unloading cable-tool equipment. Drillers were to learn in future years that the best cable tools made even fifty years later could not start to penetrate the mystery of the hill.

With the Savage brothers was a geologist named Otley. He had a definite idea that oil would be found on the hill. But Higgins was not happy over the way he arrived at his conclusions. Otley had the oil-vein theory and said the vein came into Texas from out of the Rockies and formed an oil lake when it reached the Gulf Coast.

Otley was an interesting man to talk with, however, and he entertained Higgins for hours with his stories of oil. Pitch, Otley told him, was the mortar for the walls of Babylon. It was the sealer of the round boats of woven reed that plied the Euphrates before the dawn of Christian civilization. It had lubricated the axles of the chariots that bore the Egyptian kings, whose bodies had been embalmed in a crude petroleum fluid. The Chinese, he said, used natural gas two thousand years ago for heat and light, conducting it into their homes through bamboo poles. Indians in America skimmed oil off water-filled sumps and used it for medicine and tonics, and to waterproof their canoes. As late as 1858 a Dr. Keir made a rock-oil natural remedy and then started distilling crude oil into kerosene to burn in lamps as a substitute for camphene, the dangerous mixture of alcohol and turpentine. He had sold nine barrels for $275 in New York in 1858.

Yes, Otley was interesting and entertaining, but Higgins doubted that he would be much help in conquering the hill. What the Savage brothers needed was the right equipment. Maybe after all, he reasoned, it is a blessing in disguise. Time would be lost, but more information about the formations would be gained and oil would not be found.

He was right. When the time limit was up and the Savages had gone only 350 feet, Higgins was happy. He refused to grant an extension, and his arguments were so vigorous this time that the other directors went along with him.

The forerunner of all great optimists in the oil business, Higgins now took to the streets again and started pleading with his fellow citizens to invest their money in another hole in the hill. He turned aside all arguments about the first two holes with the promise that he would make them millionaires. Untold millions of barrels of oil, he said, were there.

The town's wiseacres started calling him "the Millionaire" and he laughed with them. He tried to get Carroll and O'Brien to use their influence in the community to help him peddle his bill of goods, but they were too busy trying to beat a panic. They knew, too, that it was impractical to try to raise money in such times. So persistent was Higgins that his fellow townsmen began to fear that he was losing his mind. He realized this, but the Big Hill had become an obsession with him and he couldn't abandon it yet. Inside him he felt something tugging at his interest whenever his cause looked hopeless. Besides, he was the kind of man who fought the hardest when the odds against him were the strongest.

IV

Then came another disappointment. The directors leased all of their holdings again. The terms were the same as under the Savage lease. The lease was with the Texas Mineral Company, but the company was really the same Savage brothers. They had incorporated under the Texas law and had gone to Sour Lake, twenty-five miles northwest, and drilled for oil. They had found a piddling well that produced fifty barrels of asphaltum base crude from a very shallow depth and they wanted another crack at the Gladys City area.

Otley said this convinced him that he was on the trail of the elusive oil lake and that the vein of oil had been penetrated at Sour Lake, pointing directly to Gladys City. Jim Savage and Otley had come to Beaumont and resold their idea to the Gladys City stockholders, in spite of Pattillo Higgins' fight against a new lease.

This fight was the last act on the part of Higgins in the company. He was disappointed and dejected. He told Carroll that his stock was for sale, and Carroll bought it. There was no bitterness or rancor, but Higgins left the company before the Savage brothers started the third hole on the hill. Higgins felt that his associates were not heeding his advice and that he should not burden them further with his objections and opposition. He offered his services in an advisory capacity in any way they saw fit to use them, but bowed out of the company.

The third hole was just that. Only it didn't get as far as the first two. The Savage brothers gained nothing but experience. But they did learn that cable tools would not do the job. Their experience was later valuable to them and to the world when they turned to rotary equipment to bring in the Caddo field in Louisiana, one of the most important discoveries after Spindletop.

V

Pattillo Higgins returned to the real-estate business, but he retained his land and his interest in the hill. His idea now was to raise enough money to get the equipment he believed would penetrate the stubborn rock beneath the rise in the prairie. He would make enough money to live on and pay off some of his debts out of his business, and still have time to devote to organizing a syndicate to drill for oil. If the Gladys City company would lease to others, it would lease to him.

But first he must have confirmation that his oil theory was right. To have that, a recognized geologist must be called in. The state geologist would certainly agree with him, he reasoned, and investors might listen to a state official.

One night he wrote a lengthy letter to E. T. Dumble, the state's chief geologist, explaining in detail what he had found on the hill. He asked that Dumble come to Beaumont and look over the mound prospect with him.

The time was ripe, Higgins felt, to interest money in the hill. The panic was lifting early in 1898 and men would be more willing to invest.

Somewhat belatedly, he received a letter from Dumble, who regretted that he could not make arrangements to come to Beaumont, but would send one of his assistants, a Mr. William Kennedy.

When Kennedy arrived, Higgins kept him under wraps. He wanted this confirmation of his suspicions to come as a surprise to his fellow townsmen. He knew that if Kennedy agreed with him, as he undoubtedly would, he could raise enough money to get a good contractor with good equipment to bring in the well. After all, the disappointments up to now could have been expected. It wasn't surprising that the Beaumonters were not taking his project seriously. Three holes had been punched into the hill and, as far as ordinary laymen knew, that was test enough. What they didn't understand, and wouldn't until Kennedy explained it, was that these had served as exploratory wells. They had really proved that only one thing was lacking, and that one thing was the right equipment.

Higgins met Kennedy at the T.&N.O. station, and the two men had lunch at the Crosby House while Higgins explained his geological ideas. He told Kennedy all that had happened in the first three wells. He explained about the quicksand and the engineering problems.

"I know you will agree with my geological theories, Mr. Kennedy," Higgins said. "You will agree that as soon as we find an engineer who can get through quicksand that we will find a great store of oil beneath it."

Kennedy looked skeptical, but interested. He looked over the samples of rock recovered from the well and he listened to the story about the pocket of gas Sharp and Savage had both found at about sixty feet. He heard about the quicksand and about the gas seepages. He didn't seem too enthusiastic, but Higgins felt that he was being professional, not wanting to appear too eager with these findings.

The two went out to the hill. Higgins took Kennedy to the locations of the three unsuccessful holes. He explained in detail the troubles encountered in each. He had a log of each well, and those three logs proved his idea without a doubt as far as they went. Higgins said oil would be found around 1000 feet. Then Higgins gave Kennedy his analysis of the soil made with crude chemical sets.

Gradually it occurred to Higgins that Kennedy was not impressed. The man tried to look interested, but seemed to find this talk contrary to his own convictions. At last Higgins asked him what he thought.

"What I think, Mr. Higgins, is that you are wasting your time and your money if you are looking for oil or gas here on the coastal prairie."

This staggered Pattillo Higgins. He looked at the geologist in amazement and disbelief. Here before him stood the one man he thought would understand his findings. Hadn't he shown him exactly what he was talking about? Hadn't he explained in even more detail than he had to his Gladys City company associates? Here was an educated geologist—a man with a degree in the subject. What was wrong?

"Rock, Mr. Higgins, is necessary before you find oil. A water well was drilled at the County Courthouse in Beaumont a few years back. It went down 1400 feet and there was no sign of rock," Kennedy was saying. "Your theories are without scientific basis."

Kennedy said that there was no precedent to confirm anything that Higgins had found or contended. He said that Higgins was working on an unproved premise, that if he, Kennedy, agreed, he would be doing a great injustice to those who might invest money in the project.

Higgins stood on his hill a defeated man. His only thought was to get rid of Kennedy as fast as he could, and keep him quiet. The man was dead wrong, but his word would be heeded. Higgins realized that if Kennedy had agreed with him the money would be easy to raise. He tried to understand the thinking of this man, who had been formally trained in geology. It was too much for him. He got Kennedy to the hotel and saw that he left town on the next train.

For days Higgins was stunned. He went back and checked all of his findings with his theories. He could find nothing wrong with them. It was Kennedy who was wrong, and it was fortunate that the people of Beaumont had not heard the opinion of this blinded man.

Then, two weeks after Kennedy had left Beaumont, it happened. The one thing Pattillo Higgins was not prepared for.

In the town's only newspaper was an article signed by Kennedy telling of his findings in Beaumont. Based on a thorough investigation, he said, he was prepared to warn Beaumonters and others "not to fritter away their dollars in the vain outlook for oil in the Beaumont area."

Mr. Kennedy could have accomplished no more toward destroying the dream of Pattillo Higgins had he come to Beaumont and moved the Gladys City hill over to Russia. To this day Higgins has never completely forgiven Kennedy for not telling him that he was going to write the article for the Beaumont paper. As the months went by he understood, however, that if Kennedy felt that way, it was his duty to so express himself. The one thing Higgins couldn't understand was the reason for Kennedy's tragic error. Higgins knew that oil-bearing rock would be found under the hill, but at a greater depth than had been drilled by the three early holes. Why Kennedy couldn't understand that the three holes were too shallow and therefore inconclusive Higgins could not for the world comprehend. It left him in a daze, and at this point Higgins' disrespect for men like Kennedy was born.

As far as Beaumont capital was concerned, Kennedy had discouraged it completely. But, thought Pattillo Higgins, that was only as far as Beaumonters were concerned.

Beaumonters had not only ignored his pleas, some of them actually believed he was the victim of hallucinations and were suggesting that he take a long rest. For ten years he had wrestled with a single idea and had received the backing of Carroll and O'Brien only to meet with one misfortune after another. Yet he was like a man inspired. He would not give up. He would go outside for help.

George Carroll and Captain O'Brien heartily approved his idea to place an advertisement in a manufacturing journal. Of course, they would lease the Gladys City property to him or to whomever he might interest in the proposition. They would do even better; they would give him or his associate an option to purchase part of the land and permit the drilling of a hole during the period of the option.

He thanked his former associates and then prepared the advertisement. He stated that oil, gas and sulphur were to be found at Big Hill four miles south of Beaumont and that he desired to make the arrangements for a lease, or an option to buy acreage in the area. He specified that the person answering the advertisement should be capable of adequately financing a proposition of some magnitude, but that the prospect for making millions of dollars was most promising.

An answer was not long coming. It was the only reply he was ever to receive. That advertisement, probably the last hope Higgins had on earth for his hill, brought together two of the greatest pioneers in American history.

The letter was signed, "Captain Anthony F. Lucas."

CHAPTER THREE

The Captain

The Southern Pacific from the East was late that morning, as usual, but Pattillo Higgins was on time. He sat in Dunlap's drug store across a narrow dirt street from the station waiting for Captain Anthony F. Lucas.

He had time to think, and uppermost in his mind was the hope that Lucas would be capable of handling the obstreperous hill which had resisted the attempts of others to find its secret. Higgins knew that he must eventually abandon his own efforts, but he felt an obligation to himself and his community to see that the work was taken up by another.

Higgins regretted that his home-towners had permitted this project to get into the hands of an outsider, but he was glad that an outsider was available. He tried to rationalize the stubbornness of Beaumonters. He knew there was no real money in town. Even the lumber mills, representing the city's only industry of any significance, paid their employees in company scrip to be spent only in company commissaries. Cash was a scarce commodity. But if some of the city's people had only followed him in his belief in the hill, cash could have been plentiful.

His efforts to convince them had been futile, however, and now this stranger would probably come and find the treasure Higgins had told Beaumont it should seek on its own. Outside of thirty-three acres on the south slope of the hill and scattered lots in his undeveloped dream city, Higgins had little to gain. He had lost much. In the years he had pursued the plan for an industrial oil city, he had spent $30,000. He had to stop because he owed $17,000. He had been forced to drop 550 acres on and near the hill that he had bought for $17 an acre. The time would come when this same land would bring more than $3,000,000—to others.

These thoughts were crowding his troubled mind as he heard the whistle of the train. In a few minutes he was extending his hand in welcome to the stranger in whom he would place his hope for the Gladys City hill.

The Captain was a handsome man. More than six feet tall, he was broad, erect, mature and wore a full moustache. His countenance was a portrait of strength. His eyes were soft, yet they bore no trace of weakness. He received Higgins' welcome with a warm smile. His first words revealed a slight but interesting accent.

Captain Anthony Francis Lucas was a naturalized American citizen. He was born on the Island of Hvar in Dalmatia, of Slavic parents named Luchich. He graduated from the school of mining engineering in Gratz when he was twenty and then attended the Austrian Naval Academy in Fiume and Pola as a midshipman. At twenty-four he was commissioned a lieutenant in the Austrian navy. Before going to sea, he decided to visit an uncle in Michigan for six months. His leave was extended and he decided to apply for United States citizenship and change his name to Lucas, as his uncle had done. As an engineer he made three times his navy salary, and opportunity in America was far greater than it was for a Slav in the Austrian navy.

In 1887 Lucas married Caroline Fitzgerald of Macon, Georgia, daughter of a prominent physician. Shortly thereafter, the Captain and his bride moved to Washington. In 1893, a year after their son, Anthony Fitzgerald, was born, they moved to Louisiana, where Lucas was engaged as a mining engineer. He explored salt mines at Anse LaButte, Jefferson Island, Grande Cote, Petit Anse and Weeks' Island. One of his friends was Joseph Jefferson, the famous actor. The great masses of salt below the surface of the earth had attracted the Captain's attention. He observed signs of oil, gas and sulphur in most of them. He developed and worked on a theory that they were salt plugs around which it was possible for oil or sulphur to accumulate.

On weekend excursions from Louisiana, Lucas visited some of Texas' coastal uplifts, including those at Beaumont and High Island. He found good indications of sulphur at Gladys City. Higgins' advertisement attracted him and he decided to look at the prospect further with a view toward investing his own capital if it looked good enough.

II

Higgins and Lucas stood on the apex of the inverted saucer-like hill. Lucas explained his idea about salt domes, and Higgins told the Captain why he believed the hill would be a prolific producer. He said it would not be surprising to him if the great well 500 miles north of Baku, in Russia, which produced 100,000 barrels of oil in eleven hours in 1893 before dropping off, could be duplicated here. Higgins said that anticlinal pressure caused by this salt mass below the surface would produce geysers of oil. Lucas said he would be looking for sulphur, but that if oil were found, that would be good.

Higgins made an appointment for Lucas with Carroll and O'Brien for the early afternoon. In the meantime Lucas was interested in the kind of deal that could be made.

"You can lease the entire Gladys City company holdings or any part of them," Higgins said. "I have been offered all of the 2,700 acres of land in fee for $20 an acre. My suggestion is, however, that you take a lease and option to purchase the 600 or 700 acres on and near to the hill. This can be handled for $50 an acre."

On June 20th, several days after the Captain's arrival in Beaumont, he signed a lease and option agreement for 663 acres. He agreed to pay $31,150. Of this, he paid $11,050 cash, and signed 7-percent promissory notes for like amounts to fall due on the next two anniversary dates of the agreement. That was the deal. He had all of the Gladys City's land on the hill, as well as protection on the north and west flanks.

For his efforts Pattillo Higgins was given a 10 per cent interest in the Lucas options. George Carroll agreed to match that amount from his part of any profits, if the undertaking were successful. Lucas recorded his deal with Higgins, but Carroll's promise to Higgins amounted to a gentleman's agreement. While Higgins had originally asked 25 percent interest in the lease, he was satisfied with this compromise.

Captain Lucas took Higgins' suggestion for a location for his well. It was east of the railroad tracks on lot 44 in Gladys City, near where Higgins originally planned the company's drill site.

Before the last of June, Lucas was ready to start drilling. Higgins had seen his equipment, a rotary rig Lucas had used in his Louisiana operations, and had ventured the opinion that it was too light. Lucas said it was the best he could get, and that he believed it might work, as he knew both the contractor and the equipment.

It was early July when the hole was spudded. Lucas had planned carefully, but he was in for some surprises.

Like Sharp and Savage before him, he was soon aware that Higgins knew his hill. The going was rough from the start. Weeks passed and progress was slow. The sweltering, torrid summer turned into a freezing winter and still he was digging with little results. In Louisiana he had been able to penetrate 2100 feet in a couple of months, but this hill was different.

Pattillo Higgins watched the operation as closely as his time would permit. He told Carroll, who accompanied him to the hill one day in January, that he was afraid the Captain had about reached his limit with the equipment and the help that he had.

This was about the time that Lucas reached an oil sand and recovered three demijohns of heavy green crude. Two days later, however, the driller came running to Lucas' home with the news that the pipe had collapsed because of gas pressure.

Captain Lucas was stunned by the news. Following on the heels of the oil showing, this twist of fate was cruel. Thinking more of his family than of his theory, the Captain told Caroline Lucas this meant failure. His funds were not sufficient to start another well.

"Anthony, you have some oil from the hill," Mrs. Lucas said, "I think it will be easy to get financial help. I know your money is low, but this is such a big thing that you can share it with others."

This assurance was needed and it helped. Anthony Lucas became an oil wildcatter that moment. He would not look for sulphur, but for oil. Higgins had been right on that count, too. Now, more than ever before, Captain Lucas realized the wisdom of Higgins' advice to get heavier equipment.

That evening Lucas and Higgins met in the French Café and the Captain told of his failure. He also revealed that he was low financially and would need help if he were to try again.

"Stopping is out of the question, Captain," Higgins said. "You know what is below the hill now. I doubt it, but maybe local capital will help you. If not, you know that there are oil men who will."

Yes, Higgins was right, Lucas thought. He would try Beaumonters first. They were entitled to a chance now that they could see the oil. His efforts were futile. Those he called on seemed to cringe at the thought that here was another Pattillo Higgins to haunt them with wild talk about spouting oil wells.

He decided to take his proposition to the Standard Oil Company. He was beginning to wear the Higgins mantle well. In a few days he was off to see Henry C. Folger, a Standard executive who had agreed to give him a hearing.

En route to New York, Lucas stopped in Washington to visit friends and make a special call. He had been told that Congressman Sibley of Pennsylvania had been successful in oil operations and might be interested.

The Honorable Mr. Sibley was in a somewhat testy mood the day the Captain arrived, but he admitted Lucas to his office.

Far from being downcast now, Lucas was enthusiastic. He took his jar of oil to the congressman and talked for fifteen minutes before Sibley could get a word in. When be did, Lucas heard a lecture on oil prospecting which ended with Sibley saying, "Captain Lucas, let me warn you against the dire consequences of unsubstantiated enthusiasm. The search for oil is risky and not always as all-fired profitable as you might think. If you will assure me of several thousands of barrels of oil daily at Gladys City, I'll go along with you. Otherwise, I am not interested."

The outburst amused the Captain. He picked up his hat and thanked the gentleman from Pennsylvania for his time.

"You know, Mr. Congressman, if I could assure you the production of several thousand barrels of oil daily, I doubt that I would be here asking for your assistance," Lucas said as he departed.

III

The night before the Captain saw Folger, New York was hit by a severe blizzard. The temperature dropped below zero. This afforded Lucas a chance to test the oil under such conditions, so he left one jar outside his hotel window that night. The next morning he was jubilant to find that the liquid had not congealed in spite of its low gravity of 17° Baumé. This proved the oil could be stored and transported easily in severe weather.

In Folger's office the Captain made no attempt to conceal his enthusiasm. He told of the test and Folger looked at the jar of oil with interest.

"Mr. Folger," Lucas said, "I don't need money for myself. This is not a promotion whereby I'll take a salary and live on it irrespective of the outcome. I want an association in further prospecting and proving this oilfield and the theory of salt domes."

Folger was gracious when Lucas had finished. He admitted he was doubtful, but said that before he turned down the prospect he would have Calvin Payne, the company's expert in Titusville, make a trip to Beaumont. If Lucas could convince Payne, a deal might be made. "In fact, Captain, Mr. Payne and I recently advanced J. S. Cullinan money to start a refinery in Corsicana," Folger said. "Payne might like your deal. We could use more oil."

In late February Calvin Payne called on Lucas at his home. With him was J. S. Cullinan, the former Standard man who was now operating independently in Texas' largest oil field at Corsicana.

The three men went out to the location where Lucas had drilled his first hole. He explained the operation and how it had ended. Then he told Payne and Cullinan of his experiences in Louisiana and how he had arrived at the nascent-dome theory. He pointed to the circular elevation and how it varied in texture and structure from the surrounding sediments which made up the prairie.

Payne listened and then thought for some time before replying. He looked to Cullinan for an opinion, but Cullinan only smiled and remained silent.

"Captain Lucas, I have traveled around the world looking at oil fields in Russia, Roumania, Borneo and Sumatra, as well as most of the fields in the United States," Payne said. "The indications you have pointed out, while noteworthy and most interesting, have no analogy to any field I have ever seen produce oil. I do not believe there is any chance for oil here in paying quantities."

"But, Mr. Payne," Lucas said, holding up the demijohn of oil, "here is the proof. Here is oil that came from this hill. It isn't all I am looking for, but it certainly proves that there is oil here."

Payne shook his head and said that heavy, black oil like that could be found almost anywhere, but that it couldn't be produced in quantities that would pay for boring the wells.

"Mr. Lucas," Payne said, "I have learned enough about you to know that you are a fine mechanical and mining engineer. Why don't you go back to that profession and leave this risky and tricky business of oil to such people as Mr. Cullinan and me? You have completely misled yourself and I know it has been expensive. You will never find oil here."

For a fraction of a moment Lucas almost capitulated. Payne was regarded as one of the world's renowned oil experts, a man who had started in the oil fields as a driller, and had moved to one of the highest positions in the only large oil company in the world.

"I'm sorry you can't see the possibilities, Mr. Payne," Lucas said. "I still believe they are here and I will stay with the hill if I can get the financial backing I need. I know you have gone to an expense to see this prospect and I appreciate it."

The weeks passed and there was no sign of help. On several occasions it is likely that Captain Lucas would have taken the advice of Calvin Payne, had not his wife encouraged him to go ahead. Lucas himself was prepared to face anything, but he was not willing to cause Mrs. Lucas and his boy, Tony, unusual hardship when he could get out of Beaumont and make a good living.

In April two distinguished visitors showed up in Beaumont. They were Dr. C. Willard Hayes of the United States Geological Survey, and E. W. Parker, former chief statistician for that agency. Dr. Hayes stopped at the Crosby House and made himself available to discuss Gulf Coast geology. Captain Lucas was not long seeking him out.

Lucas called Pattillo Higgins and George Carroll and asked them to ride to the Hill with him and the two government men.

Lucas directed the party around Gladys City. Higgins was amused. He had about as much confidence in a professional geologist, especially one who worked for the government, as he had in an East Texas weather prophet. He could see what Lucas was trying to do. The Captain was covering the same ground Higgins went over when he talked with Kennedy.

Lucas had one advantage. He could explain his salt-dome theory and maybe that would impress the geologist. Higgins had little hope, however, and was not surprised when Dr. Hayes disagreed with the Lucas theory and added that there was no precedent for oil being found in the unconsolidated sands and clays of the coastal plain.

"Captain Lucas," Dr. Hayes said, "let me point out an event which apparently has escaped your notice. In Galveston County, not much more than forty miles from this very spot, a hole was drilled to 3070 feet recently and not one drop of oil was recovered or even smelled. That cost the city of Galveston almost a million dollars. It was a vast sum of money that I would hate to see you throw away here."

Lucas knew about the Galveston well. He knew that the drillers were pursuing a different idea, seeking fresh water. They had no indication of a dome structure such as this hill. Hayes called attention to the absence of an oil seepage. Lucas referred to the Herman Frasch sulphur dome near Lake Charles, where a barrel and a half of oil was being produced daily along with the sulphur. He said salt domes required no seepage indications. There was no encouragement from Hayes.

Higgins extended his sympathy to Lucas. He had been over the same ground, only Kennedy had used the water well at the courthouse instead of the one in Galveston County. Geologists had to have a precedent. They couldn't consider an original thought, he told Lucas.

"Captain Lucas," Higgins said, "those men should be asking you, not telling you. Your experience in Louisiana makes you the greatest authority in the world—probably the only authority—on salt domes. Yet these experts come and tell you this or that can't happen because it has never happened before. You believe there is oil here because there is a salt plug below, and I think you are right. I know there is oil here in greater quantities than man has ever found before. I wish I could help you, but I can't. But for God's sake don't stop because ignorant men in high places say to stop—and get your backing before that man writes a letter to the Beaumont newspaper."

IV

There was one geologist who believed that Captain Lucas' theory had merit. Dr. William Battle Phillips, professor of field geology at the University of Texas, made a trip to Beaumont to see Lucas. He explained that he did not care to go against both the federal and state geological experts, but that he believed there was something to the nascent-dome idea. Phillips suggested that Lucas go see Guffey and Galey in Pittsburgh. In fact, he gave him a written introduction to Galey.

This, the first word of encouragement the Captain had got outside his immediate family, Pattillo Higgins, and the landowners, gave him courage at a very critical time. It also gave him an idea. Guffey and Galey operated in Corsicana, and Galey might be there. In Corsicana, Galey was waiting for Lucas when he arrived. He told the Captain that he had already heard of his dome theory and also what Payne and Hayes thought of it.

"But, Captain, those gentlemen are not always right. Both my partner and I have recently brought in fine producers where the experts said there would be no oil. Tell me about your idea. I like imagination and originality," Galey said.

These were the kindest words he could have spoken. Lucas was given new hope with them. No detail of his theory was left untold and Galey was fascinated.

"Your idea is revolutionary. Let me talk to Guffey and I will write to you in a few days," Galey said. "Better still, get on the train and come with me to Pittsburgh. I might need you to explain some of this. It is a little different from looking for oil scum on a creek bank or in a farmer's well."

In Pittsburgh Captain Anthony Lucas met the other half of the great wildcatting team of Guffey and Galey. James McClurg Guffey was a genius in his field, which was raising the money for Galey to find oil with. He was a pleasant man with aesthetic features which belied his tremendous energy. Guffey was one of the stalwarts of the Democratic Party, and during the ill-starred Garfield régime had been Chairman of the National Democratic Committee. His political sideline demanded much of his time and money.

Guffey had great faith in John H. Galey, but the Hayes and Payne reports made him skeptical.

"How much land do you control, Captain?" was his first question.

When Lucas said 600 acres, Guffey replied that that was a mere pittance. The dome theory may be right and all of the oil might be on the hill, but Guffey wanted to be sure. He demanded that Lucas get all of the hill, if possible, and as many acres as he could lease around it. The entire deal would depend on that.

"Go back to Beaumont, Captain Lucas, and let me know how you come out between now and the first of July," Guffey said, "and mention this deal to no man. Guffey and Galey cannot be identified with it. If we are known, you will find land prices ten times as high as they will be for a man who drilled a dry hole."

Lucas asked if he could inform Higgins.

"Who," asked Guffey, "is Higgins?"

Lucas told him and Guffey replied that under no circumstances must anyone else know—not even Higgins.

"And remember that Mr. Higgins is not to be part of this deal unless it is to share in whatever profits you individually make out of it," Guffey said. "This will mean putting up $300,000 if we are to back you, and it is impractical to cut in everyone who ever heard of oil prospects in Texas."

Lucas was not happy about keeping Higgins in the dark, but he knew that if Higgins understood that it was necessary to get the money, he would approve.

In May, Lucas leased the fifty-acre Chaison tract in the Douthit survey and the 5300-acre Hebert tract in the Sigler survey south of the hill. On June 20th, the anniversary of his first contract with the Gladys City company, he succeeded in leasing the remainder of the hill except for about eighty acres. Another 3800 acres was leased southwest of the hill on the McClure-Collier-Cameron tract in the Hillebrandt survey. With the 2500 acres he could acquire from the Gladys City company, that would give him around 15,000 acres by his deadline. His leases gave the landowners one-tenth royalty in oil or any other minerals he found.

Lucas was quite pleased that he had acquired such large holdings before the deadline that Guffey laid down; however, the most remarkable omission of acreage from his block was the many small tracts which made up the Spindletop Heights subdivision which ran across the hill, and which was adjacent to the well location. There were other small parcels which varied from city lots to fifteen-acre tracts which were also open. One of these "holes" in Lucas' block was Higgins' thirty-three-acre tract, 100 feet from the well site.

Guffey approved the land holdings, but said that in view of the fact that he and Galey were borrowing all of the money from the Mellon interests, they would have to have most of the prospect. Lucas got a relatively small part of the partnership of Guffey, Galey and Lucas, but he had financed his hope of proving the dome theory. The terms had included the provision that Lucas was to draw no salary or other remuneration. This he had insisted on himself, in spite of his low finances, to prove his good faith. It had impressed Guffey.

Galey said he would write to the Hamill brothers in Corsicana, the firm he wanted to drill the well.

Guffey's parting shot was that while the contract called for three wells, that would hold only in the event that the first hole produced oil or looked promising. There was no obligation, he said, to drill three dry holes.

Because of Payne and Hayes, the Captain had no other choice. Honest though they both were in their opinions, it would have been far better had he seen Guffey and Galey before talking to the experts. It would have saved Payne and Hayes monumental embarrassment, too.

When Captain Lucas returned home, his family celebrated his arrival. The good news had preceded him by letter and happiness filled the big frame house.

"Carrie," Lucas told his wife, "things are going to be a little tight for us. Our funds are down to rock bottom and I don't want to borrow."

Mrs. Lucas looked around the house and pointed to several pieces of expensive furniture that had been brought from Washington.

"I have had dozens of people admire this old furniture," she said. "We'll make it pay for our groceries until the well comes in."

The Captain appreciated her willingness to sacrifice. He knew the furniture would have to be sold and replaced by tables and chairs made from egg crates and apple boxes. He knew, too, that Tony would go to school in September. This meant spending more money for books and clothes. A devout Episcopalian, the Captain had complete faith in his undertaking and believed that the Lord would help him provide for his family in the meantime.

V

The Captain was in Corsicana to see the Hamill brothers the day that John Galey came to Beaumont to stake the location for the well. Galey had only a short time to stay, so he accepted Mrs. Lucas' offer to go to the field while he marked the spot for the Captain to drill on. He took the occasion to impress upon Mrs. Lucas, as the Captain had already done, the necessity for secrecy.

On the south side of the hill and the north edge of the McFaddin-Kyle and Wiess land, Galey found a hog wallow with three rough-hewn boxes full of sulphur water. Mrs. Lucas told him the farmers and ranchers brought their hogs there to kill fleas and cure the mange. It was a bald, alkali spot surrounded by a sea of undulating marsh grass, whipped by the coastal winds and deep in the smell of salt spray. As near as he could place the stake to the southmost box, he drove it a foot into the ground. Turning then to Mrs. Lucas, John

Galey smiled and said: "Tell that Captain of yours to start that first well right here. And tell him that I know he is going to hit the biggest oil well this side of Baku. Anyway, bless you both and let me hear from you if you need anything."

John Galey drove off, telling Mrs. Lucas to say nothing to anyone about his being there. She promised, and to herself she chuckled over Galey's remark about needing anything. She knew Anthony Lucas well enough to know that no one outside his little family would know it if they were all starving.

John Galey was lucky with his stake driving that day. Had he decided to go fifty feet south of the hog wallow, he would have found himself and the Honorable James McClurg Guffey financing a dry hole. A great deal of the history of the world was tied to that decision. And, as in the case of all wildcatters, it is not known yet whether he was lucky or just plain smart.

VI

When John Galey hired the Hamill brothers to drill the well at Gladys City, he didn't do it altogether because he enjoyed the conviviality of Jim Hamill. That helped, but Galey was a smart operator. He knew from his studies of the first four holes in the hill that the job was going to be one that would require resourcefulness. And John Galey knew that in the Hamill brothers he had that word personified.

It took Captain Anthony Lucas only a few hours to realize that after he met Al Hamill, the youngest brother, in Beaumont. Al formed the one-man advance detachment for the drilling crew that would dig the Lucas well. Lucas met him at the train and Al explained that the first thing he wanted to do was line up the lumber for the derrick, and wood for boiler fuel.

The two men went to see George Carroll at his lumber yard. After the derrick lumber had been arranged for, Carroll made an offer.

"Mr. Hamill," he said, "if you bring in a well that will flow at least 5000 barrels of oil a day, the lumber for your derrick will be my present."

Al Hamill hardly took this as a generous offer. He was accustomed to "big" fifty-barrel wells in Corsicana. To him it was like offering a new hat to a mediocre hitter for slugging three home runs over a 600-foot centerfield fence in one game.

Lucas explained to Al when they left the lumber yard that Pattillo Higgins had predicted wells on the hill that would produce thousands of barrels a day and that Carroll had implicit faith in Higgins.

"It might surprise you to know that I believe you will drill that well with a free derrick, too," Lucas told Hamill.

But that wasn't the incident that caused the Captain to banish the last vestige of doubt he might have had about his drilling contractors.

Lucas had complained to Al that he could not get a car of pipe unloaded. A local contractor looked at the pipe-laden gondola and had declined the job, suggesting a house mover. The house mover had called the project an enormous one, requiring a rig and horsepower. But even before that it would be necessary to make an estimate of cost and time.

"Now, Mr. Hamill, the railroad company is crying for its gondola and it looks like it will be several days before I can return it to them," Lucas said.

Al asked where the pipe was located and was told it was on a spur line near the hill. He suggested that they go look over the problem.

When he got there, Al Hamill climbed up on the pipe, took off his coat, threw two pieces of six-inch pipe over the side to serve as slides, and told Lucas to stack the pipe as he threw it down. In a little more than an hour, Al Hamill had unloaded 500 feet of ten-inch, 900 feet of six-inch, and 1200 feet of four-inch pipe.

Captain Lucas was an Al Hamill man from that day on.

The incident illustrates, also, how unprepared Beaumont was for the industrial revolution it was soon to face. The incredulous house mover had to be shown the results of the feat on the ground. He wouldn't believe Lucas when the Captain told him why his services would not be required.

The Hamills had what they considered a very good contract. They would get $2 a foot and Guffey and Galey would furnish the pipe. With their new rotary rig, which Curt Hamill had been working with, they could drill ordinary wells for 35 cents a foot. The cable-tool method had cost them about 75 cents a foot. They had spent $400 on their new rig for a rotary, draw-works, pump, and swivel.

A week after Al arrived, the remainder of the crew came in. Curt, the derrick man, was the other brother who would work on the Lucas job. Jim Hamill remained in Corsicana to run the company. Henry McLeod was the driller and Peck Byrd was the fireman and the fourth member of the crew.

Completely without experience, the Hamills had to build a derrick. In Corsicana derrick builders did the job, but there were none in Beaumont. They simply made a pattern and laid the derrick out on the ground. When they were finished, it was perfect.

Oil stories were not frequent in Beaumont, but on October 26th, the *Journal* had one. It quoted Captain Lucas, who denied rumors that oil had been found on the hill. The Captain explained that the drillers had not even started the hole yet.

The next day, however, the hole was spudded. The Hamills solved the quicksand problem early. Curt had found that when the drilling fluid was heavy, the sidewalls of the hole seemed to hold better. He hit upon the idea of driving a herd of McFaddin's cattle into the slush pit to muddy up the water. The sixty-foot quicksand problem was that easy and with that act an idea was born for drilling mud. Without it today there would be few oil wells drilled.

Trouble came when the Hamills reached 160 feet. There, even the heavy mud would not close off the sidewalls. The formation seemed to be coarse sand and gravel up to the size of eggs.

Lucas was told about the problem and he admitted that he had no solution. The hole was being drilled with eight-inch pipe and it was impossible to proceed as long as the loss of circulation prevented the cuttings from returning to the top of the hole. This same difficulty had stopped both Sharp and Savage.

The Hamills finally decided they would try to drive the eight-inch pipe down and wash with four-inch inside the larger pipe which would serve as casing until the coarse formation was penetrated. This proved to be one of the monumental accomplishments of all time in well-drilling.

A drivehead was rigged up on the bottom of the eight-inch pipe. It was a sharply beveled bit that would simply bite into the earth. A heavy drive block was forged to use on top of the four-inch pipe in the manner of a pile-driver. Driving power was achieved by pulling the cathead line and giving it a quick slip to get the hardest blow possible. This was done by hand and the crew members took turns at the man-killing job.

As often as possible the circulating pump would be started to wash the sand from the bottom of the eight-inch pipe. Some days the crew would make only a few feet, and on other days progress would be better. It took more than two weeks to go through 285 feet of sand and gravel. Captain Lucas watched, prayed, and marveled. Henry McLeod decided there was an easier way of making a living and "retired" during the operation.

The next crisis came after the gumbo was reached at 445 feet and normal rotary drilling was resumed. The drillers had gone about 200 feet more when they hit a gas pocket. The circulating mud began to boil and flow up through the rotary table. Shortly, muddy water and gas were spouting halfway up the derrick.

The small blowout was finally controlled, but then it was obvious that to prevent future disaster it would be necessary to keep the circulating pumps going twenty-four hours a day. Until this time the three-man crew had worked only in the daylight hours. Every third day now one of the crew had to work an eighteen-hour shift. The night man did not try to drill. He merely kept up steam to keep the pumps in motion and the drill pipe rotating slowly.

Captain Lucas visited the well one cold day in early December and Curt Hamill told him the pipe was stuck due to gas pressure. There was a hundred feet of sand in the pipe and it seemed impossible to go ahead. This was happening every time the counter-pressure exerted by the pump was stopped to put on another joint of pipe. Various suggestions were offered, like going over the six-inch pipe with larger pipe, but the larger pipe would also stick.

No greater problem had been encountered. Lucas was distressed and the drilling crew was afraid it had reached the end of its resourcefulness.

Caroline Lucas heard her husband say that it seemed the second failure was inevitable. She offered encouragement, but it didn't seem to relieve his mind. There was no sleep for Anthony Lucas that night. He turned and tossed and wrestled with his problem.

As he lay there, he began to wonder how a boiler having a one hundred-pound pressure could be pumped full without any water escaping. Suddenly the answer came. It was because a boiler was equipped with a check valve.

He jumped from his bed and threw his clothes on as he dashed out of the house. His wife and son feared that the mental burden had been too much for him. He rushed to the woodshed and picked up a pine box and a discarded rubber belt. He hurriedly hitched his buggy and drove to the hill where Al Hamill was doing his eighteen-hour shift.

Excitedly, he told Hamill of his idea. Soon Curt and Peck were on the job and a check valve had been rigged up out of a pine board with perforations in the center and a small rubber belt underneath. It was placed between the couplings of the casings and the trouble was overcome.

Spindletop Heights was a real-estate development which extended like a long, pointing finger into the center of the hill proper. In August Captain Lucas had leased 122 acres of this land from Guy W. Junker. In November he had leased another fifteen acres from J. M. Page. Off to the west of the periphery of the hill he had leased 834 acres in the Rowe and Stivers surveys. As late as December 1st, he had closed a deal with J. F. Keith, one of the city's leading lumbermen, for 4800 acres in the Arriola league several miles north of Beaumont in Hardin County. Wherever and whenever he could, he was leasing land to protect his partnership in the event oil was found.

One December morning, while talking to Curt Hamill, the Captain took a sudden interest in a lump of clay found on a fishtail bit. Examining the clay closely, he saw a piece of rock the size of a small egg.

"That explains why the drilling has been so hard lately, Curt," Lucas exclaimed.

Curt looked puzzled and the Captain explained further.

"You have drilled into the dome structure proper. This proves we are right."

Then he showed young Hamill limestone with calcite intercalations. He also pointed out fragments of dolomite and sulphur.

"This is the best thing that has happened, boys," Lucas exclaimed to the crew. "Watch now for something good any day. And say a little prayer."

The Captain rushed home with his "great find" to show Caroline and Tony. They were as puzzled over the evidence for his happy excitement as the Hamills had been, but they were delighted to see him enthusiastic again.

That night it was Al Hamill's turn for the eighteen-hour shift. About three o'clock in the morning he noticed the pump working more freely than it had for days, and the rotary was turning easily. Al began to let pipe down the hole. Still the pump and rotary responded freely. He had let almost an entire length of pipe down when he detected a gassy odor.

He tried to investigate, but the light on the rig was not bright enough. Soon, day began to dawn and he could then see an oil scum on the ditch and in the slush pit. Curt and Peck Byrd showed up about that time and Peck was sent running for the Captain.

Lucas was excited when he arrived. Peck had told him about the oil.

"What will she make?" Lucas asked Al.

The Hamills thought a fifty-barrel well was a whopper. It was the biggest Corsicana had in an area where the average well was good for ten barrels a day.

"I'd say fifty barrels," Al replied with his tongue in his cheek.

Lucas then ordered another joint of pipe to test the depth of the formation. Soon another thirty-five feet had been drilled and the drilling became harder. The pipe was resting on hard rock at 880 feet.

The Captain said he would wire Galey to come at once. In the meantime he ordered the crew to set four-inch drill pipe as a test string.

Galey arrived a few days later, and the men started bailing the well. There was a small flow of oil. Then the bailer was run again and it was found that 300 feet of soft sand had heaved up into the hole. For the next week efforts to bring the well in were fruitless. The four-inch pipe was pulled and six-inch was landed on the top of the hard formation at 880 feet.

While this was going on the *Beaumont Journal* came out with a story about the well. It told of oil being discovered and then lost, but suggested that Captain Lucas had met with some success. Without using Galey's name the newspaper told about the "expert" from Pennsylvania who had seen the well and declared it lost because of salt water in the heaving sand. Some doubt as to the future of the well, and, indeed, the entire prospect, was expressed. The story posed a question about what Captain Lucas would do next. It stated that his present concern was saving pipe that was in the hole and worth some $4,000.

Winding up on a sad note, the story said, "But all is speculation mingled with disappointment to Captain Lucas which is too keen to be appreciated and too delicate to find expression in words."

This story didn't bother Lucas and Galey. It gave them a great advantage. They knew now that they could make an oil field on the hill. Whether this well could be completed or another well would have to be drilled nearby was the only question. What no one knew was how big the well would be. Even Al Hamill was dubious about his fifty-barrel guess, and the grade of oil seemed far below that of Corsicana. But everyone knew enough to know that more acreage had to be obtained to keep the situation from getting out of hand when the well did come in. Galey said if this well would not produce, a second would be started at once.

On the day before Christmas John Galey called Curt, Al and Peck Byrd together and told them to put the well in shape and go home for the holidays. He advised Captain Lucas to do what he could about closing up the gaps in the land situation. He gave the Captain an almost impossible job.

Landowners and courthouse clerks were occupied with Christmas activities.

On New Year's Day, 1901—the first day of the twentieth century—the two Hamill Brothers and Peck Byrd were back on the job. They didn't know how far they had to go, but they knew they needed help. Efforts to recruit labor were not successful. Big, healthy boys and men would come to the well and watch the strange proceedings. But when they were asked if they wanted a job, they always had an excuse. They were leary of the work on the hissing, clanking, rattling contraption the Hamill brothers called a rig.

It was January 2nd, and rumors were rife again. The skies in the area of the hill were brilliantly illuminated, and Beaumonters believed that this was due to gas burning at the well. The Captain admitted the gas.

"Bless you, yes, we have gas," Lucas was quoted in the *Journal* as saying. "Enough to stock a book agent. But the illumination was apparently the light of St. Elmo's fire."

On January 9th, the Hamills were still perplexed by the mysteries of this strange hill. They had gone through 140 feet of solid rock to a total depth of 1020 feet. There the bit seemed to hit a crevice, and again problems that seemed insurmountable arose. When Curt tried to rotate the pipe it would jerk the rotary chain to pieces, but he kept grinding away with no apparent headway. Galey had ordered that the well be taken to the contract depth of 1200 feet, and, if nothing were found deeper, to back up and perforate the pipe in the 845-foot sand and try to complete the well. Failing in that, he said, a second hole would be drilled.

Beaumont had no supply house, so Al wired Jim Hamill for another fishtail bit and some new rotary chains, to be picked up the next morning.

Captain Lucas was worried. He knew he had an oil sand, but the pressures and sands and gumbo were obstacles never encountered in oil-well drilling before. He was not sure the hill would ever produce, in spite of John Galey's cheerful optimism. The words of Calvin Payne kept haunting him—the black oil from the first hole could be found anywhere, but it had no value.

After supper Anthony and Carrie Lucas were sitting in the living room of their home. Suddenly, the hill seemed to light up with a fantastic glow, and then the great light seemed to gather into one large ball of flame and come to rest on the crown block of the derrick. The Hamills said it gave off a low hissing sound for a few minutes. It was the St. Elmo fire, which for centuries had visited the hill as if beckoning men to a great treasure. It was the last time the phenomenon would ever be seen on the hill.

The Captain told Carrie what it was.

"Doesn't that have a special meaning for men of the sea?" she asked.

"Yes," Anthony Lucas replied, still gazing at the hill. "It means their ship will come safely into harbor."

CHAPTER FOUR

Geyser of Oil

There wasn't a trace of a cloud in the sky. The weather was cold and invigorating and smoke was rising from every chimney in Beaumont on the morning of January 10, 1901.

Pattillo Higgins rode off into the north wind toward Hardin County to complete a deal that would get him out of debt. He had located a strip of timberland that Frank Keith would buy.

Al Hamill was in the freight depot early to pick up the new fishtail bit from Corsicana. It was barely daylight when he and Higgins exchanged greetings as they passed each other on Park Street.

After a brief visit to the well, Captain Lucas returned to his home on the way to town to tell Caroline he would be in Louie Mayer's store on Crockett Street.

The morning *Enterprise* gave its usual reports of the local, national and world events. The district attorney, who had been supported by George Carroll in the recent election, would start a war on gambling. A big diamond discovery was reported from Capitan near El Paso. Dr. Walter Reed announced his famous discovery of the carrier of yellow fever. Old Tom Sharkey was crying for another crack at Kid McCoy. William Jennings Bryan was due to visit Houston, and Al. G. Fields' minstrels and Sousa's band were booked into the Goodhue Opera House. Mayor Wheat returned from Washington without selling the city's improvement bonds. Governor Sayers was to open the new session of the state legislature in Austin.

Beaumont was not prepared for the dramatic excitement that was now only hours away. Its 9,000 inhabitants were satisfied with conditions as they were. Beaumont had a chamber of commerce, solid citizens, culture and magnolias. It was as cosmopolitan as any city in the South. A fourth of its citizens were Negroes. Many of its successful merchants were Jews. Almost every other white man and most of the Negroes spoke a Louisiana patois. It had a healthy immigrant population, particularly Italians. There was a Dutch settlement just south of town called Nederland. Beaumont was more Southern than Southwestern, but it did have a few cowpokes. It was a pleasant place to live. It had few animosities and a minimum of prejudices. All in all it was a model American small town.

II

On the hill the crew of three had put on the new fishtail bit. That done, the drill stem was lowered back into the hole. With the pipe down about 700 feet and Curt Hamill steering it from the double boards forty feet above the derrick floor, something began to happen.

Mud started to bubble up over the rotary table. Al and Peck backed away when suddenly the force increased and mud spurted high up the derrick. Curt, drenched with mud and gumbo, grabbed for the ladder and slid down it to safety. All three scampered in different directions. This was a new experience for these old hands of the Corsicana field. As they ran, six tons of four-inch pipe came shooting up through the derrick, knocking off the crown block. Then the pipe leapt, like activated spaghetti, on over the top of the derrick and broke off in sections, falling around the camp like giant spikes driven into the earth.

Then everything was quiet. The Hamills and Peck Byrd cautiously returned to the derrick floor. It was a shambles, with mud, muck and water standing a foot deep. The disgusted crew looked over the situation, started cleaning up the debris, and expressed themselves in a manner of eloquence reserved for men of the oil fields.

"What the hell are we going to do with the damn thing now?" Peck Byrd asked Al as he shut off the boiler fires.

"Well, Peck," Al was saying, "I guess we'll just have to shovel this mud away and see if. . . ."

His words were interrupted by a roar like the shot of a heavy cannon. Then again the flow of mud started up through the hole, followed by a terrific column of gas. The startled crew scattered again. Peck missed his footing and tumbled headlong into the slush pit. Within seconds, the gas was followed by a solid flow of oil—green and heavy.

"Peck, run to the house and get the Captain," Al shouted, "while Curt and me try to figure this thing out. It looks like oil! Hurry! Hurry!"

The mud-soaked Peck Byrd ran to the Lucas home. When he got there he was out of breath and sat holding his side, panting a few minutes, before he could deliver the message to Mrs. Lucas.

"Get the Captain! Tell him to come right now!" Peck shouted in excitement. "Look, Mrs. Lucas, look," he said, pointing to the well. But before she could find out what had happened, Peck was off on a run back to the well.

She looked toward the hill and saw a great plume of black liquid spouting over the derrick. The sight was fantastic. She could not explain what had happened, but she implored the Captain to lose no time in getting back to the hill.

"Hurry, Anthony, something awful has happened. The well is spouting," she shouted into the telephone.

The Captain turned and fled from the store without explanation. He mounted his gig, as Louie Mayer watched in astonishment, and stood on the floorboards whipping his horse as he raced out Park Street, past the O'Brien and Carroll homes, out Highland Avenue and past his own home without even looking toward his wife, who was trying to attract his attention by waving from the porch.

The phenomenon was in full view now. It was frightening to the Captain. His eyes had never beheld such a sight before. Could it be oil?

When he reached the hill, Lucas' excitement was too much and the horse was too slow. At the apex of the hill, he tried to jump from the buggy and tumbled down the slope. Al Hamill saw the fall and started toward him, but the Captain rolled forward and came to his feet on a dead run.

"Al, Al," he was shouting, "what is it? What is it?"

"Oil, Captain! Oil, every drop of it," the jubilant Al replied.

Grabbing Al Hamill by the waist and swinging him around, Lucas looked up toward the gray skies and said, "Thank God. Thank God, you've done it! You've done it!"

"It came in at ten-thirty, almost an hour ago, and it has been shooting a steady six-inch stream of oil more than a hundred feet above the top of the derrick, just like it is now. I can't understand it," Al said. "But I don't think we are going to pay George Carroll for that derrick."

Captain Lucas was exultant. He stood under the shower of green oil, felt it, smelled it and tasted it to make certain he wasn't dreaming.

Then he backed off and looked up to the top of the great plume. Oil, shale, and rocks were raining down. Almost to himself he whispered hoarsely, with a rising inflection, "A geyser of oil! A geyser of oil!"

III

Farmers, ranchers and everyone living within sight of the great geyser started converging on the hill. They were amazed and puzzled. They were coming afoot and by horseback, wagon, buggy, carriage and bicycle.

Charley Ingals, a carpenter-farmer, stood under the well a few minutes, then mounted his horse and headed for Beaumont. Like an oil-saturated Paul Revere, he rode past houses shouting "Oil! Oil, on the hill!" and more people came out of their houses, looked south and started for Gladys City. As he rode down Pearl and Crockett Streets he continued shouting his message, "It's oil! On the hill! And the damn stuff has ruined my home and farm," he yelled at the townspeople.

The news rocked Beaumont as if it had been hit by an earthquake. People rushed from their half-eaten meals, from homes and cafés. They came out of commissaries, stores, barber shops and saloons and, like feathers being drawn by a giant vacuum, started toward the hill. Every available mode of conveyance was filled. The livery stables were emptied. Those who couldn't get a ride began to walk. The courthouse, Beaumont's only tall building, was crowded with men, women and children climbing out on its roof and into every window. The well was clearly visible from the upper floors.

In the wake of the excitement, stores and shops were left abandoned. Half-shaven customers from barber shops ran down the street. In the south end of the town a teacher at a blackboard was deserted by a class, including young Tony Lucas, who had heard and seen the well when it roared in.

Panic-stricken livestock scurried and stampeded over the prairie away from the hill. The superstitious saw and heard the well and ran in the opposite direction, some of them shouting that the world was coming to an end. Passengers on the Sabine & East Texas train saw the well and were curious but disappointed as the train kept moving.

By early afternoon hundreds were gathered around the hill. They were coming from Beaumont and Port Arthur and every village and hamlet in the county. Perry McFaddin, one of the landowners of the well site, began to recruit workers from the spectators to help dig a ditch around the site, keep people back, and prevent smoking. The Hamills warned of the danger of fire, which could turn the well into a holocaust.

At the moment few realized they were watching an event far more important to the progress of civilization than most of the wars of the world combined. Nowhere else on earth had such a sight ever been seen before except in Russia.

Carrie Lucas had followed her excited husband up the road to the hill. There she joined him in his jubilation. When they were back home the Captain sent a telegram to John Galey, urging him to rush to Beaumont and see the geyser of oil.

By early afternoon Beaumont was teeming with excitement. Everywhere men were gathered in small groups talking about the hill and how they were going to get there. Many farmers and businessmen who were struggling for a living would be wealthy within a few days. They were the millionaires-to-be that Pattillo Higgins had talked about while they scorned and, later, pitied him. Now they realized that his predictions had come to pass. It was Captain George O'Brien, who, after listening to reports and discussing them on the post office corner, turned to the group there and said slowly, but seriously, "Pattillo Higgins told all of us this would happen. I am ready to take my hat off to him."

The others agreed. Beaumont was proud, at last, of this native son whose interest had never flagged, and whose determination always matched the resistance to his efforts.

Captain Lucas was the man of the hour. His struggles and disappointments had become street gossip. Some who had virtually invited him out of their offices when he sought local capital now claimed his friendship. No longer was he the silent stranger the newspapers had warned against leasing land to a few weeks back, while the chamber of commerce had appointed a committee to help J. A. Paulhamus get leases. The newspapers had said editorially, "The leases are not for bona-fide development, but for the Standard Oil Company—to serve its own purposes—and retard development."

Those days were all over. Captain Lucas had succeeded where others had failed. He was a genius, a gentleman, a developer and a godsend to this community. Even if it was Standard that was backing him, what of it? Today Beaumont recognized a man most of its citizens had ignored and avoided for a year and a half.

IV

It was a cold and weary Pattillo Higgins who heard the news of the geyser of oil from Jim Collier. Higgins was undemonstrative, but he was more excited than he let Jim Collier think he was.

Riding down Pearl Street toward his home, he was hailed by the little knots of men gathered on every corner. They spoke to him with a respect that approached reverence. Several of his loyal friends shouted, "They can call you 'Millionaire' now without laughing, Bud!"

That night Pattillo Higgins looked over a proposed plan for the Higgins Oil Company. He had listed the men he would ask to go into the venture. His thirty-three-acre tract, which he bought with the settlement for his undivided interest in the Gladys City company years before, was 200 feet north of the Lucas well. His company would not be a promotion. The associates he had in mind were men who had the cash that he did not have to put in for operations. It would mean letting his partners have a majority of the stock, but it would be a company that would be solid and a credit to Beaumont. He would sell his thirty-three acres to this company for $5000 and take a good block of the stock for himself.

Pattillo Higgins considered another plan in his office that night. It was a plan to file suit against both Captain Anthony F. Lucas and his old friend, George Washington Carroll. He didn't like it and he hoped something would happen in the next few days to make it unnecessary. But he was aware of being left out of the new Lucas-Gladys City deal and did not intend to stay in the dark much longer. His former associates, who had neither consulted with nor informed him of the new arrangements, would either give him an explanation or the courts would provide one.

V

The rest of the world was not prepared for the news that was now flowing out of Beaumont in volumes equal to the oil from the spouter on the hill. The first flash went out about one o'clock, based on Charley Ingals' eyewitness account. Later there was confirmation from others, including farmers near the site, who were called by reporters. Finally the newsmen went to the well to see for themselves.

Long-distance telephone calls from Beaumont swamped the meager switchboard facilities. The telegraph offices were overtaxed.

The result was that the evening trains brought the greatest off-loading of passengers in the little town's history. It was the vanguard of an invasion force that would continue to grow by the hour.

Beaumonters, long hungry for excitement and now almost satiated with it in a matter of hours, made the Crosby House their gathering point. It was across the street from the railway station where the new arrivals could be met and greeted. Late into the night there was a hubbub and an activity which was the inauguration of an atmosphere that would grow into a crescendo of shouts and bids and chaotic confusion as the days and nights passed.

Every saloon in town kept its doors open after hours. Several, including the Crosby bar, didn't close. They could have thrown away their keys, because from this night forward they wouldn't need them.

By morning the details of the Lucas well were being read in newspapers around the world. As if the giant vacuum had increased its range, the railroads of the nation became arteries of activity pointing toward Beaumont. Large newspapers ordered staff members to go immediately to see and report back the facts on this wonder well. Its appeal was greater than that of the California gold rush or the Klondike. It had human interest and it portended industrial potentialities of unlimited scope. The Beaumont newsmen had performed nobly in telling the first news of the incident. And they had done so without resorting to exaggeration. Their early dispatches said the well was producing 30,000 barrels. There would be lower estimates later, but even that was less than a third of the 100,000 barrels a day it was actually flowing.

It was some time after midnight when a special train arrived from Galveston and Houston bringing, among others, David R. Beatty, who would later become one of the most fabulous characters in the history of early Texas oil development.

VI

Captain Lucas was at the well before daylight, and so was a reporter from the *Journal.* Asked for an estimate of the flow, Lucas said 6,000 barrels a day. He had never heard of a larger well in America. Then he pointed to the diminished flow, indicated by the oil now spouting only slightly over the top of the derrick, and expressed the hope that the well might soon be controlled.

As dawn was breaking the Captain told Al Hamill that Mrs. Lucas had insisted that he come home for breakfast. None of the crew had been able to leave the well since it broke loose. The invitation was accepted after Curt assured Al that the situation was well in hand.

Mrs. Lucas was serving the coffee as the Captain showed Al two giant cabbages he had received the evening before.

"They are from an Italian friend of mine who sold a lease for $5,000 yesterday and gives me credit for making him rich," Lucas laughed. "He has a bad conscience. Two days ago I met him downtown. He told me that if I struck oil it would make him rich. I agreed, and told him I had left my purse at home and would like to borrow two dollars. He refused. So now he feels bad about that and happy over his fortune, so he sent me the cabbages."

At this point the Captain heard a carriage pull up in the front yard and looked out the window. Getting out were Joseph S. Cullinan and two other men. Cullinan was the most important oil man in Texas. A former Standard man, he had gone to Corsicana upon the invitation of the city officials who were anxious to get an oil man to develop the industry. After failing to get backing elsewhere he had called on Payne and Folger, two old Standard associates, who had agreed to back him. The assumption, natural enough, was that Cullinan was Standard-controlled.

In company with Cullinan was T. J. Wood, another of the state's leading oil magnates, and Samuel M. (Golden Rule) Jones, the former Socialist mayor of Toledo who had opposed and defeated both the Republicans and Democrats.

Ostensibly the visit was for Cullinan to offer his congratulations to the Captain and to bring a personal message from Calvin Payne.

"I talked with Mr. Payne last night after hearing about the well," Cullinan said, "and he asked me to extend his congratulations. To use his own words, 'you certainly showed us.' "

Cullinan asked what depth the oil was flowing from. Captain Lucas thought a few seconds before answering. Then he said 1,160 feet. Al Hamill was not certain whether the Captain was deliberately misleading the Standard man, whether be actually believed that, or whether he had merely made a mistake in his almost uncontrolled excitement over success. Hamill knew the oil was flowing from the bottom of fifty-one joints of twenty-foot pipe and that the oil sand could be no deeper than 1,020 feet, but he kept his silence. Whether it was intentional or not, Lucas' error in the total depth he gave Cullinan was the first misrepresentation of a report on a well in the Gulf Coast—and it lived throughout the years to be emblazoned forty years later on the monument located on the sight of the Lucas well.

Cullinan and his friends had breakfast at Carrie Lucas' insistence. When the meal was over, the party rode out to the well. As they approached the derrick the Captain was surprised to see that the oil flow was apparently stronger, instead of continuing to diminish as he had anticipated it would do.

Peck Byrd explained the situation to the Captain.

"She was getting weaker and weaker for awhile, Captain," Peck said. "Then I'll be damned if she didn't stop altogether for almost a minute. I figured the show was over and was walking up to kiss her good-bye when the old fool blasted out again like the *Maine* blowing up. Then a solid stream of oil started up and has been shooting stronger and higher than ever before."

Cullinan looked at the well with deep admiration. He said it was the most magnificent thing he had ever seen. Lucas asked his advice about capping it and Cullinan said he would not give such a suggestion if he had one.

"It's too beautiful to stop, Captain," he said good-naturedly. "Let it flow like the Russian wells at Groznyi and Baku."

VII

Captain Lucas and his family were sitting down to Sunday dinner when the colored maid screamed and came running out of the kitchen.

"Mistah Captain! Mistah Captain!" she shouted, "the oil well is on fire!"

The Lucas family rushed to the south window of the living room overlooking the hill. A great mushroom of billowing smoke was rising, apparently from the well. Anthony Lucas looked and dropped to his knees for a moment of fervent prayer. Rising quickly, he dashed out the door to his horse and rode to the field. As he got closer he could see that it was not the well, but waste oil, that was burning. Several hundred spectators were fighting the flames away from the well. The Captain joined them. Curt Hamill had started fighting the fire with his jacket. Then an unidentified man who was crossing the hill in a wagon with his family jumped out with a blanket and started swamping the flames, and horsemen, using their saddle blankets, joined in.

Black smoke rose high in the clouds and swept over Port Arthur ten miles to the south. Beaumonters could see the great column of smoke and flames and feared the worst.

The blaze was under control in a short time, but not before it taught Lucas and the Hamills a lesson. From now on there would be no smoking. The fire had started from a discarded cigar. Thereafter no one was permitted within fifty feet of the spouter.

VIII

John H. Galey barely had a chance to report on his Beaumont trip to Jim Guffey back in Pittsburgh when the wonderful news of the geyser of oil reached the offices of Guffey and Galey. Guffey hugged the lucky old oil hound, as he called Galey, and danced him around the office.

"Now, get yourself back to Beaumont and let me hear from you exactly what it is," Guffey said.

"But, Jim, aren't you coming with me? This thing sounds big enough for both of us," Galey rejoined.

"No, John, no," was Guffey's reply. "If it is what it sounds like, those Mellon brothers are going to get a chance to finance an oil company that will make old John D. Rockefeller sick. Now, hurry."

All the way from Pittsburgh to Beaumont the old wildcatter had stuck his head out the train window at every station, large or small, to buy the local newspapers and keep up with the progress of the big well. When he got to Beaumont he was met by the Captain and Jim Hamill. He insisted on getting a drink to celebrate. The Captain said he didn't drink. Then he offered to buy him the biggest cigar in town. No thanks, the Captain didn't smoke.

"Well, I'll be damned," Galey said.

"And watch your language, John," Jim Hamill admonished. "The Captain doesn't swear, either."

"I guess I can forgive him for his pious character, since he can damn sure find oil," Galey, himself a teetotaler who was quiet, modest and deeply serious, said, with a rare resort to profanity.

When Mike Welker, the ace reporter for the *Enterprise,* asked for an interview at the well, Galey strenuously objected. His resistance worn down, however, he said that the well would mark the beginning of the liquid fuel age.

"We must demonstrate the permanency of supply and accumulate stocks, however, to be able to contract with fuel users for fifteen or twenty years before we can expect them to change their boilers over from coal to oil," be said. "This will mean the investment of millions of dollars. It will mean that this well, the most wonderful thing I have ever seen in my life, must prove itself. Right now our problem is to get the flow under control. This waste can't go on."

Galey told the press that he believed the flow was coming from an oil pool below the apex of the hill.

After talking with the Hamills, Galey and the Captain went to see Caroline Lucas, who had prepared dinner. Galey told the proud woman that he gave her credit for the well.

"You know," he said, "I have no doubt that if it hadn't been for your determination, the Captain would have given up before he came to see me, and several times afterwards."

The Captain agreed.

IX

The Hamills met with Lucas and Galey at the Crosby House the night of January 14th to discuss harnessing the well.

Lucas presented a sheaf of telegrams and letters he had received offering suggestions for doing the job. It had been reported that Lucas was offering $10,000 to anyone who could control the well. The story was pure fiction, but Lucas had many responses. Fees asked ranged as high as $100,000. Some replies were from crackpots, but others were genuine.

Jim Hamill said that he and his brothers had an idea for trying to stop the flow and that since they had brought the well in they would like to have a chance to complete the job.

Galey agreed that they were entitled to the chance. Their plan was outlined and approved. The necessary equipment was ordered from Corsicana that night.

The Hamills realized they were taking on a job which involved a serious risk to their lives, as well as their reputations. They were not fools. They didn't cherish a flirtation with death. They were simply challenged by a problem that had never been encountered before. Along with other famous drilling teams like the Sharp brothers and the Sturm brothers, they were pioneers in oilfield ingenuity.

One of the first things they did was to work out a set of signals by which they could communicate with one another in the midst of the well's deafening roar. They also realized that they would have to have protection from the oil and the noxious gas. Their outfit consisted of goggles, gauze shields for their noses, and plaster over their ears.

The Hamills built a carriage inside the derrick. This was composed of two light railroad irons attached to the first girt above the floor. Then they bolted two-by-eight-inch plank supports to six-by-four-inch boards to constitute a frame. Off to the side of the well the gate valve was assembled with an eight-inch collar and an eight-by-six-inch swedge nipple with a six-inch tee. There was another nipple for the upright gate to be used for release. When everything was in readiness, the apparatus was to be launched against the column of oil. This was the critical part of the operation.

A gate valve was placed over the casing to increase the diameter of the flow, leaving an area of "play" around the six-inch pipe. The carriage was then successfully drawn over the well by block and tackle in spite of the violent impact of the oil column. The assembly was drawn down by turning long screw bolts until the short nipple with an eight-inch tee could be attached. This done, and the oil freely flowing through the vertical pipe, the gate was gradually closed, diverting the stream into the horizontal pipe. This gave the crew a chance to work around the well, within the derrick, and place foundations for anchorage to hold down both the apparatus and the casings. Old rope was calked into the larger pipe around the six-inch and secured with heavy wrought-iron clamps, tightened with set screws to prevent the six-inch pipe from moving upward. Finally, the gate valve on the horizontal pipe was gradually closed and the flow of oil was completely shut off. It was a masterful operation and a demonstration of intelligence and ingenuity.

A large mound of sand was thrown up over the wellhead assembly as a precaution against the well being destroyed by fire.

When the operation was completed, the hundreds of people standing around the well, watching what was probably the construction and operation of the first oilfield "Christmas tree," as the wellhead valve assembly for controlling flow and pressure was called, let up a loud roar of applause. The weary and oil-saturated Hamills still had enough strength and sense of humor left to line up and bow to their audience. Today the American oil industry is full of men like the Hamill crew. In those days such outfits were scarce. Their pioneering on Spindletop Hill, aided by the genius of Captain Anthony Lucas, was one of the greatest contributions to the industry that was born there.

Pattillo Higgins didn't originate the name Spindletop and he didn't like it much. It was the name given to a subdivision that was in proximity to and in competition with his Gladys City. But when he told reporters where he would stake his first well, he unintentionally gave the field the name that it would live with from that day forward.

Higgins has always referred to the field as the Beaumont oil field, in honor of his home town. Captain Lucas, out of appreciation for the cooperation given him by Carroll and O'Brien, preferred and used Gladys City field. The newspapers ruled out Big Hill when it was realized that three other coastal mounds bore the same name, one of them in Jefferson County. Higgins Hill was once suggested, but was condemned by Higgins himself.

After Pattillo Higgins said he was going to drill in Spindletop Heights, that was it. In a very few weeks Heights was dropped.

The field became Spindletop, a name that would go down in history as the site of the greatest oil wells of all time and a living symbol of the oil industry.

It was a few days before the well was capped that the word "gusher" came into use. Up until that time this well, the first of its kind ever seen by anyone outside of Russia, was referred to as a “spouter” or “geyser of oil.”

A roustabout working in Perry McFaddin’s crew building the levees turned to one of the reporters and simply said, “Mister, that’s some gusher, ain’t it?” From that day on the well was referred to as the Lucas gusher and the dictionaries soon had a new application for the word.

CHAPTER FIVE

Birth of a Boom Town

The Lucas gusher aroused the nation for nine days until it was controlled. A sprinkling of oil leaders from all over the country headed for Beaumont, and throngs of people flooded into the city from Texas and Louisiana. There was much talk but little action.

A flurry of sensational deals was recorded soon after the well came in, but a number of factors held off an immediate boom. For instance, it seemed significant that Standard Oil officials had swooped down on Beaumont almost immediately, but had withdrawn without entering the field. Even John Galey had expressed surprise at the early excitement, stating that it was unjustified because the product was not illuminating oil. Naturally enough, Galey didn't want too much activity at that point. Equipment and transportation were woefully short. Wary property owners took their land off the market or placed their prices so high that no one would consider them.

But probably the most widely circulated condemnation of all was contained in an interview given by E. Steiner, a West Virginia oil man. The statement, first made to the press in New Orleans, gained wide circulation over the country, and only the Beaumont newspapers took the time to answer it. Steiner said that the Beaumont field was a colossal accident, that the gusher was a crevice well, and that no other wells were likely to be found in the area. Furthermore, he said the oil was not marketable, and that the cost of drilling wells, about $5,000 apiece, was exorbitant.

During all of this time, however, Beaumont wasn't exactly being deserted. Hundreds of people were making their way there every day. They were mostly the curious and the cautious. But there were some who did more than look and belittle.

Pattillo Higgins organized his company almost immediately. The best drilling contractors from Corsicana were being brought in. Of the outsiders, D. R. Beatty and the Heywood brothers were optimists in action. They disregarded the cautions and took a gamble while the odds were still long. They, along with Higgins, lost no time in assembling men, materials and money. Shortly after the gusher was capped Guffey and Galey had started two new wells. Beatty and the Heywood brothers were quick to acquire leases and start digging.

It was Beatty who was to have the honor of actually opening the eyes of the world to the real meaning of Spindletop. He was a short, slender, energetic man in his early forties, accustomed to long hours of work. He was a Galveston railroad and real-estate promoter who had spent enough time in Corsicana to get oil in his veins and make valuable friendships with Texans in the industry. Beatty lost most of his possessions in the great Galveston hurricane which occurred four months before Spindletop was discovered. Since then he had been working his usual long hours on relief and rehabilitation committees in the devastated city.

On the afternoon of January 10th he was in the office of the *Galveston News* with a committee report when the telegraph operator rushed a dispatch to the editor. The message told of the geyser of oil four miles south of Beaumont which was flowing an estimated 30,000 barrels of oil daily. Beatty was as excited as the editor over the news. When a special car left the island that night with newspapermen and others interested, Beatty was aboard. The banks were closed when the news came in and he didn't take time to get more cash than the $20 he had in his pockets.

Early the next morning he was at the well watching the phenomenal flow of oil sweep the skies and come raining down over the countryside. His imagination was fired, but he felt helpless with only a handful of money. He overheard Lige Adams say that he lived only a half-mile north of the well on a farm. Beatty didn't want to make Adams an offer there because he knew others might overhear and outbid him. He waited until the young man left, and then followed him home.

In the Adams home be found a little family that had moved to Spindletop Heights only a few months previously when Lige had been fired from his job as a millwright in Port Arthur. He met Mrs. Adams and their little daughter. Lige had paid $200 for ten acres and was going to try farming. Right now he was out of money and needed some kind of work to pull him through the winter.

Beatty told him that he would like to lease his land, but didn't have but a little more than $10 with him. Lige said he wasn't interested in a bonus as much as he was in a well.

"Mr. Adams, I will get a well drilled here immediately if you will give me a lease," Beatty said. "In fact, I'll agree to start operations within thirty days. And I'll give you one-eighth of the oil."

"That's a deal," Adams said, "on one other condition. Your crew will need a cook and I need a job. Sign me on as cook when you start and you can have the lease."

Adams refused the $10 offered him, but Beatty turned to the little girl and gave her the money for a new dress. He returned to Galveston, and obtained half of the backing he needed. He went to Corsicana and got the rest of it, plus one of the most famous and colorful drilling teams in the state, the Sturm brothers. The big job was getting the equipment to Beaumont by the deadline. On the last day Bill and Jim Sturm managed to get the derrick and rig ready to go. It was a fight, because they heard that Adams already had a much better offer waiting if the thirty-day requirement were not fulfilled.

Actual drilling began before the deadline, and after more than a month's operation, an hour before daylight on March 26th, Jim Sturm was blasted off the derrick floor and knocked out by a terrific charge of gas. Lige Adams was overcome by the fumes that drifted into the cooking shed. Both of the men were revived in time to see the column of oil start up and over the derrick for a producer almost as good as the Lucas gusher.

The calumniators were left choking on their words and there were no more conservatives from that moment on.

II

The happiest man in the world besides D. R. Beatty that day was W. Scott Heywood. Spindletop, which was the cradle of the modern oil industry, would produce hundreds of fabulous characters, but few more so than Scott Heywood.

One of four famous Heywood brothers of vaudeville and music, Scott was an adventurer. When the Klondike opened, he left the entertainment business to seek a fortune. With a little stake from that he went to California and invested in oil. There he learned something of the business and made a little more money.

On the morning of January 11th Scott Heywood was having breakfast in a café in San Francisco when he learned of the Lucas gusher. The news story popped out at him and he made up his mind immediately that this was the greatest opportunity on earth for a man who would act fast. He took time to send a telegram to his brother Dewey in Chicago to join him in Beaumont, but he didn't check out of his hotel or pack a trunk. The first train for Beaumont was leaving in thirty minutes and he was determined to be on it. Twenty-four hours might be the difference between a fortune and a failure.

It was on the day and almost the hour that the Hamills were capping the Lucas well that Scott Heywood arrived in Beaumont. After checking into the Crosby, he hired one of the old surreys to take him to the field. There he found the well almost deserted, except for a large crew that was cleaning up around it. The workman he approached would not let him through the fence to see the well, but did call Elmer Dobbins, who identified himself as a driller. Heywood told Dobbins he was an oil man from California who was getting ready to drill on the hill. He wanted to look at the well, and, if Dobbins were a driller, he might have a contract for him. Dobbins broke the rule and Heywood got all of the information he wanted. Dobbins, who had been lured by the bait all drillers snap at—an opportunity to become a contractor—later got the job Heywood promised him.

But Scott Heywood had trouble for a while. He found a fifteen-acre tract owned by Keith and Ward directly north of the well. He would have got it if he had had any money, but he missed out when Beatty gave $5,000 cash and 50 per cent royalty. When, after a few days, Scott heard nothing from his brother Dewey, he became worried. However, Dewey showed up in a week. He had gone to Beaumont, California, when Scott failed to specify Texas in the telegram.

Even then, however, the two didn't have enough money for the lease. They sent a telegram to the other two brothers, Alba and O. W., for help. The money came back with a telegram which indicated their blind faith. It said, "Don't bother about details. You are on the ground. Play ball. Be careful at first base, but play ball."

Now, with enough money to lease another fifteen-acre tract from the Higgins Oil Company, they took an option on the lease. Beatty was trying to tie that up, too, but Scott convinced the Higgins company that it would be to their advantage to have a new operator in the field. Beatty, he said, already had leases, and might not drill as many wells as soon as another operator would.

It was at this point that Captain W. C. Tyrrell came into the picture. Captain Tyrrell was a prosperous businessman with holdings in Iowa, the Dakotas, Minnesota and Texas. He was in Port Arthur inspecting some of his property when the Lucas well broke loose. Knowing little or nothing about the oil business, he kept alert for a good opportunity. Overhearing and observing the Heywood brothers convinced him they were dependable men who knew something about the business. The Captain approached them one night and told them if they should need his financial help, he would talk with them.

The next day they were in his office explaining their problem. They had purchased the Higgins lease with a thirty-day drilling obligation and needed $10,000 cash for equipment and a crew. If more were required, they would furnish it. Tyrrell gave the boys a $1,000 check as earnest money and said he would sleep over it. If he decided to go with them he would give them a check for $9,000 the next morning. If not, they could have the $1,000. The next day Tyrrell gave the check for $9,000 and the first Heywood well was started.

When the Beatty well came in, the Heywoods and Captain Tyrrell celebrated. They had good reason. Their first well was drilling exactly on a line halfway between the Lucas and Beatty gushers. They had nothing else to worry about.

Scott Heywood then returned to California, got southwestern rights on an oil-burning stove and heater, the first of its kind outside of the Pacific coast. When he returned, his well was in and the famous Heywood Brothers Oil Company was formed, with Captain Tyrrell as president.

III

In the meantime Guffey and Galey had brought in two more wells and on April 18th the first Higgins well came in. Six wells had been drilled, every one a gusher.

There were dozens of other success stories going out over the news wires. There was one about a commissary clerk who had recently bought four acres of land with his $60 savings to keep from spending the money imprudently. The boom came and he sold out for $100,000.

A Negro farmer with a small tract of land near the hill had been trying to sell out for $150 for three years. When the Lucas gusher came in he was north of Beaumont visiting relatives with his wife and children. Returning to Beaumont, he was puzzled by the turmoil. As he neared his home, he was met by a man who offered him $20,000 for his farm. The necessary papers were already made out and all he had to do was sign and take the cash. When he reached home, he found another man waiting with $50,000 in cash, but it was too late. The early bird sold to the man waiting at the house making $30,000 in fifteen minutes. The same tract brought $100,000 after the Beatty well came in.

A Mrs. Sullivan became known over the nation as "Mrs. Slop." She had a small pig farm on the hill and made the daily rounds in Beaumont collecting garbage in an old, dilapidated buckboard wagon. She sold a lease on her place for $35,000 one day, and the next day she resumed her garbage collections.

A business failure from Missouri came to Beaumont with $20 and bought a lease on an acre. He sold it the same day for enough to retire on and live comfortably for the rest of his life.

Tragedy and fortune struck one family a simultaneous blow. The head of the family got $50,000 for his small acreage on the bill and immediately went stark mad.

Beatty sold his first well to C. D. Pullen of New York for $1,250,000, with a quarter of a million for his share, and the other million for his associates, all of whom became wealthy as the result of a total investment of less than $10,000. Beatty was an indefatigable worker, who negotiated deals in the millions every day for months. His friends said he aged fifteen years in six months under the stress of hard work and that the average day of a New York broker was a quiet pastoral one compared to his.

It was said that no man ever engaged in business with Higgins, Lucas, the Heywoods, or Beatty who didn't become a millionaire—or at least extremely wealthy. Yet none of these ever entered into the frenzied stock schemes that were to follow. Lucas went so far as to throw two men out of his office when they proposed giving him a million dollars worth of stock in a company for merely using his name. They admitted their land holdings were probably no good, after Lucas pointed out that fact to them, but they said that any one would buy stock in a company named after him and in which he was a director and officer.

IV

Pattillo Higgins filed two important suits in May of 1901. The first was against A. F. Lucas et al. for the one-tenth interest he believed he was entitled to in the Lucas well. In this suit he asked for $4,000,000. One of his contentions was that the first well Lucas drilled could have been brought in, but that it was capped instead.

Later in the month he filed suit against George W. Carroll, contending that Carroll had already made $2,000,000, of which Higgins was entitled to 10 per cent, in accordance with their agreement. He contended that Carroll's deal with Lucas was based on Higgins' prediction that oil would be found in inexhaustible quantities.

There were countersuits and in the end a settlement was made to the satisfaction of everyone. In all of the legal contentions, however, there were no apparent hard feelings between Carroll and Higgins, who remained fast friends throughout. Higgins and Lucas, however, had no further relations, either good or bad.

The Higgins suits did one important thing. They indicated for the first time in dollars the great value of the Lucas discovery. They were highly publicized and people outside Beaumont paid little attention to any of the details except the figures. Carroll, in three months, had made $2,000,000. And Higgins claimed that Lucas owed him $4,000,000 which was only 10 percent of the value of his holdings. These figures were highly exaggerated, of course, but everyone reading about them didn't realize that fact.

Then, shortly after the sixth well came in, some amazing facts were set out in conservative articles in leading manufacturing journals. Statistics are usually cold and uninviting, but the country was fascinated by the picture Spindletop presented.

Half its six wells were capable of flowing more than the 68,000,000 barrels annually, or 185,000 barrels daily, that Russia was producing as the leading oil country of the world. Obviously, as the field progressed, American leadership in petroleum would become more pronounced. This awakened a new national pride which was tonic for the nation. Russia had pioneered the fuel-oil field, particularly by powering steamships with oil from the Baku region. Now America would follow and go beyond that example not only in ships, but in railroads, factories, and the home.

As far as this country was concerned, there was only one oil company, and that was Standard. The others existed by sufferance of Standard. The Rockefeller monopoly had not hurt the general public, but it was a trust, a monopoly and contrary to the principles of independence. Furthermore, at Spindletop it had proved that, as such, it lacked imagination or the will to venture by turning down the prospect on the hill and even failing to get in early after Spindletop's real significance became evident. Those who have nothing want something and will explore, invent, work and gamble to get it. Standard had everything, and there was no incentive to expand unless doing so was a cinch—for Standard.

V

Now the statistics spelled doom for Standard's monopoly. Before Spindletop, Standard directly controlled 48,000,000 of the 58,000,000 barrels of petroleum produced annually in the country, and, by virtue of that fact alone, directed the disposition and price of the other 10,000,000 barrels. The eastern fields of Pennsylvania, West Virginia, Ohio, New York and Indiana accounted for 53,000,000 of America's 58,000,000 barrels of oil. Standard actually produced 22,000,000 barrels of this oil, and purchased 85 per cent of the remainder at a fair average price of $1.13 a barrel. California produced 4,000,000 barrels, and Texas produced another million barrels, mostly at Corsicana. There was a little production in Kansas, Colorado, Kentucky and Wyoming. Outside of Russia, in the remainder of the world, there was oil production in small amounts in the Dutch East Indies, Austria-Hungary, and Romania. That was the world and national oil situation at the end of 1900, ten days before the Lucas gusher.

Now the picture had changed. Not only was America to become the leading oil nation with the first six wells in Spindletop, but it would completely crack the oil monopoly. The Lucas well alone was capable of producing as much oil as 37,000 eastern wells, six times as much oil as California, twice as much as Pennsylvania (the leading oil state), and at least half of the nation's total output. With five additional wells, those figures could be multiplied until Spindletop's dominance became apparent to even the most difficult to convince. Russian oil, 600 miles from tidewater, and with a 46-cent tariff on every barrel, could not compete.

Spindletop could produce more oil in one day than the rest of the fields of the world combined!

These facts were staggering, yet true. And the great natural phenomenon of a mineral, worth millions of dollars, gushing hundreds of feet into the air more freely than the geysers of hot water at Yellowstone, was enough to move a people to action and a feeling of new independence and national strength.

The Beatty well had done the trick. Beaumont became the mecca for every man who yearned for wealth. It was the door opener for a boom where every man had a chance to make millions or go broke. It gave birth to the land of the big rich.

CHAPTER SIX

Pandemonium

There were no strangers. Every man was a boomer. The carnival spirit prevailed. It was like the stock market during a crisis, a battlefield during the attack, and a faro game where a fortune was won or lost on the turn of a card. This was no ghost walk or mere spectacular show. It was real. Deals involving millions of dollars were as common as popcorn sales at a fair.

This was Beaumont, the home of Spindletop, from April, 1901, until no man knew when. The brains and the brawn, the daring and the hopeful, the decent and the depraved, the young and the old, mingled and mixed. They spoke of oil and dollars and land and leases. Most of them had no knowledge of the subject they were discussing, but they were on the ground floor. They were on the spot that the whole world was talking and reading about.

No man was too big or too little. Anyone might have an option or an idea. Wealthy men slept in garrets and panhandled fresh food at nearby truck farms. Street urchins sold whisky flasks of oil for a quarter until the chiselers cut the price to a dime. Men walked around with signs on their hats like giant press cards advertising land deals. Others took corners like newsboys and hawked leases and options. Hack drivers got rich charging $10 to $20 a person for trips to the hill in six-passenger surreys and buses. Even buckboard wagons were pushed into service. The S. P. station and the Crosby House were ringed with buggies, surreys and wagons.

Men pushed and shoved and jostled each other good-naturedly, shouting, "Howdy, Boomer" as they collided. There was a scramble and a rush for space on trains to Houston, Port Arthur and Orange every evening. Hundreds walked the streets when they found no place to sleep. Everywhere there was a sort of insanity.

Every walk of life was represented. Every state and almost every land on the globe had some delegate present. It was a curious, carefree, oil-mad band of fortune hunters. On the registers of Beaumont hotels were senators and governors and cabinet members. There were names that were legendary to the average small-town Texan, names like William Jennings Bryan, George J. Gould, John W. Gates, Andrew Carnegie and the Rockefellers.

II

As the days passed, more thousands poured in. The population rose above 50,000. Houston, eighty-five miles to the west, became the gateway to Beaumont. Six trains daily were scheduled and specials were running frequently. The favorite train was the all-Pullman that left Houston at ten o'clock at night and arrived in Beaumont at six o'clock the next morning. Men would catch early afternoon trains back to Houston in time to return again the same night. They bought thirty-day tickets in order to hold their reservations.

The Crosby House became a center for this madness. It was an old frame building with two great galleries where men gathered day and night. The bar and the café became twenty-four-hour operations along with the remainder of the hotel. It was here that most of the traders chose to assemble. They would stand on tables and chairs and offer to buy or sell leases. One night a man stood on a chair in the center of the lobby waving a hundred $1,000 bills, which he was offering for a single acre in proven territory. The crowd laughed. That was the price a twenty-foot lot would bring next to an oil well.

The brokerage business became a new field of opportunity for the uncapitalized. All it took was shrewdness and energy, and it paid great dividends. The brokers would sell stock, leases, or land, for a commission. Many of them became wealthy without investing a nickel or owning a drop of oil. The map vendors hawked their wares on the streets. They bought rough blueprints of the hill area for a dime and sold them for as much as $3. It was a cinch business. No man could operate without a map, and the maps didn't last long with the usage they were getting. Hundreds of thousands of them were sold.

Land and leases were sold without abstracts or titles, and resold over and over on the same basis. They were sold solely on the word of the seller, backed by a small-scale map, where a slight error could mislead a buyer by several thousands of feet. There was seldom any effort at deception. The seller was usually selling his lease or property on the same basis that he had bought it, sight unseen. All deals were strictly cash. There were no time payments. If a man's credit was beyond question his check or draft would be honored. Otherwise it was greenbacks all the way.

Money was a cheap commodity. It came into town in carloads from all over the nation to pay for stock. Silver dollars were stacked like cordwood in the banks and railroad stations. Men would come in and scoop it up in shovels and count it in back rooms. Trading, all transacted in cash, was done with notes of large denominations. It was not unusual to see a trader throw a five-dollar bill away when it got mixed up in his $100, $1,000 and $5,000 notes.

There was no tie that bound. Old Jonas, the candy man who had held forth in the Crosby lobby for years, had to give way to progress and madness. The flower and rose garden around the Crosby was cut up into six-foot squares that were rented for $100 a month each for office spaces, with simple two-by-fours for partitions between them. Million-dollar corporations took them over. Oil companies moved into every barn and abandoned shack in town and painted them red so the traders would know they were business offices. Packing crates were fashioned into desks and set up on the curbings. Business houses that were not highly profitable gave way to new tenants. Even corners in saloons were rented out to oil corporations and promoters.

III

Crockett Street moved west and got rough. It became Deep Crockett, the haven of the demimonde, and the most notorious red-light district in the western hemisphere, if not the world. It was a street of assignation, with brothels over every saloon, dance hall and gambling house. One vaudeville house advertised its cribs for prostitutes off the balcony. Its risqué and vulgar acts served as teasers for those who needed them. The girls would do the rest.

The town's saloons did a thriving business. The Crosby bar was six and eight deep all day and all night. The others were as busy, although the class of trade was seldom as high. Mosso, a saloon keeper on Highland Avenue, made himself something of a local saint when he cleared the place every Sabbath morning to let a Sunday school class hold meetings on its sawdust floors. As the meeting ended the front of the place was always crowded with thirsty boomers who rushed in as the last child left. Every saloon keeper in town gladly paid a $50 fine each Monday morning for staying open on Sunday. Beaumont was drunk dry only once, and that was the Saturday after the Lucas well came in. After that half the whisky sold in Texas was consumed in Beaumont.

Gambling halls were over every saloon with dice, poker and faro tables running wide open. The small law-enforcement agency was unable to cope with the situation and for months did not even try.

George Washington Carroll said many times that he would rather have lived forever without the wealth that came to him from oil than to see Beaumont become a city of iniquity. The men of Beaumont would not permit their wives or daughters to go into town without adequate escort. Many of them sent their families away and rented the spare rooms to the homeless. There were a few female clerks and stenographers and some woman lease promoters. There were hundreds of men for every woman in the daily turmoil of the streets. But most men were hellbent for fortune and had little time to think of companionship.

Probably the most annoyed of all Beaumont's citizens were its bankers. They kept their doors open for twelve and sixteen hours a day, turning away thousands nightly even then. They seldom went out for a meal, and their work never ended. Yet what they did was done for practically nothing. There was no way to make a profit on deposits without loans, and no one wanted to borrow money at first. In spite of this a half-dozen new banks opened in one year.

Men walked the streets or slept in the sawdust piles at the mills because they could find no other accommodations. Every one of the squalid little hotels was filled to capacity. No man had a room alone. Every hotel room had from four to twenty cots, and the halls and lobbies were lined with cots or bare mattresses. Men slept on pool tables, in barber chairs, on roof tops, in pup tents, pyramidals, wall tents, and in lean-to shacks made of flimsy lumber. They slept on porches, in store windows, and wherever they could find a place to lie down.

There might have been a dozen baths in Beaumont's hotels, but no one recalls them. Men who had been reared in fastidious surroundings went for weeks without bathing rather than use the filthy tubs in barber shops.

Beaumont's cistern water was not potable. Doctors warned the thirsty to drink whisky or boiled water. This led to a new business. On street corners vendors were selling boiled water out of wash tubs for a nickel a drink and gallon jugs for $1. But even this didn't solve the problem. Soon most of the visitors and natives were stricken with a particularly vexatious form of diarrhea that gained recognition the world over as "the Beaumonts." This, naturally, led to other problems. The sanitary facilities available were almost medieval. Behind the Crosby were a half-dozen two-seaters before which lines of as many as twenty-five to fifty were standing constantly. Many a small boy made as much as $10 a day lining up and selling his place to perturbed customers as they approached the door that led to the throne of relief.

Queues were everywhere. In front of the post office, banks, the express office and cafés. The cafés were filled to capacity every hour around the clock, and still all could not be fed. The prices were low but the waiters expected big tips and when they didn't get them, the items on the menu became scarce. The low tippers became marked men. A party of four might pay $2 for four full-course dinners, but if they tipped less than $5 they were thereafter ignored. Many families opened soup kitchens on their porches.

Madame LaMonte established herself in the Cordova Hotel, a local bandbox, and began to foretell to the gullible, at $10 a prophecy, where to buy and when to sell. Within a month she tried to buy the hotel and the block it stood on.

When her predictions started to turn sour, however, she departed with two valises of cash.

IV

The stories that were going out of Beaumont by mail and wire to the newspapers of the world were fairly accurate. But those that were being sent out of Dallas, Austin and San Antonio by writers who had never seen the place were lurid and fantastic. They were responsible for many of the millions of dollars invested by those who knew nothing of the true situation. The larger newspapers sent their own correspondents and, for the most part, got excellent, accurate coverage. The truth was enough to stir people, but the pipe dreams led to confusion.

Beaumont newspapers almost stopped once, however, due to the boom. Through a series of trades one night in a saloon, a Beaumont printer pyramided his weekly pay check into $30,000. He got every printer in town drunk and the newspapers virtually stopped. They advertised for out-of-town printers, but as they arrived in town, they were met by the local craftsmen and invited to the party. It took two weeks to spend the $30,000, after which everyone returned to his type case and press. The local newspaper situation revived faster than its printers did from their hangovers and the wrath of their women.

Spindletop was all things to all men. The Fords, Oldses, Packards, Duryeas, Hayneses and even the Wrights saw in it the answer to their greatest problem. President McKinley and Teddy Roosevelt saw it as the dawn of a new age for America based on a limitless source of energy. Railroads and steamship operators looked upon it as opening new opportunities in trade by drastically reducing the cost and increasing the comfort of transportation. John W. Gates said that the discovery, coupled with automotive advancements, would bring all Americans together as neighbors through a system of good roads. Only the coal barons and Standard Oil magnates looked upon it with misgivings. They saw their monopolies threatened.

V

As the weeks rolled by the swindlers rolled in. The fake stock company became the bane of Beaumont's existence. Companies were formed on nothing more than a lease on a quarter of an acre of land somewhere in Texas. Million-dollar corporations became the order of the day. Four such corporations were formed on one quarter-acre tract with a single well on the hill. The pattern was for some man without a cent to organize a million-dollar corporation, sell stock, and set himself, his relatives and friends up in jobs with fabulous salaries. They took money from the poor, the feeble, and the lame with impunity. Some investors bought land which, when investigated, proved to be far out in the Gulf.

Within a year after the field was discovered there were more than 500 Texas corporations doing oil business in Beaumont. Hundreds of others were chartered in other states.

Most of those were companies headed by men with no other intention except bilking the public. The real oil men would have nothing to do with them. Men like Higgins, Heywood, Cullinan, Lucas and the others did not put their stock on the market. They constantly urged the public to beware of stock promotions. The heads of the promotional companies knew nothing about the oil business. They had no idea of its possibilities and cared less. They were in the money racket. They knew only that men bored holes in the ground, got oil in great quantities, and that it was supposed to represent wealth. They didn't know and didn't tell their shareholders that there was no market for the oil or that the price was dropping lower every day.

Lithographing companies in Houston, New Orleans and Galveston were working twenty-four hours a day printing stock certificates, and still could not keep up with the orders. Men were paid fancy salaries to do nothing but sign the certificates after filling them out. Some of these certificate men worked for a half-dozen companies, getting paid on the basis of the amount of stock they signed. Many of them received executive titles, such as secretary, treasurer or vice-president.

The newspapers of the nation were flooded with full-page advertisements of "gilt-edge" oil stocks. *Boyce's Monthly Magazine* gave away a share of stock in some hopeless company with every subscription, promising wealth for nothing.

Probably the most ludicrous promotion of all was one by a group of Texans. They advertised young George Fenley of Uvalde as the boy with the X-ray eyes who could see through the strata of the earth and find oil. Incredible as it seems, thousands of shares of stock were sold in the company promoting Fenley. Even the most respected of the news services was sucked in when the company actually found oil at 1100 feet where Fenley had "seen" it. The story neglected to tell that it was at that depth that almost everyone else found oil, and that the Fenley location was surrounded by existing producers.

One of the most successful companies was headed by Colonel E. M. House of Austin, later adviser to President Wilson, and a group of northern capitalists. They purchased the streets and alleys from the Gladys City company for $90,000. That gave them a perfect gridiron of two-thirds of the hill. The effect was that the company did not have to drill to prove its acreage. Anywhere anyone else drilled would do that. There were few smarter ideas ever conceived. The company was capitalized for $1,000,000 and the stock was sold out in less than thirty-six hours. The sale of dedicated streets and alleys finally led to legal pyrotechnics, but not before it provided a fat dividend for the Gladys City stockholders and added a fascinating chapter to the crazy quiltwork of the Spindletop picture.

The hectic speculations of this period are typified by the experience of a railroad brakeman who came to town early, paid $1 for a lease on a quarter of an acre, organized a multimillion dollar corporation, and put himself on a $10,000-a-month sinecure. Or by that of a reporter for the *St. Louis Post-Dispatch,* who stepped off the train and was met by a man who offered him a lease in the Bullock survey for $1,000. Knowing nothing of the land, the reporter hesitated. Another St. Louis man behind him bought the lease. The next day the two met on the street and the reporter asked the purchaser if he considered his action wise. His fellow townsman replied that he certainly did, because he had sold the lease two hours later for $5,000. He said he was not wise for selling so soon, however, because he had seen the lease change hands again within a matter of hours for $20,000.

Every conceivable type of stock company was being formed. Some of them were legitimate, but they were in the minority. A group of Beaumont and New York women organized the Young Ladies Oil Company and threatened to build one of the greatest organizations in the field by their aggressiveness. They actually did go farther than most others and very little was lost by the stockholders.

There was a Lucky Dime Company, organized by a group of Galveston men who sold stock for 10 cents a share. Within a few days there was a One-Penny Oil Company selling its stock for a cent a share and bringing down the wrath of the oil men who saw in this an unholy method of extracting pennies from the children and the childish.

Order came out of chaos to some extent when Sam Park and others organized the Beaumont Oil Exchange. There, at least, those who wanted to have protection from the swindlers could get it. The exchange set up offices in an old store building at Orleans and Laurel Streets and announced it was open for one hundred members. Some of those who hadn't been wealthy long enough to forget the value of a dollar objected to the $3 monthly dues. Park told them he preferred more active men, anyway, and took in others. When the conservative old Beaumonters, including many who had ignored Pattillo Higgins years before, saw the exchange was going to succeed without them, they decided to come in, but it was too late. All of the seats were sold. Pattillo Higgins was elected an honorary member in "recognition of his great service to his native city by locating the enormous wealth under its surface." The exchange lasted only a year, but it inspired oil exchanges in Houston and also New Orleans.

VI

Excursion trains were coming into Beaumont in an endless chain. One Sunday in May more than 15,000 poured off of trains and traipsed through mud, gumbo and oil. There were men, women and children in their best clothes. In their excitement they were oblivious to the grave danger they faced. At times rocks and shale rained down around them like flak from antiaircraft weapons. There were times when the mere striking of a match could have engulfed the entire mob in flames. As it was, some passed out from the gas fumes, but the others paid little attention to that in their enthusiasm for the phenomenal display they were viewing first hand and which had been built up by publicity, full-page advertisements, brochures, circular letters and word-of-mouth salesmanship. When the excursionists boarded the train to return home they were in the hands of professional stock salesmen. Their only question was: How fast can I get rich? When things didn't pan out as they expected, they called the great oil field "Swindletop."

The excursions, from the East particularly, were sheer promotions organized by outfits like the King-Crowther excursion company. The ride didn't cost much, as the stock companies paid most of that. Many stock companies sold out completely with a single excursion.

In spite of the fact that every man in Beaumont with anything to rent, sell, or lease was getting richer by the day, the home-towners grew weary of the boom long before it was over. When the rains came and swamped the streets with mud, making it necessary to cross them with rowboats on occasion, there was some hope that the end was in sight. But nothing stopped the mad pace. Wagons and horses were almost lost in the mud. On some occasions locomotives would tie onto vehicles to extricate them while men sat around betting on whether the wagon would come out whole or in half. Men, delirious with the desire to get rich, waded waist deep in the bog. When it was too muddy to ride to the field by horse or horse-drawn vehicle, men actually walked the four miles through mud and mire. Al Hamill frequently rode a horse from the hill to George Carroll's home on the edge of town. Then he walked the rest of way on boardwalks. The last mile was too tough for horses on the mud streets.

VII

Beaumont was an amazing place until the day the boom broke. Robert E. Lee, the barber, had twenty chairs in his shop across from the post office. They were never empty. When the shop doors were opened at seven o'clock every morning seventy-five to one hundred men were clamoring to get in. Barbers made $100 a week in commissions and virtually doubled that in tips. Lee had to keep change for $1,000 bills, which he frequently got. Men would pay to spend the night in his barber chairs and would padlock suitcases to their legs. The suitcases frequently contained as much as $100,000 in cash.

One day D. P. Wheat, Beaumont's rotund mayor, who usually sported a top hat, cane, gloves, ascot tie and a large gold watch fob, called a meeting of the citizens. Something, he said, had to be done for the visitors. Before the meeting was over, the old auditorium was turned into a hall of cots where from 200 to 300 could sleep at one time in six-hour shifts. And the ladies of the Christian Church set up a coffee and sandwich bar in the old post office building. The W.C.T.U., horrified by the doctors who warned people to drink whisky in preference to Beaumont cistern water, established free watering corners, providing boiled water for those who preferred it to hard liquor.

Even the errors at Beaumont were fabulous. One company, by mistake, sold a million dollars worth of stock based on a lease which was found not to exist. No one got his money back when the company failed. Another time a promoter organized a company and sold every share of stock in it before he discovered that the land he had was worth twice as much as the company was capitalized for. His stockholders took over the company and kicked him out, presumably for using bad judgment. One day Jim Hogg picked up a sulphur pyrite blown out of one of his wells, facetiously announced that it was gold, and the next day it was all Beaumont could do to keep from being invaded by a gold rush in addition to all its other troubles. The story got so good that Hogg, momentarily taken in by his own doings, seriously considered organizing a gold-mining company.

The native Beaumonters always did things in the grand manner. When the new Kyle Opera house, one of the finest in the entire South, was opened, Beaumont's new rich went upstage. The men would come in from the field covered with mud and oil and change into white tie, high hat, and tails for an evening at the opera.

It was shortly after the discovery well came in that the city council passed an ordinance against drilling inside the city limits. This ordinance kept many Beaumont small homeowners from getting rich quick. Within weeks every acre of land within a thirty-mile radius of the hill was under lease or had been sold. Farmers who were not stubborn or stupid made more money in one deal than their farms could be expected to produce in a lifetime of toil.

Calder Avenue was Beaumont's silk-stocking row, the home of the first families, but it extended beyond the city limits. When Sam McNeeley announced that he would drill for oil on his four lots along the swanky boulevard, a mass meeting resulted. He sold the land for his own price immediately after the meeting.

All of this Pattillo Higgins watched with justifiable amusement. In order that others might not forget, he placed an enlargement of his old Gladys City Oil, Gas, and Manufacturing Company letterhead of 1892 in the lobby of the Crosby House. There were the storage tanks, the smokestacks, the oil derricks and the activity. Had he been able to sell the stock in that one company, it would have controlled everything.

Beaumont was the mecca of the fortune hunters, but for every man who got rich there, hundreds lost every dime they had.

CHAPTER SEVEN

Hell on the Hill

A switch engine belched out a blast of coal cinders that fell into the grass on the west edge of the hill, igniting a small fire. A narrow rivulet of oil, overflowing from the lake created by the Lucas gusher, was lighted like a fuse. Suddenly, the fire slithered to the main body of oil in the flats.

Minutes later the lake was afire with towering flames leaping toward a column of black smoke. The smoke reached a low-hanging layer of stratus clouds and gradually spread over an ever widening area, enveloping the countryside in nocturnal darkness. Great bursts of flame would occasionally flood the hill in blinding light.

Men and animals were thrown into panic. A horseman dashed into Beaumont with the message that hell had broken loose on the hill. A shifting wind overcame more than a dozen men with smoke fumes, but they were rescued by the heroic action of field workers who pulled them to safety.

Cap Forney, the Guffey and Galey field superintendent, saw the fire moving like a tidal wave toward the east. He saw that the oil lake was doomed, and decided that a counter-fire would shorten the life of the conflagration. Jumping into his buckboard wagon, he raced to the opposite edge of the overflow, and set fire to the oil there. This created a blaze as spectacular as the first one, and the two towering walls of fire began moving toward one another.

As the space between the fires narrowed, a vacuum was created. Periodically a suction seemed to lift quantities of unconsumed oil high above the ground, where it would ignite by combustion and explode, and the oil would burst into flame like gigantic star shells. The effect was weird and indescribable.

The climax came when the two walls of fire met with an impact that shook the countryside. As this happened streaks of fire shot up through the low-hanging clouds and then rained down. The main blaze was choked out, but a series of scattered fires continued to illuminate the otherwise smoke-darkened hill.

The Negro churches in the vicinity were crowded with frightened and superstitious worshippers. Many left Beaumont that day never to return. That night, when the excitement subsided, ministers, both Negro and white, met to urge the discontinuation of oil activities on the hill. Their theme was "The earth is the Lord's and the fullness thereof." They predicted dire consequences from this invasion of the Lord's domain, and said that the great fire was a warning. They told their congregations that the town would eventually blow up if drilling were not stopped. The next catastrophe, they said, would be vast underground fires that would burn until the county collapsed. Others predicted that the four wells then drilling, if they came in out of control, would submerge the entire coast under a sea of oil which would ignite and destroy all living beings.

This fire was the first of many that the hill would see in the next year. The toll was not great. The Daugherty boarding house was destroyed. Guffey and Galey's long frame building, which housed its eighty workers, was burned to the ground. Three carloads of lumber and pipe were lost, and Walter Sharp's derrick on the McFaddin tract was a casualty. The Hamills had time to move their rig before the flames reached it, and the Beatty, Heywood and Higgins outfits were not endangered. Probably a million barrels of oil went up in smoke and flames, but that was no appreciable loss, as it was unlikely that it would have ever been salvaged and tanked.

The great inferno gave the hill a true baptism of fire. Witnesses would never forget that morning of March 3, 1901. The fire had its good points as well as its bad. The danger of the lake of oil exploding was gone. It provided more ammunition for the press at a time when things were otherwise at a comparative standstill. The stories were exaggerated into fantastic nightmares. Some reported hundreds killed and injured, although the total casualties were actually confined to horses, cattle and a few hogs. The Lucas gusher, while it was flowing, would certainly have been destroyed by this fire. But because the Hamills had covered it with a mound of water-saturated sand it was undamaged by the flames. Thereafter, waste oil was burned every Sunday at Taylor's Bayou to prevent a dangerous accumulation.

II

Spindletop had neither brokers, promoters, skin-game artists, nor the stock-market atmosphere of the Crosby lobby or the oil exchange, but it had its own kind of confusion. For instance, the post office was called Guffey. The railroad station was Gladys City, and the oil field was Spindletop. It was after the Beatty well came in that the area started to fill up with job seekers. There were not many wells being drilled at first on the hill itself because land prices were prohibitive, but for miles in every direction derricks could be spotted by the plumes of smoke rising from boilers alongside them.

The wildcatters and promoters believed that oil could be found anywhere near Beaumont. They listened to the government geologists who came to town and proclaimed that the entire Gulf Coast plain was underlaid with oil. They ignored Pattillo Higgins who said there would be no oil found except where nature's signs indicated it. One by one they bit into the dust until finally the land boom was over. That led everyone to the hill regardless of land prices. Price tags of a quarter of a million dollars an acre seemed reasonable enough then.

That was when the hill gained its own population. A town began to grow up around the post office and the depot. The first saloon that opened there, however, was closed the same day. George W. Carroll reminded the landowners that the property would revert to the Gladys City company if whisky, wine, or beer were sold on the premises.

This situation forced the establishment of a second and more tolerant center of activity. Along the south edge of the hill on the McFaddin land, a few hundred feet east of the Lucas gusher, Clint Grinnell built the Log Cabin saloon. Within a few weeks there were boarding houses, restaurants, supply shacks, offices and saloons. In the back room, on the second floor, or on a balcony of each saloon was a gambling room. Doors were never closed.

Spindletop provided an outlet for the worst as well as the best in men. Cheap prostitutes, both black and white, opened shop around the hill in tents and shacks, catering mostly to the common laborers, roughnecks and pipeliners. This competition was met by the "Deep Crockett" girls, who kept their business alive by riding horseback around the field to make bookings with the drillers and pushers. Drillers frequently went to town in parties of six or eight and took over some of the best houses for a night or two. Neither Spindletop nor Beaumont ever reached the depths of degradation that some boom towns of the future were to reach. But it was no tea party.

Jefferson County was blessed with better than average law enforcement. Ras Landry, the Louisiana-born sheriff, was the town's most colorful western character. He was fearless, yet he was moderate. He didn't set himself up as a dictator, and he didn't try to impress people with his reputation. Landry was naturally colorful. He wanted as much law and order as possible under the circumstances, and he succeeded quite well. He was a tall, angular man with a broad handlebar moustache, and a grim countenance that could melt easily into a friendly smile. He wore fancy boots, a white hat with a broad brim, and two pearl-handled pistols that he was capable of using when the occasion demanded. Because he was firm and yet tolerant, he was highly respected. Landry would let things go so far, and then he would crack down. In that way he kept the situation fairly well in hand. He finally put a temporary jail on the hill because he thought it unwise to try to navigate the four miles to the courthouse after dark with prisoners in a buggy, and inhuman to chain men to a tree for the night.

The hill was a workingman's realm. The men with their names on the leases and the paychecks would come out during the day, but it would take a blowout or fire to get them out at night. The hill was unpleasant. Slimy, black, oil-soaked earth, normally three feet deep in mud, was a constant invitation to a pratfall. The dudes who visited the hill were the sightseers, the curious, the excursionists and the slick promoters who would lead droves of suckers off trains and across the field to look at the gushers. They made their visits short.

When things settled down to something like normal, there were three distinct living areas. The most popular was on the

McFaddin land around the Log Cabin saloon. Men with families chose Gladys City where the rough stuff was held to a minimum and a drunk was bound to wind up in the arms of the law. South Africa, across the tracks to the east, was where the Negroes and Mexicans lived. It was populated by the team drivers, tank builders and ditch diggers.

Before long the hill became fairly well organized. It had everything except a church. There were Sundays when the Reverend Mr. Smart from George Carroll's Baptist Church would hold services in a store. The response was never good, but the opportunity was there. There really were no Sundays in the field. Every day was the same. Men worked twelve hours out of every twenty-four, and one day was like any other until pay day, and the few days after, when the hospitals and morgues would fill up with the casualties from the wild spending sprees.

It was a hell of a hill. Its water couldn't be drunk even when it was boiled, because it was full of sulphur. It was as bad on bellies as it was on boilers. Water brought $6 a barrel, while oil was 3 cents a barrel, a practical application of the law of supply and demand.

Tents and long wooden sleeping shacks, called bull pens, dotted the hill. Every man had a place to sleep and eat. It wasn't good, but it was cheap. A cot in a tent or bull pen usually cost 50 cents a week. Meals at Fuller's or Tobe Hahn's restaurant cost 30 cents. An eight-course dinner was 40 cents, and a whole chicken pot pie with all of the trimmings was 75 cents. The chicken pie was the favorite dish of the gamblers and promoters.

III

Spindletop was the birthplace of a new breed of men. Most of them didn't know any more about an oil well than a mule knows about a holiday. If they got off the train in Beaumont, got their lungs full of sulphur gas and the oil spray from the hill, didn't flinch when a stray hog knocked them down on the streets, stood their ground when the promoters and money-mad boomers jostled them, and were able to stand the ride to the hill, they had passed the first test. Things got tougher on the hill, but those who came through Beaumont without getting on the next train to go back home were initiated. Once on the hill they got the second degree. Usually they started off with a fight over a cot, stood by while someone got shot, or almost drowned in a mudhole. If they stayed two days and two nights they had what it took.

They came from the farms and ranches and from the towns and cities. Most of them were native Texans or Louisiana Acadians. But there was a sprinkling of others. You could spot a West Virginian by the bag of Mail Pouch on his hip. Or a Pennsylvanian by the Pollock stogie between his teeth. They were there with their experience, but it was not very useful. They brought cable tools and found they wouldn't work. They had to learn about rotary drilling.

The attraction on the hill was twofold. First the wages for inexperienced helpers were from $2 to $3 a day. That was twice the average pay for labor anywhere else. Drillers, who were the aristocrats, got from $5 to $15 a day, depending on their skill and background. Then there was the lure of working in a place the whole world was talking about. Men were fascinated by the crack of the bull whips, the bark of the exhaust pumps, the roar of the wild well, the clink of poker chips and the whirl of the roulette wheel. These men were sons of pioneers, endowed with a love of danger and hard work. Most of them came for the adventure and the money, but before many days passed, they had oil in their blood and knew they would never make a living any other way.

Just living on the hill was a gamble. It was an arena of action where men were shot, knifed and beaten to death every day. Even the timid who avoided the fights had their chance to die. Occupational dangers involved death by fire, gas, falling, or stopping something that was falling. It was an experience not unlike that a combat soldier finds in battle. And it welded the participants together in much the same fraternal way. Most of the hill workers were single and between the ages of seventeen and twenty-five. The few older and married men were usually the skilled workers or the superintendents and foremen.

These men were here and they would stay. Not necessarily on the hill, but in the industry that was being born here. Those who could stand the gaff would become drillers, contractors, independent operators and even executives in the large companies that would push monopoly off the American scene and replace it with competition.

It was on this hill that a well borer first became known as a driller, a skilled helper as a roughneck, a semiskilled helper as a roustabout, and a beginner as a boll weevil. It was here, too, that a spouting oil well was called a gusher, and a cable-tool driller first heard himself referred to as a "rope choker." Old-fashioned mule skinners learned to answer when called "hardtails." Spindletop was opening new ways of language as well as thinking. It was on this hill that a "shoestringer" would "poor boy" a hole down by splitting his interest with his crew, the landowner, the boarding house, the supply house, the saloon keeper, and sometimes the madame at his favorite bawdy house. Many times when he finally brought in a gusher he found that he had little or no interest left for himself.

No one knew much about the rotary drilling rig, yet it was the only instrument that could dig into the quicksands, rocks and gumbo of the hill. There is no record of cable tools ever starting and finishing a well there. And there were few men outside the Hamills, the Sharps and the Sturms who knew much about rotary, and even they didn't know too much. This led to the use of initiative and invention by almost every serious-minded man in the field, regardless of his job. It was the dawn of a new day in production techniques. It was also the beginning of a new spirit of mutual respect and cooperation among the men in the field.

IV

Weeks passed and derricks went up everywhere on the hill. Three particular spots of unusual activity were created by the sale of infinitesimal tracts of land to promoters in the Hogg-Swayne, Keith-Ward and Yellowpine districts. Higgins, Guffey, Heywood, Lone Star and Crescent, National Oil and Pipeline and others kept the wells sparsely spaced on their tracts. But the promoters were drilling to satisfy stockholders. There was never any oil sold from 90 per cent of the wells. Oil that was sold went for 3 cents—$2 less than Pennsylvania oil prices. Still, not one wildcatter let this economic obstacle stand in his way. This was a new kind of oil for which there was no market. It was the beginning of an industry. The stock money was not entirely invested in vain, however, in the long run. The stock buyers and promoters were unwittingly providing millions to finance feverish activity and work which would train and condition an army of men for the oil conquests of the future.

Contractors hit a bonanza. They found operators who knew nothing about oil, but who were willing to pay as high as $10 a foot for wells. One such contractor made enough money to realize an ambition he had long cherished. He bought a barrel of Guckenheimer whisky, had it delivered to his tent, and proceeded to drink all of it. He died on the most glorious jag any man has ever known.

Hardly an hour passed when someone didn't yell "fight." It was the signal for a gathering of all unoccupied hands in the field. They were seldom disappointed. The fights were beauties. The participants enjoyed them as much as the spectators. Usually the gladiators would beat one another to a pulp and then saunter off arm in arm to the nearest saloon, where the loser would set up the crowd. The nights were equally hilarious. The Log Cabin saloon was the scene of as many as six or eight fights at one time. In fact, they were so commonplace that only the most violent attracted attention. Jack Hunter, the chief bartender, would occasionally fire a shot out a window to break up a bloody battle. Gunplay was not too frequent, but it was usually started by some two-bit gambler or a weakling who couldn't stand the pace. The gunmen got the silent treatment from the men in the field and eventually left when they found themselves ostracized. The law was virtually powerless to handle many of the cases, except where actual murder was involved. Most of the gunmen were gamblers or sharpies of some kind. The Texans were usually quiet farm or ranch boys who resorted to shooting only as a last resort.

Easterners were largely responsible for the fact that Negroes did not work on the wells. They contended that Negroes had not worked in the fields in the oil regions, and they believed they would prove a nuisance in Beaumont. There was no great objection to this by anyone, especially the Negroes, who had no particular desire to defy death in a dozen ways every day. There were ample openings for them, but they preferred driving teams, stacking pipe, building tanks and digging ditches to working immediately over a drilling hole.

Inexperienced help working around boilers accounted for numerous explosions, some of them fatal. Escaping gas sometimes caused derrick men high above the ground to lose their senses and fall fifty feet to the derrick floors. The hospitals were constantly filled with men blinded by gas.

As the derricks increased in number, the dangers increased. One day a party of New York newspapermen were guests of a group of promoters. Three gushers were turned on for their benefit and one of them sprayed a nearby boiler, igniting the oil. Within a few minutes the journalists had a story they couldn't have dreamed up. A gusher burst into flames and the sight was phenomenal. It was the first flowing well that had caught fire. For a half hour the entire field was endangered, until one of the workers devised a long-handled wrench and succeeded in shutting off the vertical valve.

At four o'clock on the afternoon of June 24th, a Guffey well blew out and tore everything in its way to particles. There was a terrific roaring noise as gas and water shot into the air. The heavy drilling rig was lifted off its moorings and hurled to one side. The derrick was torn to splinters and 400 feet of pipe shot more than 2,000 feet into the air. Gassed men fell all around. By eleven o'clock that night the wild gasser bridged over and choked itself off. The rig, derrick, pipe and hole were all totally lost. That was the first major gas blowout in the field, but there was no fire.

Nothing in the way of equipment that wasn't nailed down was safe in the field. Some called it "borrowing," because everyone participated. The practice was condoned and charges were seldom filed. There was considerable thievery, however, and one so-called supply house dealt principally in stolen goods.

The tank-car shortage was a vexing problem. The Southern Pacific got a corner on them and for some time enjoyed a commanding position. The Heywoods once demanded some type of transportation. A harassed clerk for the railroad sent them four box cars. The Heywoods were dismayed, but made the best of the situation. They filled the cars with oil and returned them to the railroad with the complaint that they would not hold oil. Of course, after that the box cars wouldn't hold anything, and were destroyed by the company.

An outstanding demonstration which typified the courage of men of the field came in August of 1901, when lightning struck a Heywood tank that was being filled with oil at the rate of 1,000 barrels an hour from a nearby well. Lightning ignited the gas that was escaping from a vent on top of the tank. A tremendous blaze shot above the tank, but the oil was not ignited, due to the strong force of gas pressure. The foreman chose to continue rather than cut off the flow; the fire was kept above the tank, but it shot more than 100 feet into the air and spread wildly at the top. Four roughnecks and roustabouts from other wells saw the danger, rushed to tents for blankets, soaked them in mud and water, and smothered the blaze. Even a slight slip on anyone's part could have blasted them all into eternity. Located as it was near a forest of derricks, the property damage could have mounted into the millions of dollars, and hundreds of lives would have been in danger.

The most dangerous trick of horseplay came to a sudden end in August. It was the custom of some drillers to initiate "boll weevils" by making them ride the rotary, which usually made them ill and sometimes resulted in injury. A big German boy from a farm in central Texas was given the treatment and injured his back. A few hours later he returned to the derrick with a six-shooter, quietly ordered the driller onto the rotary table and let him spin until he collapsed from exhaustion. That was the last recorded instance of the rotary riding trick.

Wanton waste was indulged in frequently by the promoters to the utter disgust of the oil men. One day in September more than 15,000 excursionists and visitors from over the country cluttered up the field. A dozen gushers were turned loose for their entertainment and inducement. It was on this occasion that several of the promoters, apparently under the influence of liquor, started gambling on how high their respective wells would spout into the air.

The workers in the field seldom knew who, besides the contractor, they were working for and cared less. They had no fear of being fired because they knew they could get another job the next day. Moreover, when they were fired, they got paid. Otherwise they were paid only once a month.

V

In spite of the fact that the off-the-hill territory was found to be unproductive, rumors of imminent discoveries kept coming in. Two phantom wells showed up in 1901. A man with a pair of binoculars in Port Arthur claimed he had seen a gusher halfway between the Sabine Lake and the field. It turned out to be a tall tree standing in front of a newly painted white house. The most exciting rumor of all was one about a gusher at El Vista, the Guffey shipping station south of the hill. Tom Woods, a most dependable contractor for Guffey, reported it. He said he saw oil spouting over a hundred feet into the air. Captain Lucas reasoned that it might be a secret operation. He had every reason to rely on Tom Woods. After a two-day search, nationwide news coverage, and great local excitement, a pumper for Guffey at El Vista reported that the pipeline had broken temporarily and that the oil had shot high into the air. That solved the mystery, because the break was in the exact spot where Woods had seen the oil shooting up.

The first year in the field was a rough one. It brought wealth to many and it impoverished many more. It made men and it broke them. But out of it all was born an industry, and the men to man it.

CHAPTER EIGHT

The Onion Patch

"Boys, she measures exactly two hundred and seventeen and four-tenths feet and there's not another well in the field that can touch her."

Scott Heywood was talking. He had just made an exact instrument measurement to determine how high the Heywood No. 2 was spouting. It was the greatest gusher in the world up to the morning of June 1, 1901, and since that date no one has challenged its superiority.

The day before that, the Kiser-Kelly well in the Bullock survey north of the hill had been abandoned as a duster and off-the-hill land had fallen in value from $50,000 to $2,000 an acre in twenty-four hours. Most people now took it for granted that oil would not be found anywhere except on the hill proper.

Significant incidents were commonplace on the hill between 1901 and 1903, but it would be difficult to point out three more meaningful occurrences than those which happened within a week of one another, unless the Lucas gusher itself is considered.

First of these was the Kiser-Kelly dry hole; next was the champion Heywood No. 2 gusher. The third happened a week before and its full importance was not recognized until the impact of the first two had settled on the hill. It was the transfer of the J. M. Page fifteen-acre lease from the J. M. Guffey Company to the Hogg-Swayne Syndicate. The Page tract was the only lease Captain Lucas had been able to get on the hill outside of the big Gladys City and McFaddin-Kyle-Wiess leases. Why Guffey permitted it to get out of his hands is anyone's guess. It might have been because the titles were clouded and Willie Campbell of the syndicate had the key to clearing the clouds, or it might have been that Guffey considered $180,000 a fantastically high price for the mineral rights.

Guffey had a well being drilled on the land when the deal was made with the syndicate. The syndicate purchased the hole and the drilling contract along with the mineral rights. They paid Page $105,000 for the surface rights, and settled certain claims to clear the title with others. The entire deal cost them $310,000. On the basis of their good names, members of the syndicate, including ex-Governor Hogg, James M. Swayne, W. T. Campbell, A. S. Fisher and judge R. E. Brooks, had pooled most of their assets to finance the undertaking for $40,000. They still owed $270,000. This for a tract of land Page had purchased for $450 in 1897 with a $150 down payment and two years to pay the remainder. Before this deal, Swayne, without knowing about the Lucas lease or the claims against the land, had been negotiating with Page to form a $2,000,000 corporation whereby Page would have received $500,000 for his land. Lawsuits discouraged prospective investors and that deal fell through.

With every other landowner on the hill refusing to sell at any price, Hogg hit upon the idea of getting out from under the $270,000 by selling off part of the tract in small blocks. The first sale was for two and one-half of the fifteen acres for $200,000. The whole debt was then wiped out when the Texas Oil and Development Company paid $50,000 for one-twentieth of an acre, and Judge Brooks and associates purchased a twenty-fourth of an acre for $15,000. From that point on the syndicate was on velvet. The syndicate members made tremendous profits in the next few weeks selling parcels of land in quarters, eighths, sixteenths, and thirty-seconds of an acre for small cash payments and the remainder out of oil. The purchasers formed companies and divided up their already infinitesimal holdings to confuse the situation further.

The syndicate never sold more than half of its fifteen acres, but about five acres were cut out of the Keith-Ward tract and George Carroll's Yellowpine tract in Gladys City to add further zest to the boom. Actually only a few acres were involved in the three islands of jammed-up derricks.

Whatever caused Guffey to sell the Page lease, whether it was to get Hogg into the field or as protection against Standard and for political goodwill assurance, it was a monumental mistake. The resulting frenzied drilling program ruined the hill economically. It caused prices to drop to 3 cents a barrel, and hundreds of unnecessary holes dissipated the reservoir energy, resulting in the early end of flush production. Because they held 90 per cent of the leases on the hill proper, Guffey and Company suffered far more than anyone else from the Hogg-Swayne plan.

Guffey blamed Lucas, but the Mellons blamed Guffey for the tragic error. The error was tragic, that is, for Guffey and those who had the other eighty acres on the hill. It was the Hogg-Swayne deal, however, that caused the drilling boom that gave hundreds of men the opportunity to learn the oil business from the ground up. Furthermore, it was the demand for oil built up during the period of overproduction, plus the sudden cessation of gushers, that inspired the mad search for other domes.

Had Lucas succeeded in his efforts to cover the dome with leases, or if the Page lease had not come under the syndicate's control, it is likely that there would have been no uncontrolled drilling boom. There would have been no Hogg-Swayne, Keith-Ward, or Yellowpine districts on the hill.

It was these three "districts" that gave the hill its tremendous boom. Without them there would have been no cause to drill hundreds of wells, where a handful would have sufficed. Without them the money would not have been forthcoming to finance the Spindletop University of Roughnecks and Roustabouts.

Every wildcat and legitimate company that could afford land on the hill got into the play. Within a few months wells were so thick in the "districts" that they looked like three newly filled toothpick holders. Between the "districts" were great open spaces with no more than one well to every acre or two. Pattillo Higgins looked on the sight and said the old hill looked like an onion patch. That was what the workers called it thereafter.

II

The hill continued to prosper. Its tremendous activity soon affected every section of the nation. There was hardly a county in Texas where "experts" were not looking for oil. Activity in California increased. States where the subject had never been given a thought before were being explored. Alabama was considered the area most likely for the next strike. Louisiana, free of antitrust law nuisances, was attracting a big play. Colorado had a boom. Lucas was prospecting in Kentucky, South Carolina and Georgia. John Galey probed in a half-dozen other states.

Texas was surprised when the Houston Oil Company was chartered for $30,000,000. The company's incorporators were S. Bronson Cooper of Beaumont and Joe Eagle and H. F. Bonner of Houston. Cooper and Eagle were members of Congress. Newspaper headlines implied that John Henry Kirby, fabulous East Texan, was the guiding spirit behind the deal. Kirby was a promotional genius who later became the lumber king of the Southwest. He lived a Horatio Alger life. Born in the backwoods, he was thirteen before he saw a railroad. He was still picking cotton and digging potatoes at nineteen and could barely read and write when Bronson Cooper made it possible for him to get into Southwestern University. That was his first schooling, but he completed a law course there by the time he was twenty-three. On the same day the Houston Oil Company was formed, the $10,000,000 Kirby Lumber Company was chartered. Later Kirby revealed that he was the largest single stockholder in the Houston Company, and the owner of the majority of the Kirby Lumber Company stock.

The Houston Oil Company immediately purchased a large block of stock in the Higgins Oil and Fuel Company. This gave new prestige and financing to that company and made it one of the important oil companies for the next thirty years.

As the onion patch grew, important things happened. Guffey started building a refinery in Port Arthur; Jim Sturm found a new oil sand at 960 feet; the price of oil dropped to 3 cents a barrel; the small companies tried to amalgamate, but were denied the right by the attorney general's antitrust law ruling. An organization of raiders known as the "White Cappers" flourished for a few weeks until Ras Landry could cope with the situation. The Klanlike organization made the mistake of taking a prisoner out of Landry's jail one night, and he saw to it that its activities subsided after that.

In October the greatest gasser the world had ever known came in on the McFaddin tract. The pipe shot more than a thousand feet into the air, and spouted water and thirty-pound rocks, creating a new interest in gas as a fuel. In November, the Guffey Company loaded the *Cardium,* the first oil tanker to call at Port Arthur. It took on 60,000 barrels of Spindletop oil that had been desulphurized to prevent explosion.

The *Beaumont Journal* reported seventy-nine pound pressure on a Paulhamus well, and stated that it indicated a serious drop for the field in October. The very next day the Yellowpine No. 10 gusher came in with 349 pounds pressure recorded on an improvised gauge. The hill was as mischievous as its founder, Higgins, had been in his younger days, and about as unpredictable.

Interest lagged somewhat in the field for a couple of months, due to the 3-cent price and the absence of a market for fuel oil. In December, however, there was a new surge of activity. Guffey's announcement that high-grade commercial gasoline could be made from Spindletop crude was big news. No one stopped to think that there was also little market for gasoline.

When the end of the year came there were 138 gushers on the hill and forty-six rigs were digging feverishly for new oil, and still there was no big market. It was estimated that $235,000,000 had been invested in oil in Texas due to the boom, most of it in spurious companies, and the year-end report revealed that $4,371,000 had been invested in wells and facilities, not including land and leases on and around the hill. Considering that Standard Oil was capitalized for $100,000,000, the Texas oil investment was significant.

One interesting part of the first year's report was that $294,000 was invested in eighty-four rotary well drilling outfits. Fifty years later that would be the approximate price for one such outfit.

III

The second year of Spindletop's operation was celebrated around the bars on January 10, 1902. The two months before had been the biggest in the field history with twenty gushers in November and twenty-two in December. But this month would top them all. Walter Sharp set a record by drilling a well in twelve days, even after spending two days in hard rock.

St. Patrick's Day brought the field its greatest hilarity. The Irish had a field day. The Orangemen and the Sons of Southern Ireland squared off for the greatest free-for-all fight for fun, in the history of the Southwest, at least. When it was all over, the landscape was decorated with bleeding noses and black eyes, but everyone was happy. The Irishmen retired to the saloons and drank to old Erin.

As the days went by, drilling continued, but low oil prices were strangling all except those, such as Higgins, Heywood, National, Lone Star and Crescent, Guffey and a few others, who had storage, pipelines and markets. In January gushers were sold at from $18,000 to $20,000, and in early February the Oil Exchange was the scene of a disturbing incident. R. W. Griswold, a broker, announced on the floor that he would sell a gusher in the Yellowpine tract for $8,000. The offer was immediately accepted by John D. Cameron of the Equitable Company of St. Louis. Cameron had, only a few months previously, purchased 5,000,000 barrels of Spindletop crude to be delivered over five years. That purchase had contributed more than anything else, probably, to increased activity in the field in December. The Oil Exchange officials were infuriated over the newspaper accounts of the sale. The local newspapers defended their right to report the news, and confirmed the sale. The gusher was located on a tiny parcel of land ten by twelve feet. This was a far cry from $1,250,000 National Oil and Pipeline had paid to D. R. Beatty for the second gusher ten months before. It indicated the panic of some of the small operators, but it presented an inaccurate picture. Gushers were still worth many times that amount.

On the same day as the $8,000 gusher sale, the price of oil was advanced from 9 to 10 cents a barrel. That was the typical inconsistency of the hill.

In February, also, two other important developments came to light. The French navy announced that it would use oil from Spindletop in the form of briquettes. This was followed in two days by the announcement that the United States Navy had asked for a $20,000 appropriation to finance tests with a view toward using Beaumont oil. George J. Gould returned to New York with great and glowing reports of the Texas situation and pictured the Gulf Coast as the industrial center of the future. He immediately backed up his words by ordering the International and Great Northern Railroad to take immediate steps toward equipping its engines for fuel oil to replace coal.

There was unpleasant news with the good. Dallas insurance underwriters warned the Houston and Texas Central Railroad that insurance would be canceled wherever large storage tanks for oil were built.

The M.K. & T. reduced freight rates on coal 15 per cent in order to combat oil competition. The L. & N. then reduced freight rates from $1.75 to $1.10 on the haul from Mobile to New Orleans to try to keep its coal-carrying business from vanishing.

In May there was real consternation in the field. Most of the wells stopped gushing. This was immediately attributed by some geologists to the Central American earthquakes. In that same month 300 oil companies, operating in the Beaumont area, lost their charters when they failed to pay franchise taxes to the state. This, plus the drastic oil-reservoir pressure drop, had the immediate effect of boosting the price for oil to around 20 cents. Due largely to the activities of such men as Charles Wallis of the Higgins Company, a former Galveston grocer, the market for oil was improving.

There were some dismal days, but wells kept coming in and prices for leases, although lower than when the small parcels first went on sale, were inordinately high. They would fluctuate, however, with reports of oil showings in wells off the hill. As such reports got warm, the hill prices went down, but as each of these proved to be either sheer promotion or unfounded enthusiasm, the Spindletop land prices would go up again. The hill was still capable of producing more oil than anyone could possibly use. It was the general feeling, however, that one well off the hill would destroy Spindletop's land values. But it never came.

Beaumont, in the meantime, was taking a serious blasting from critics throughout the country. Hundreds who foolishly lost their money in the wildcat stock schemes were bitter. The coal barons, who were reeling from oil competition; the railroads of the East, which were afraid of losing their coal-hauling business; the Standard, with its tentacles reaching into most of the industrial and financial institutions; and oil men who failed to get a foothold on the hill were behind the attacks. Not only was the product castigated as a farce if not a menace, but Beaumont itself was described in bitter terms. The town was bad enough, with its mud, murders, overpopulation, saloons, "Deep Crockett," gambling dens and uncontrolled scenes of wild speculation, without exaggerations.

None of this deterred the steady march toward the development of refineries, pipelines and other facilities necessary to an industry. Beaumont had oil to burn in spite of anything the skeptics could say or do. Its oil had solved the problem of cheap fuel for America. Sometimes the critics used the argument that there was too much oil. Beaumont was inclined to go along with that argument. Three barrels of oil had the heating quality of a ton of coal. Coal was priced at $3.50 a ton and its equivalent in oil, at 20 cents a barrel, was 60 cents. That was only the heating-cost saving. Other advantages were equally important. Liquid fuel offered high heating power, small bulk, cleanliness and economy. Furthermore, it offered ease of manipulation under pressure, and tremendous savings in labor and maintenance. The Southern Pacific railroad, the first large-scale user, announced that it had saved $5,000,000 in one year using oil.

The coal barons were being forced to release their stranglehold on American industry, particularly the railroads and manufacturing enterprises. Industries that had for years been forced to drag their weary way, existing, as it were, instead of profiting by capital and time invested, could now see the light. The mechanical, industrial and motor-development potential was unlimited. The fuel problem was no longer without a solution. Spindletop meant the unleashing of industrial and mechanical possibilities that the world had never dreamed of before.

A dramatic demonstration of the value of oil was announced by British shipping interests. The number of stokers had been reduced from one hundred to four on a typical steamship by using oil. Passenger business had increased with the elimination of soot and foul smoke. Ship movements were increased by the fact that oil could be loaded on a ship in hours by one man where it took days and a hundred men for coal loading. Cargo space was increased considerably by the elimination of coal-storage space.

On the other hand, the lignite-coal business of Texas, which was at that time beginning to blossom, was set back to such an extent that it has never revived.

IV

None of the significant occurrences or press reports were a cure for "petrofobia," the excitement which gripped all men who got close to a gusher. The teeming activity of the hill was slowed down only by the rain, mud and fires. Even then eight-mule teams were equal to the situation. The gas got worse as the days went by and it was not uncommon to see mules keel over and die from the fumes.

Pattillo Higgins contended that there would be deeper oil on the hill. In 1902, Jim Sturm decided to find out. He made plans to drill a well deeper than the sand just below 1000 feet. In fact he planned to go to 2000 feet or more, if necessary. There were some who doubted the Higgins theory, but they kept quiet. The well was unsuccessful because it was impossible to get through the highly charged oil sand to the required depth. Years later the Higgins theory was proved correct, but the sands were on the flanks instead of on the hill itself.

Beaumonters coughed through the night on November 13th. The odor of oil and gas was strong enough to keep them awake. The next morning they found their houses yellow with oil mist. A dense fog, wafted by a steady breeze from the Gulf, had floated thousands of barrels of oil in minute particles from the field to the town. The ground was covered with a thick coating of oil. Not a house or building in the community was left unsprayed. The oil film over the town was not unusual, but normally it was very light.

One incident in 1902 served to confirm Pattillo Higgins' advice to Lucas. The C. E. Jones Development Company brought in a gusher in lot 44 on the exact spot where the original Lucas well collapsed after finding oil at 575 feet. The well was in the area where Higgins recommended drilling for the Gladys City company, within a few feet of the railroad tracks. It was drilled for H. A. Perlstein, the town's blacksmith, and R. M. Mothner. From Perlstein's profits would come Beaumont's first skyscraper.

Spindletop raged with a fire for a solid week in September when the T. J. Woods well ignited from a cigar carelessly discarded by a driller. The well was gushing high above the derrick top when the flames reached it. There was no chance to close it in, as valves had not been installed. The fire was an awesome spectacle, colorful and belligerent. It marked the first use of steam and sand in fighting fire.

In late October the Hogg-Swayne tract was completely wiped out by a series of fires. Twenty-six derricks and pumping units were destroyed in the first blaze, but few wells were lost, due to the fact that most of the valves were closed and the wellheads covered with sand before the flames reached them. The fire started when a small wooden tank in block 38 collapsed and the oil spilled over a boiler. Among the gushers lost were the Lucky Dime, the Live Oak and Wild Gusher wells which turned into blazing fountains of oil. The wells lost were all located on less than an acre of land.

This fire was almost under control when the second started in another section of the Hogg-Swayne tract. As a workman lifted a lantern to blow out the light the gas fumes ignited and set off a tremendous blaze. A roughneck, trapped between walls of fire in the first few minutes of the excitement, was burned to death. Wooden derricks, some seventy-five of them, were quick fodder for the inferno. J. S. Corbett's giant settling tank caught fire and added to the spectacle.

Hundreds of citizens joined the field workers in battling the flames, but by the next morning the Hogg-Swayne tract was a smoldering ruin, a shabby sight for a train of excursionists to see. There were no gushers for the promoters to show that day.

The last burning embers of the blaze were cooling when lightning hit a Guffey tank during a thunderstorm. The flames leapt to an adjoining tank and carried on to the thick patch of wells in the Keith-Ward tract. Great walls of flame, a pall of smoke and flashing lightning combined to produce one of the weirdest spectacles of Spindletop. Hundreds braved the heavy storm to climb the hill and watch the fireworks. Lightning struck a number of installations on the hill, including a Negro church in the South Africa area where a funeral was being held. A mourner killed by the lightning was the only casualty of the day. The heavy rain drenched the fire. Its waters created a blinding steam that choked off the flames. When the twelve days during which the hill was a constant hellfire finally came to an end, only the Yellowpine district stood intact. Work was started rebuilding and in a few days little evidence of the destruction remained. The safety committee, however, issued a field ruling that as soon as wells were completed in the future derricks would be removed, and brick housing of the type introduced by Lone Star and Crescent earlier would cover them. This ruling destroyed the picturesque onion-patch effect, but it gave new protection to millions of barrels of oil.

By October there were 440 gushers on the hill. In the three "districts" they were spaced on an average of twenty wells to the acre. There were millions of barrels of oil in storage, and field rules forced those without storage to hold their oil. The gusher for fun and promotion days were over. The bugaboo of low pressures was almost forgotten when a well in the Keith-Ward tract came in in December with a deafening roar and a new record in pressures. A few days later the Yellowpine No. 10 came in and the pressure gauge recorded 200 pounds. A pipeline gauge was attached and the needle went around to 340 pounds. That was three times the pressure of the Lucas gusher. Again the old hill had confounded its critics.

As the year ended the demand for oil was steadily increasing. It was being used in locomotives, sugar mills, factory furnaces, breweries, residential stoves and heaters, ships, smelting plants and on roads. Power plants began using oil, and the age of electrical power started a tremendous expansion. At Sulphur Mines, Louisiana, the answer was found to the greatest problem in producing sulphur. Oil as a fuel enabled Herman Frasch, the sulphur genius, to get the fullest benefit of his hot-water production method. Coal, wood and other fuels had hampered Frasch, but now oil provided the perfect answer, and another of the world's great natural resources could be obtained in quantities sufficient to provide for the abundance that was to come.

V

It was the day-after-day excitement of new gushers that continued to increase the Spindletop tempo. For Captain Lucas the sight of his gusher coming in was almost enough. All that followed only helped to complicate his life. First there was the Higgins suit, then the sale of his interest to the Guffey Company, and now people were urging him to run for governor.

Beaumonters had shown their appreciation to the Captain by presenting him with a Tiffany-produced medal of esteem. It was a solid gold watch charm larger than a silver dollar. On one side was a replica of the Lucas gusher with the derrick in tiny gold bars, and inlaid onyx depicting the oil shooting over the crown block. The capacity of the well was stated as 53,700 barrels, a figure that was low, but probably as correct as any other used. On the reverse side was a five-pointed star with the word "Texas" spelled out in the spaces between the points. A large diamond was in the center and smaller diamonds tipped each point of the star. The inscription on that side was "Beaumont to Lucas from One Hundred Friends."

The Captain heard several speeches at the presentation. Men said that his great success had come in the face of opposition, discouragement and ridicule "which was somewhat concealed out of admiration for the man's perseverance."

A few days after that an Englishman stepped up to the Captain and said he wanted to make his own presentation.

"I heard about your well the day before it came in. I was in Calcutta and the international dateline favored me," he said. "I rushed here and in a few days I made $200,000, thanks to you."

The Captain was so astonished when he was handed a large diamond scarf pin that he did not even learn the donor's name. The man from Calcutta boarded a train and was gone.

Lucas was the name everyone identified with the Beaumont oil discovery. Higgins was lost in the shouting. John Galey, the man whose persuasion had sent Guffey to the Mellons for the money, was scarcely mentioned. Higgins and Galey were too busy to be bothered by an absence of recognition. Even Carroll and O'Brien, the men who first gave encouragement to Higgins, were forgotten in the concentration of praise on Lucas.

The Captain was a modest man and the excitement, plus the acclaim, was too much for him. He accepted Guffey's offer to look at other prospects and went to a dozen areas in Texas, then to Kentucky, Georgia, Alabama, North and South Carolina, and Louisiana. Wherever he went he was met by the curious and the well wishers. The preposterous stories that he had made $40,000,000 caused people to want to see him. His trip was virtually a triumphal procession, and every acre of land he visited went up in value many times.

One morning the *Atlanta Constitution* carried a most fantastic story. It was a mournful, sob-sister, rags-to-riches treatment. Lucas was described as a former railroad conductor whose wife had come to the *Constitution* office with two little boys several months before looking for her husband, Captain Anthony Lucas, a conductor on the Georgia Midland Railroad. Nothing had been heard of the Captain, the account related, and it was assumed he had vanished, until the great Lucas gusher came in. Now, it continued, he was rolling in wealth while his wife and children were still struggling to exist. The canard was copied by the *Birmingham Telegram* and forwarded to the *Chicago Record-Herald.* From there it was picked up by other newspapers and some magazines. It turned out that the conductor Lucas was another man who, at the time the story was written, was back with his family in Montgomery. Months later, journals and magazines usually highly regarded for their accuracy, such as the *National Oil Reporter,* continued to circulate the story.

The Captain was not bothered as much by that, however, as he was by an article that reported he was certain that oil would be found in Charlton County, Georgia, because he had found the "rare oil bloom" growing in profusion. It quoted the Captain as saying that the flower was a definite indication of oil.

When he first read the story he was amused, and reared back in uproarious laughter. Suddenly, he stopped, and realized what so ridiculous a statement might do to his professional reputation.

"Good Lord, I hope none of my friends read this as coming from me," he said. "They will think I have gone crazy. How in the world could a flower indicate the presence of oil?"

He rushed out of the house to the newspaper office to make a correction. But again, the harm was done. One by one the newspapers and magazines picked up the story. The denials always followed, but the Captain never got over his embarrassments. He felt that fame had too many penalties.

Lucas returned to Beaumont in September. He stayed a few weeks, but soon tired again of the boom, which was worse than ever. He was a scientific man and the hectic confusion, the lawsuits, the promoters and the mud and mosquitoes were more than he cared for. He left one day late that year and returned to the scene of his great accomplishment only once more, two years later. His trail had led him around the world and eventually back to his Washington home and office.

Lucas was confident oil would be found on Spindletop's flanks. He said, however, the world would have to wait until equipment was developed which could penetrate the necessary depths.

VI

Pattillo Higgins had his own ideas and they did not fall into the groove that accommodated those of his partners in the Higgins Oil and Fuel Company. He didn't like selling the majority of the stock to the Houston Oil Company. So Higgins sold his own stock and retired from the company.

He had an idea bigger than all of his former ideas combined. Pattillo Higgins decided to form a "standard" oil company. A standard company was regarded as one which would produce, transport, refine and market the product. Texas had no such company, and there was some doubt as to the legality of one under the state's antitrust laws. The Higgins Standard Oil Company, Limited, was chartered in November of 1901, and came into existence publicly early in 1902. The president was Pattillo Higgins. His associates included D. Call, president of the Beaumont National Bank, and I. D. Polk, a realtor and Higgins' friend of long standing. Other directors included capitalists from Lake Charles, Houston and Lawrence, Kansas.

The most elaborate promotional brochure ever produced for an oil company was made up. It was eleven by fourteen inches, buckram bound, and contained seventy-two pages with stories of the company, its promoters, anticlinal pressure, the origin of oil, dozens of pictures and illustrations, a chapter on "The True Story of the Beaumont Oil Field," and another titled "Nature Paints Her Own Signs." Major gushers in the field were shown in full-page photographs.

The company was capitalized for $10,000,000, and stock purchasers were given an opportunity to buy $100 par value certificates for $50. Higgins said the stock was being sold for half its value and that the company's holdings were worth five times the capital stock.

In the introduction he wrote, "I have made enough money to retire from business and keep me in a sumptuous way all the days of my life. I am not selfish, therefore, a retired life would not suit me. I want to live for the good of others. I have a talent for big things. If I hide my talent, I will be responsible for the things which are left in darkness and not developed."

Higgins announced his intention of building a large refinery in Houston, and another across Sabine Lake in Cameron Parish, Louisiana. His company had 155,000 acres in fee lands and 42,000 acres more under lease. He called Spindletop Higgins Oil Field No. 1, and then spotted Higgins fields No. 2, 3, and 4. The second great field, he said, would be 23 miles east of Houston at Barbers Hill. The third would be located on the Cameron Parish lands, and the fourth in San Augustine and Sabine Counties north of Beaumont. A network of pipelines would connect all of these fields.

He said other fields had to be developed; otherwise Spindletop, due to the abuse it had received from promoters, could play out and leave all oil companies in a critical condition.

For the company's letterhead he adopted the one used by the original Gladys City company, with modifications. The picture of little Gladys, who was now one of Beaumont's most beautiful belles, was left out. Gushers were placed on either side of the industrial layout. There was also a tank steamer and a tank car, each labeled "Higgins."

In the "Story of the Beaumont Oil Field," Higgins lowered the boom for the first time on all his fellow townsmen. He called them "two-by-four-headed Beaumonters" and he said of his directors in the Gladys City company, "if we wanted to go to New York from San Francisco we would have to ride there on the bare backs of long-eared jackasses without bridles."

The full measure of his wrath, however, fell on geologists, particularly the government breed. He devoted almost a page to a diatribe against these "learned men of science," as he called them, by concluding that: "There are many geologists filling high positions who ought to be out on a farm making rails and following behind long-eared mules."

Pattillo Higgins' proposed company failed to materialize. Some said he devoted too much space in his brochure to condemning others for things that would have been better forgotten. But the most likely reason his company failed to raise the necessary capital was that the wildcat promoters, chiselers, and stock-scheme artists had disgusted the nation with oil stock. A few months before, his standard-company stock would have been in greater demand than any on the market.

When the venture folded, Pattillo Higgins, in a philosophical mood, said all wasn't lost. He said he had been able to get a few things off his chest that had been troubling him a long time.

"And anyway," he said fifty years later, "those mosquitoes in Cameron Parish would have eaten me alive and I would be dead, like most of those men who were great successes in the Beaumont oil field. The work involved was too much for one man."

One feature of his brochure was worth the thousands of dollars Higgins put into his company and lost. It was the reproduction of a letter giving him full credit for the discovery and development of Spindletop.

The testimonial was signed by thirty-two of Beaumont's most prominent citizens. Among them were W. C. Averill, O. B. Greeves, J. F. Keith, M. K. Fletcher, J. C. Ward, Congressman Bronson Cooper, W. B. Dunlap, John N. Gilbert, C. T. Heisig, I. D. Polk, R. M. Mothner, Leon Levy, John H.

Broocks, and a half dozen others who made fortunes as a direct result of Higgins' persistence.

The document was attested to by the county clerk on December 3, 1901, and it gave the story as completely as it would ever be told. The document read as follows:

> To whom it may concern:
>
> This is to certify that we, the undersigned citizens of Beaumont, Texas, are personally acquainted with Pattillo Higgins of this city; we have known him for many years, and believe him to be perfectly reliable and trustworthy. He is a native of Beaumont, Texas.
>
> We know within our personal knowledge that Mr. Higgins discovered the Beaumont Oil Field in the year 1892, and he said when the field was developed that it would be worth millions of dollars. He said that single wells would flow thousands of barrels of oil per day. He located the exact spot where all the big gushers are now found.
>
> Mr. Higgins organized a company in the year 1892 for the purpose of developing the oil field which he had discovered, and he styled the company Gladys City Oil, Gas and Manufacturing Company. His company bought a large tract where the big oil gushers are now found, and they contracted with a well contractor to have a well drilled to a depth of 1,500 feet. On account of the well contractor being unskilled and having inferior machinery, he drilled the well to a depth of 300 feet and could not go any deeper, and he abandoned the work. Mr. Higgins tried to get his company to make other contracts to drill wells, but he could not influence them to do so, and confusion arose among the directors, and the company remained in idleness for a number of years. Mr. Higgins bought lands individually in the oil field and commenced to induce others to go in with him and develop the oil field. He finally

> made a contract with Capt. A. F. Lucas to come and develop the field, and Capt. Lucas came and commenced drilling and he brought in a well on the 10th day of January, 1901, and the well was called the Lucas well.
>
> Mr. Higgins deserves the whole honor of discovering and developing the Beaumont oil field.

That admission of facts and establishment of credit was worth more to Pattillo Higgins than a dozen Tiffany medals. It was the first and the last recognition his fellow townsmen have ever given him. But it was sweet recompense for years of toil, heartbreaks and disappointments. The prophet had found some measure of honor even in his own home country.

CHAPTER NINE

Guffey Goes Gulf

To tell the story of how the Mellons got into Spindletop it is necessary to go back to that midsummer morning in 1900, described in Chapter 3, when John Galey introduced Captain Anthony Lucas to Colonel James M. Guffey in the Pittsburgh offices of Guffey and Galey.

"Captain Lucas has a revolutionary idea about the possibility of oil on salt domes," Galey began. "I have looked over his prospect and am in agreement with his theory to some extent. There are surface indications of oil on the land he has under option south of Beaumont, Texas. The location has the advantage of proximity to tidewater that isn't enjoyed by any other field in the United States, or, so far as I know, in the world."

Guffey listened to Galey with the respect and the attention he always paid to his recommendations, and then asked

Lucas more about his theory. The Captain explained at length with intelligence and enthusiasm. He told of his first well and the oil he had trapped before the pipe collapsed in the hole. Then he explained his various efforts to get a new test financed, and the type of deal that he could make with the Gladys City company. Guffey sat back a few minutes to contemplate.

As they sat there, Captain Lucas was intrigued by this man. His name was known throughout the oil world along with that of John Galey. He was a picturesque figure with long, white, curly hair, blue eyes and a healthy, ruddy complexion. His features were almost delicate. He wore a Prince Albert coat, a dazzling waistcoat, a handsome, pleated shirt, with a wide lay-down collar and a Windsor tie. The wide-brimmed, black felt hat resting on the desk completed the ensemble of this Pittsburgh version of a western dandy. The one incongruous note in his otherwise faultless attire was his uncreased trousers. Guffey, Lucas thought, was a strange type of man to be associated with the modest, quiet Galey, but probably they formed a balanced team. He knew that by reputation Guffey was a shrewd promoter, who did things on a grandiose scale. He was obviously a combination exhibitionist, politician and capitalist.

Guffey studied Galey's map of the Texas prospect and commented that there was no oil production nearer than Corsicana, some 200 miles away. Finally he seemed satisfied in his own mind, apparently having worked out a plan of procedure.

"I'll make an appointment with A. W. Mellon of the T. Mellon and Sons Bank," Guffey said. "This afternoon we will know what we can do. I would not start such a project without sufficient funds for three wells, storage and transportation facilities. If we start, we must assume we will find oil. The amount I will want, about $300,000, may be hard to get.

"Naturally, Mr. Mellon will want to know the details. I propose a partnership," Guffey continued, "based on five-eighths interest for myself, a quarter interest for John Galey, and the remaining eighth for you."

He was talking directly to Lucas. The Captain said that he had hoped for a better arrangement for himself.

"Captain Lucas, this proposition has been turned down by the Standard Oil Company, the people of Beaumont, and everyone else you have approached. Furthermore, state geological officials and the United States Geological Survey have condemned it outright. In addition to that, four holes have been drilled and your jar of oil is the only tangible result to date," Guffey said. "This is a risk I would not consider under any circumstances were it not for John Galey's faith and recommendation. You have had your gamble and lost. Now you have a chance to recoup your losses and make a profit on my gamble, depending on what we find. If you want the deal on that basis, I will present it to the bank that way. It is your decision to make."

Lucas could not answer this argument. Every point was well taken. Whether he did or not, he could have recalled that less than a year ago he had given Pattillo Higgins even less interest in a proposition which involved scarcely 10 per cent of the amount Guffey proposed to spend. Guffey was not interested in the deal Lucas had made with Higgins, stating that such a deal was purely the Captain's personal worry and not the partnership's. Lucas was disappointed, but he had no alternative. He accepted the Guffey terms.

Galey left such matters entirely in Guffey's hands. As far as he was concerned, that was Guffey's part of the business. He understood that the Colonel was proposing that the prosperous partnership of Guffey and Galey would borrow the money from the Mellons and, in effect, lend it to a new and separate partnership of Guffey, Galey and Lucas.

The Mellons had respect for Guffey, particularly since his partnership had been highly successful in recent years, but they based their loans entirely on Galey's reports. They not only considered John Galey the greatest oil explorer in the business, they regarded him as a friend of the family. They were happy, however, that Guffey was the businessman in the partnership.

Andrew Mellon heard Galey's ideas on the prospect in Texas, backed by Guffey's opinion that the project was well worth the risk involved in view of its nearness to tidewater.

"If we should hit oil at Beaumont in sizable quantities, which John thinks highly probably," Guffey said to Mellon, "there would be no limit to our opportunities. I prefer that no one know that we are behind this venture, however. We intend to let it appear that Lucas is continuing independently with borrowed money."

Guffey said that if the loan were made he would urge complete silence as far as the Mellon bank was concerned. Mellon said that if the loan were made, of course, that would be understood.

It was later in the afternoon that Guffey and Galey returned from Mellon's office with the good news that a loan had been approved. The details were all that remained. The partnership of Guffey, Galey and Lucas was formed under the name of The Guffey Petroleum Company.

II

Within a month Galey had made arrangements with the Hamill brothers to drill and then went to Beaumont himself to stake location for the first well. He took to this task like an old bird dog heading for good quail country.

Galey was born near Cherry Run, Pennsylvania, in 1840. From almost the very day that the famous Drake well came in as America's first commercial oil producer, he was in the business. He was far too active in the search for oil to be annoyed by the Civil War. It was in the '60s that he discovered the famous Maple Shade well in Pleasantville. Even the fact that Lee's armies had invaded Pennsylvania did not turn him from his task of seeking new oil.

Galey probed the earth around Clarion, Armstrong and Butler Counties, and followed the scent of oil to Stump Creek Island, where he discovered oil in the middle of the Allegheny River. There his famous "Island Queen," "Island King," "Mellon" and "Andrew" wells, the latter named for his friend, A. W. Mellon, are still known in petroleum history books. He developed a large portion of the Bradford field before joining forces with Guffey in 1880 to open the McDonald field with the famous Matthews gusher, the greatest of all producers until the Lucas gusher took over supremacy. Then Galey's nose for oil led the partnership to the discovery of the Sand Fork and Kile pools. At one time Guffey and Galey's production was in excess of 40,000 barrels a day, establishing them as the greatest producers in the world. Even after he heard the unimaginative John D. Archbold of Standard vow he would drink every gallon of oil produced west of the Mississippi, Galey moved in to establish the Neodosha field in Kansas. When water well drillers found traces of oil in Corsicana, he moved there to develop the potential before Cullinan was called. He drilled the first wildcat in Osage County, Oklahoma, missing the great Glenn Pool by a bare half-mile, and then took the 186,000-acre lease there that Guffey sold to Theodore N. Barnsdall for too little. Galey drilled in Mexico near Tampico, where he lost vast sums of money seeking the oil that was too deep for his equipment. There were few spots he missed, drilling one wildcat in the center of the Mojave Desert and another in the city limits of Washington, D. C.

Out of his intrepid diggings came some of the greatest of the world's oil companies, such as Sinclair Prairie, Standard of Kansas, Barnsdall and others, in addition to those that were born on the hill at Spindletop. Yet with all of this wealth that he helped create, he was a man with a complete disregard for money. He threw away millions in his never ending search for oil and regarded money only as a means to pursue his wildcatting aims. John Galey never looked over his shoulder. His serious eyes were always set straight into the future. What he made or lost yesterday was never a concern to him.

III

The fact that there was oil on Spindletop hill did not surprise Galey. He never looked for it in a place he didn't expect to find it. But the magnificence of the Lucas gusher virtually overwhelmed him. It constituted a fitting climax to the most illustrious career of wildcatting in the annals of the industry.

He arrived in Beaumont three days after the well came in. Already the town was a milling mass of humanity. Because the well had come in without warning there had been no time to lease surrounding land on the hill or even to clear the titles of leases already made. Lucas, overcome with excitement, had failed to wrap up such tracts as the Ingals, the Adams, the Keith-Ward, the Higgins, or the scattered tracts in Gladys City when the opportunity to do so was ripe. When Galey arrived, all of these tracts were gone, and he knew the Guffey Company was in for trouble.

It was Lucas who made the first sale of oil. He entered into a contract with a company operating in Louisiana under a New Jersey charter for mining and dealing in salt, sulphur and other minerals. The contract called for a minimum of 150 barrels of oil and an average of 2500 barrels a day at 25 cents a barrel. The contract was signed on February 16th and called for deliveries to start on March 1st. Strange as it would seem in the years to follow, this contract was with a firm incorporated in New Jersey under the name of the Gulf Company. Within a few weeks that company, with which Lucas had formerly been associated in his mining work in Louisiana, changed its name to the American Salt Company.

IV

Back in Pittsburgh excitement was almost as high as it was in Beaumont. Overnight Colonel Guffey had been transformed into the Napoleon of oil who had risen to challenge the empire of Rockefeller. Guffey, the promoter and showman, had conveyed his enthusiasm, to some extent, to the banking firm of T. Mellon and Sons. But he had not overpowered the imperturbable Andrew W. Mellon. Day after day Guffey made his way to the Mellon bank urging great sums of money to start a new company. He wanted a refinery and more wells, more miles of pipeline, millions of barrels of storage and other facilities that the titanic new oil discovery demanded. But Mellon was reluctant to let him have the enormous sums until all doubt had been dispelled about Spindletop. The accounts were glowing, but they were also confusing. Already the coal barons and the other oil interests had begun to underrate the Lucas gusher.

It took the Beatty well and the next two Guffey wells to convince Mellon. With the evidence in, Andrew Mellon and his brother, Richard B. Mellon, decided to help finance a corporation that would take over the holdings of the Guffey Petroleum Company. It was to be named the J. M. Guffey Petroleum Company and would be capitalized for $15,000,000 with 150,000 shares at $100 each. It being necessary under Texas law to pay in at least 10 per cent of the capital in cash, it was decided that 50,000 shares would be sold for $30 each to provide $1,500,000 for the purchase of the Guffey Petroleum Company and its assets. Guffey was to get 70,000 shares and the remaining 30,000 shares were to go into the treasury.

Guffey's plan, as discussed with Mellon, was to purchase the interests of his partners. He was to pay Galey $750,000, and Lucas $400,000. When he approached Galey, the old wildcatter permitted himself to be talked into dealing for

$366,000 and a handful of loose mining stocks Guffey had in his safe. Lucas was not so easy, but finally A. W. Mellon got him to settle for the $400,000 plus 1,000 shares of Guffey stock. He also agreed to keep Lucas in the company to do some additional exploration work in the salt-dome areas as well as in Kentucky and the southeastern states.

The 50,000 shares of stock were purchased by the two Mellon brothers, who took 10,000 shares each, and by a group of prominent Pittsburgh capitalists who each took 5,000 shares. These men were judge James H. Reed, counsel for Carnegie Steel and the Pennsylvania Railroad; Senator William Flinn, Pittsburgh's political boss; J. D. Callery, bank president; T. H. Given, manufacturer, and Joshua Rhodes and M. K. McMullin, capitalists. As the deal wound up, Guffey had 69,000 shares of stock and $734,000 cash, and was president of the new company.

On May 16th, when the charter was issued for his company, the colorful Colonel paid his first and only visit to Beaumont. Local newspapers described him as a man of "great good humor and hospitality, with eyes that gleam with determination and quickness." Guffey told the press that his company would rank as the greatest fuel-oil firm in the world, occupying the same relation to fuel oil that Standard did to illuminating oil. He offered no objection to comments on the remarkable fact that the greatest oil man in the United States (meaning Guffey) and the greatest oil field in the world had been brought together by a series of most interesting circumstances. Guffey said that because of Spindletop and his organization, "the coal trust can well afford to be uneasy now."

A few weeks later the additional 30,000 shares of J. M. Guffey Company stock was sold at $66 to a group of new capitalists who came into great wealth by virtue of the sale of the Carnegie Steel to J. P. Morgan, who was forming the United

States Steel Company. This had the immediate effect of doubling the value of Guffey stock, giving Guffey a stock interest valued at more than $4,500,000.

In June it was realized that a separate refining company would be required. The directors decided to name the company the Texas Oil Refining Company and directed J. C. McDowell, the manager of the Guffey properties, to take out a charter in that name. McDowell replied that a name nearly like that had been preempted by the Texas Fuel Oil Company and suggested that the name "Gulf" be substituted. The Guffey owners believed that a name like "Texas" or "Gulf" would pay dividends in local pride and goodwill. In November the Gulf Refining Company of Texas was chartered. The company was capitalized for $750,000, and the stock was taken largely by the same men who owned the Guffey stock. There were 150,000 shares at $5 each and Guffey became the largest stockholder and president with 41,673 shares. Again the second largest stockholders were Andrew and Richard Mellon with 16,483 shares each. This company saw the addition of such names as Charles M. Schwab, Lawrence Phipps and James Galey to the list of stockholders.

Early in 1902 Guffey succeeded in talking the Mellons into floating a $5,000,000 bond issue. The Mellon bank took $2,500,000 of the issue and persuaded the Old Colony Trust of Boston to take $1,500,000. The other $1,000,000 was left unissued.

During all this time the Mellons insisted that their relationship to the company remain on a banking basis; they were reluctant to enter the oil business, because they had been in it before to their sorrow. Because of a difference existing between William L. Mellon, a nephew of the Mellon brothers, and Guffey, the younger Mellon, who was a seasoned oil man despite his youth, stayed out of the Guffey company. He preferred to have nothing to do with Guffey's enterprises regardless of their success, and the arrangement seemed to be all right with Guffey. It was obvious to all, however, that the business in Texas was not getting along too well. The price of oil had dropped to 3 cents and the Guffey company, a large producer, was suffering.

V

William Larimer Mellon, nephew of the Mellon brothers, was in his thirties, and preparing to retire from business for a much needed rest in August of 1902 when his Uncle Andrew walked into his office late one afternoon.

The young man saw that his uncle was troubled even before he spoke a word.

"Will, those wells in Texas have stopped flowing," he said. "I'm worried. Someone who knows something about oil should go down to Texas and look into this, and I think you are the one to go."

Some thirteen years earlier, as a young man of twenty, Will Mellon had been lured by the oil business. He had spent six years building up a company, starting in Economy field. During that period he had learned every phase of the business. After developing properties, he had made contracts with a French purchaser that were profitable until the Pennsylvania Railroad raised its freight rates to the point where every barrel shipped represented a loss. Then a contract was made with Reading Railroad with the result that the president was fired and the new executive refused to honor the contract. It was at that point that the pressure of Standard was recognized, or at least suspected. Will and his brothers then decided to build a pipeline to loading facilities at Marcus Hook, on the Delaware River. Their troubles were untold. Fights between railroad and pipeline crews blocked the way for months. Finally, through sheer perseverance, they succeeded in reaching tidewater with the line. Their business increased with other foreign orders, until the day came that Standard had enough. Mellon oil properties were sold to Standard for a profit of some $2,500,000. When the deal was over Will Mellon agreed to spend some time with Standard acquainting that company with his operations. It had been a most successful undertaking, but the Mellons had had their fill of the oil business and competing with the Rockefellers.

At twenty-seven Will Mellon had made a fortune and gone into the streetcar business. Now he had spent seven successful years in that field and had sold out. He was ready for a rest when his uncle asked him to go to Texas.

His report, when he returned, was gloomy. The Guffey company was probably the most botched-up affair he had ever witnessed. The position of advantage as the field discoverer had not been properly exploited. Leases that should have been taken had been missed. Vast sums had been spent on worthless leases. Titles were in bad shape and lawsuits by the hundreds could be expected. Much money had been squandered unnecessarily and necessary money had not been spent. The refinery units were inadequate and required more capital to be put on an efficient basis. Oil would have to be brought in from other new fields, such as Sour Lake and Jennings.

It was the opinion of the two Mellon brothers and their young nephew that the deal needed between $12,000,000 and $15,000,000 in new money as soon as possible. The Mellons had a bear by the tail and wanted to let go.

Andrew Mellon made an engagement with Henry H. Rogers and John D. Archbold for a meeting at the old Holland House in New York. Carefully and in minute detail the situation was explained and an offer made to turn the company over to Standard if the Mellons could recover most of their investments and those of their friends and the Old Colony Trust. Now it was Rogers' turn to talk, and he was brief.

"We're out," he said. "After the way Mr. Rockefeller has been treated by the State of Texas, he'll never put another dime down there. But it's all right. You have our best wishes."

Now the Mellons were back in the oil business whether they wanted to be or not. But at least Standard had given its blessing. Trouble with the oil trust could be avoided.

VI

William L. Mellon became the executive vice-president of the J. M. Guffey Petroleum Company and the Gulf Refining Company. He took into this job many outstanding qualities, including a soaring imagination, a capacity for making good decisions, and the ability to judge men. He recognized his job from the outset and knew that to be successful the company must have ample production.

His problems were even greater than he had anticipated. For instance, he found, upon moving to Beaumont, that Guffey had made a contract in June of 1901 with the Shell Trade and Transport Company for 4,500,000 barrels of oil over a period of twenty years at 25 cents a barrel. Early in 1902 the prices had increased above that point and were rising rapidly. This contract alone could strangle the company out of existence in a short time. Something had to be done. Shell was a trading company which entered the petroleum trading field at the insistence of Colonel Guffey, who thought he had made the greatest deal of his life. The company, on the strength of the Guffey contract, had purchased tankers and other facilities for handling oil in England.

Andrew Mellon made a trip to England to see the Shell officials and successfully negotiated a new contract. He convinced the Shell people that the Guffey contract would bankrupt the company and leave Shell without the oil to fulfill its own commitments. A new contract calling for a large amount of oil at a fair price over a period of six months was agreed upon. Shell's interest in the oil industry was born of the

Lucas gusher and Spindletop, and the future would prove the good fortune of that birth.

The changes the new executive vice-president had to make were bound to throw him into conflict with his old enemy, Jim Guffey. The difference between the two men had started long before Spindletop, when Guffey had taken an oil deal to the Mellon bank. The brothers had called W. L. in for advice, and he had recommended against the Guffey proposal. Guffey was furious and thereafter blamed young Mellon every time the Mellon bank refused him a loan.

As soon as he arrived in Beaumont, Will Mellon decided that personnel changes had to be made. He let out most of the men that Guffey had put into jobs and began hiring experienced oil men and business managers. McDowell, for instance, general manager for Guffey Petroleum Company, was a politician like Guffey, although a Republican. But Mellon had problems that politicians were not capable of handling. He engaged the services of H. C. Markham, a vice-president of Southern Pacific, to head the company administratively in Texas and Louisiana.

Mellon found out that George H. Tabor, one of Henry Rogers' protégés, was dissatisfied in his position with Atlantic, a Standard affiliate, and hired him for the Gulf Company. Tabor was a self-taught chemist who came from an old New England whale-oil family. Though irascible, he was a most competent man and equal to the multitude of problems that Gulf's refinery faced in Port Arthur, then a small settlement some ten miles south of Spindletop.

George Craig was hired to take over production, and he brought along John H. Fisher to handle pipelines. Both were excellent men.

Gale R. Nutty was the best salesman in the business, and Mellon, knowing that getting rid of the Beaumont crude was one of his monumental tasks, engaged his services.

One day Will Mellon and his wife stopped in Beaumont for a brief visit and checked their baggage at the station. The station agent became confused and misplaced the baggage. Another man stepped up, took over the checks, and in a few minutes cleared up things with courtesy and efficiency. Mellon introduced himself and made a note of the man's name and his position. He was Frank Leovy, district passenger and freight agent, who had been sent to Beaumont from New Orleans as a trouble shooter. Mellon, on the lookout for good men, hired Leovy, who later rose to the vice-presidency of the Gulf Oil Corporation.

With these men as a nucleus, Mellon began to make some progress with his problem company. He was receiving terrific competition from the Texas Company, Sun, Higgins, Heywood and others, including the Burt Refinery, a company that he strongly suspected of being Standard in spite of Mr. Rockefeller's determination to stay out of Texas. But under experienced and forceful leadership, Gulf and Guffey continued to improve.

VII

As the days passed into weeks and months and years, Mellon continued to wrestle with the hill and the other fields that had come into being after Lucas had shown the way with his nascent-dome theory.

Guffey, bad manager that he was, continued at the head of the company and was a constant obstacle to Will Mellon. In the meantime his money affairs had gone bad and he owed the Mellon bank alone more than a million dollars in principal and unpaid interest. He owed much more to other Pittsburgh banks. The Mellon bank held 24,000 shares of Guffey stock as collateral.

In 1907, when the Glenn Pool came in in Oklahoma, Will Mellon saw the chance to make the Guffey and Gulf properties highly profitable, if they could build a pipeline from Oklahoma to the Gulf. In spite of the protests of Guffey, the company was reorganized again and the Gulf Oil Corporation took over the J. M. Guffey Petroleum Company, the Gulf Refining Company of Texas and the recently created Gulf Pipeline Company. The Gulf Oil Corporation was capitalized for $15,000,000 and authority was voted to float $15,000,000 in bonds. Guffey, miffed, decided to get out and was paid more than $2,500,000 for his stock interest. The Mellon bank, the Old Colony Trust, and other creditors were paid off. Andrew W. Mellon was happy again. He was president of the new company for two years. In 1909 his nephew took over the job to hold it for the next thirty-five years, during which time it would become one of the great petroleum enterprises of the world.

Within a short time after the sale Guffey found himself in the hands of receivers. He had tried to corner the coal market and had met with dismal failure.

Galey, the great old wildcatter, continued to stick his inquiring nose into oil sands. Like most wildcatters, he spent all he made seeking hidden reserves. His last days were spent with his favorite nephew, Thomas M. Galey, who traveled over the continent with him. John Galey's last venture was financed by Al Hamill, his old driller from Corsicana and Beaumont. The day it failed and the two parted company, Galey confided to Hamill that he was poorer than he had ever been in his entire lifetime.

John Galey died at Joplin, Missouri, in 1912, still looking for oil. Old Colonel Guffey came to the funeral, looked at John Galey for the last time and recalled how John had led him into the greatest oil discovery of the world's history.

"Lillian," he said to Galey's wife, "we are burying the best man I have ever known."

CHAPTER TEN

A Star Is Born

ONE night in 1901 six men sat in the lobby of the Crosby House. They were to be principal members of the cast in one of Spindletop's most absorbing dramas.

They were Joseph Stephen Cullinan, ex-Governor James Stephen Hogg, John Warne (Bet-A-Million) Gates, Walter Sharp, Arnold Schlaet, and James Roche, men who would soon band together to create one of the two most important oil companies in the world that grew out of Spindletop hill. Each of them except Roche, represented a group. Roche, the lone wolf, was a charming, penniless Englishman who had come to Beaumont to find fortune and adventure.

Each had a definite contribution to make toward the beginning of what would be known as the Texas Company, and each is entitled to proper introduction.

II

Joe Cullinan, sometimes known to his friends as "Buckskin Joe," was a man who believed that doubts and fears are man's worst enemies, and that as long as a man doesn't know he can't do a thing, there is nothing he can't accomplish.

Cullinan was a daring and restless man, a gambler who mixed caution with boldness, and who was probably the nearest to an all-around oil genius ever born. Athletic and agile, with quick, searching eyes and a clear, vigorous voice, his very handclasp inspired confidence. He was tall, handsome and distinguished, with cleancut features, a short-cropped moustache and a head of thick, well-groomed hair. A man of decision, he possessed an active, intelligent mind of the type given only to leaders.

The road to Spindletop was a natural one for Joe Cullinan. He was born in Sharon, Pennsylvania, and he had grown up in the midst of the petroleum industry. When he was only twenty-two he went to work for Standard on a small job. Thirteen years later, after he had been made manager of the big company's natural-gas interests, he resigned and organized the Petroleum Iron Works to manufacture oil tanks. Then oil was discovered in Corsicana. Guffey and Galey took the situation over, but moved out because their business was finding oil, not refining and marketing. One day Joe Cullinan visited the Texas State Fair in Dallas en route to California. There he was met by the governor, the mayor, and a virtual posse of leading Texans who practically shanghaied him to Corsicana to take over the industry. He reluctantly acceded to the demands and a did a magnificent job, with the help of friends in Standard's family.

But the morning he saw the Lucas gusher he knew that Corsicana's day was over. He organized, with his brother, Dr. M. P. Cullinan, and a friend, H. L. Scales, a $50,000 corporation which he called the Texas Fuel Oil Company, and, almost a year after the Spindletop discovery, severed his Corsicana connections and headed for Beaumont.

III

Texas never had had before, nor has it had since, a governor like James Stephen Hogg. He was the first native son to hold the high office. He was a genuine trust-buster and octopus hunter. It was at his behest that the state's antitrust laws were made strong and enforceable. Jim Hogg had a manner about him. He could charm any individual or any group. A giant of a man, he stood over six feet in height and weighed more than 300 pounds. He was voluble, vigorous, and buoyant. His personal magnetism was overwhelming. He was a jovial raconteur whose stories are told and retold to this day. In the eyes of his people he could do no wrong, even when he himself became, for a while, a one-man trust and admitted to being something of an octopus.

Jim Hogg had never been to Spindletop until Jim Swayne, his best friend, and the man who had been his floor leader in the state senate, took him there, not long after the discovery. Hogg was more interested in oil on his West Columbia farm than anywhere else. He went to Fort Worth to ask Swayne to accompany him to West Columbia, where he was to talk with a group of New Yorkers about drilling on his land. The deal didn't pan out, so Swayne induced Hogg to go on to Beaumont with him.

Once in Beaumont, the Governor couldn't understand why he had been so long getting there. Even if there was no business for him, there were people, and they were excited, milling and happy, and that was the way he liked things. He drew almost as much attention in town as the gusher did on the hill. Whether he was riding a skiff over flooded streets from his suite in the Oaks on fashionable Calder Avenue to the Crosby, dressed in a bright green slicker and covered with a brighter yellow umbrella, or holding forth in the Crosby lobby telling stories, Jim Hogg was in his element.

The Governor seldom went to the hill after his first visit. He let Jim Swayne and that other human dynamo named W. T. Campbell, a man almost as big as Hogg himself, handle his business. They took in two other friends and formed what Swayne called the Hogg-Swayne Syndicate.

"Call it Hogg-Swayne et al., Jim," Hogg told Swayne at first. "I don't feel too comfortable being associated with that word syndicate."

But it was still the Hogg-Swayne Syndicate. The other original members were Campbell, Colonel A. S. Fisher, and Judge R. E. Brooks. The syndicate was never chartered or incorporated; it was simply a group of friends banded together. Business was all done the way Jim Swayne or Willie Campbell suggested. They were honest and honorable men, so there was no sense in a lot of paper signing.

The story of the Hogg-Swayne Syndicate has already been told in Chapter 8. The "door mat" sales and leases which they made to raise the money brought on the boom, the wild speculation in stocks and land, the irreverent dissipation of the natural resources, the fires and the uncontrollable chaos.

IV

Wherever the wheels of fortune spun, there you would find John Warne (Bet-A-Million) Gates. He was the kind of man who enjoyed a fight. It wasn't Spindletop that took him to the alligator-infested, mosquito-ridden swamps that are now the thriving industrial city of Port Arthur. He was there to promote a city which would be the southern terminus of his Kansas City Southern Railroad. He tried to get the land he needed at Sabine Pass, but the Kountze brothers had their own ideas and all of the land there. Then, with the illustrious Arthur Stillwell, he platted the city of Port Arthur and planned its future. He told the Kountze brothers he would throw dirt in their faces building streets in Port Arthur, and that is virtually what he did.

He built a beautiful colonial home on Sabine Lake where Port Arthur now stands, and his faithful associate, Ike Ellwood, built a home of elegant Italian architecture, which he called Pompeian Villa. Gates owned Round Lake, which he converted into a private fishing and hunting club. The great and near great of the nation were his guests there even before the great gusher erupted a few miles to the north.

Gates was more attracted by the lush gambling palaces of Beaumont at first than he was by the oil boom itself. Daring gambler that he was, he was too smart for the wildcat stock promotions, but he knew the boom was exactly what his K.C.S. railroad plan needed. He immediately ordered it completed to Port Arthur.

The world looked on John W. Gates as a fabulous character and he was that. But he was a more solid citizen than the newspapers painted him. Gambling was his obsession, but he played the game well in business or in faro. He was fascinated by the hill north of his adopted home, but decided to hold his cards until he could size up the game and the players. He wanted to know what use could be made of the type of petroleum Spindletop was producing. His friends, among the most prominent men in the country, held off at his suggestion until the time was ripe.

V

When the first well was drilled on Big Hill, as it was then known, for the Gladys City company and Pattillo Higgins, Walter Sharp directed the operation. It was he who had the subcontract from Loonie, the sewer man who talked to Higgins first. Sharp's well was a failure because he didn't have adequate equipment and he was dealing with a geological condition that no man had encountered before. His failure on the hill was no disgrace, but the Lucas gusher was a source of almost unbearable embarrassment to him.

Walter Sharp barely missed getting in on leases in Spindletop before the gusher blew in. One of his old drillers, George Rainey, told him in Dallas during Christmas week that the Hamills had gone home so that Lucas could buy up leases. He said that the oil field was already a certainty. Sharp, normally a healthy man, became ill after arranging to go to Beaumont on January 1st, and was not able to get there until after the well came in.

When he arrived in Beaumont on January 12th, there was little chance for leasing on the hill. With Ed Prather, an old friend who had been treasurer of Dallas County until the close of 1900, Sharp decided to lease land on the line between Spindletop and Sour Lake, where he had already found oil showings. He leased thousands of acres and as the scramble for land increased, he and Prather each made a small fortune. His rigs were busy drilling on and around the hill throughout the first year of the boom.

Walter Sharp and his brother, Jim, were perfectionists who took their drilling seriously. Their contributions to the progress of rotary drilling had already made history, and their future in the field would be even more impressive. Sharp, a rangy man, was a tireless worker and his active, inventive mind was constantly on the alert for new and better ways to do things. He was receptive to new ideas and joined the Hamills, the Sturms and others who developed the methods of modern oil production. Later he was associated with Howard Hughes, Sr., in important inventions and other deals.

Cullinan depended heavily on Walter and Jim Sharp in his plans. He knew they were the kind of men who would be necessary in a sound operation of the type he had in mind.

Arnold Schlaet was a German and a brilliant man with financial power. He was the spokesman for the Laphams, who controlled the leather trust. Schlaet had won that position by his handling of a difficult negotiation in Europe a few years before Spindletop.

He went to Beaumont early in the boom, but waited for speculators and gamblers to have their day before he acted. Like most men connected with a trust, he was an ultra-conservative, almost a pessimist, but he knew that the impact Spindletop had made on the world was only beginning to be felt. Somewhere there was something for him and his associates, and he left Beaumont only for urgent business, always returning within a few days to see if the opportunity he was seeking had developed.

Arnold Schlaet was the fifth member of Cullinan's supporting cast, but by no means the least important.

VI

The acorn that grew into the mighty Texas Company oak was planted by Cullinan when he organized his $50,000 Texas Fuel Oil Company. The development that caused him finally to sever his connections with Corsicana was the 3-cent price at Spindletop after the Hogg-Swayne small-tract pattern had resulted in tremendous waste and overproduction.

He went to Beaumont in January of 1902 and started purchasing oil contracts calling for delivery starting in June. He took a million-barrel option off the hands of Roche, whose resourcefulness knew no limits. Cullinan announced that his company would be a common carrier and would take anyone's product after the proposed pipeline was built. In this way, those without their own transportation facilities could dispose of their product. His contracts called for the delivery of millions of barrels of oil over periods of from one to three years, and some for the life of certain wells.

This meant that Cullinan would have to build storage, loading and shipping facilities and pipelines, calling for huge sums of money which he was not immediately prepared to invest. His first transportation arrangements limited him to 2,000 barrels a day by rail from Gladys City to Sabine Pass. There it was taken by Tidewater Oil Company, Standard Oil and miscellaneous barges to the Louisiana sugar mills. His delivery was limited by the fact that he was able to contract for only eleven tank cars. He did the most with what he had by making arrangements for continuous crews that ate and slept in the train's caboose. There were no demands for premium wages because Cullinan was exceedingly generous with the hard-driving railroaders.

While this was going on, the Hogg-Swayne Syndicate was beginning to run into trouble. Many of the syndicate's land sales had been made on the basis of nominal cash payments and the remainder out of oil. But there was no market for the oil and the shoestringers were caught short and, consequently, so was the syndicate. Hogg, Swayne and Campbell decided something had to be done. In his travels over the state and nation the Governor had heard much of Cullinan and decided he was the man to solve their dilemma.

Hogg proposed to Cullinan that the syndicate purchase half of the Texas Fuel Oil Company's stock at par value for $25,000, and make certain loans to start more widespread operations, including a pipeline. In the meantime Walter and Jim Sharp had promoted the organization of the Producers Oil Company on the strength of a million-barrel contract with Cullinan.

In Port Arthur the news of this amalgamation of interests caused some excitement. James Roche, the Englishman, was living comfortably at the sumptuous Sabine Hotel. He knew that land in both Port Arthur and Sabine was at a premium and that the competition between the Kountze brothers and the Gates people was at a critical stage. Either Port Arthur was going to be a city or Sabine was, not both of them. And it depended on which one got the industries, specifically the oil refineries.

Roche let it be known that he was securing an option on land for a refinery and hinted that Sabine was making a good offer. Shortly he was called in by George Craig, a Gates man and president of the Port Arthur bank. Craig told Roche that he knew of his plans and said that he and another man owned a brick kiln located on land that would be suitable for a refinery.

"How many acres will you let me have, Craig?" Roche asked.

"As many as you need," was the reply.

"Forty acres?" Roche fished.

"Yes," Craig answered directly.

"How much an acre?" Roche continued.

"A hundred dollars," Craig said.

"How much down?" was the test question put by Roche.

"Nothing," Craig smiled.

"Will you put that in writing?" Roche asked with some suspicion.

"Yes," said Craig as he drew out a contract form already made out except for the number of acres, which was filled in in ink.

The forty acres on which Roche took a sixty-day option was sold a few weeks later to the Texas Fuel Oil Company as the site for its first refinery. Craig, as a matter of fact, negotiated the deal with Roche for his own land but he paid several times the $100 an acre.

VII

Arnold Schlaet saw his opportunity at last and decided to invest some of the Lapham, leather money in Cullinan's new Texas Fuel Oil Company. He enjoyed the complete confidence of his employers and was able to invest as he saw fit. They knew that he would not move until he saw the proper opening, and that is exactly what happened.

Now it was decided that even more money was necessary and that the Producers Company, which would become the source of supply for the Texas Fuel Oil Company as well as the production operation, should be bolstered. George Craig was asked to go to New York and invite Gates to serve on the board of Producers Oil Company. A great and lasting friendship and mutual respect had begun to weld Joe Cullinan and John W. Gates together.

In New York Craig explained the entire deal to Gates and said that Cullinan, Hogg and Schlaet wanted him on the board of directors of the Producers Company.

"What about the refining company?" Gates asked.

Craig explained that he believed that could be financed without additional help.

"If my party comes in, it will be in both companies," Gates said, "and I want at least half interest in each."

Craig said that he was authorized to speak only for the Producers Company, but that he believed the other deal could be arranged. Actually Craig knew that syndicate people as well as Schlaet were anxious to keep Gates out of the refinery company at first. Gates then sent a telegram to a dozen friends, most of whom he had made wealthy, and explained the situation, asking if they would join him and in what amounts. He suggested that the replies be sent to Craig.

Gates and Craig returned to Port Arthur. They were joined by another of Gates's friends, James Hopkins, president of the Diamond Match Company. At Spindletop a few days later Gates and Hopkins were shown one of Sharp's gushing wells. A few days later the important members of the cast were together. Roche sold back the refinery site he had taken an option on on credit from Craig. All of Gates's telegrams had produced results, and he and his friends owned half of both Producers and Texas Fuel Oil Companies.

Work was started on a dozen giant storage tanks at Garrison Station in Iowa Colony between Beaumont and Spindletop. A contract for a six-inch pipeline to the refinery site was let to Jack Ennis, a colorful reformed gambler, who was destined to make and lose two fortunes of his own.

In the next few weeks disaster struck. The hill virtually stopped flowing. Most of Sharp's wells went dead and two of them started making salt water. Within a few days every type of oilwell pumping device known to man was being rushed to Beaumont. Soon the price of oil shot up to 75 cents. This gave tremendous value to Cullinan's oil purchase contracts when pumping proved successful. It would have spelled doom, however, for the Producers Company except for the fact that it had Gates's money and Cullinan's influence behind it.

In early April Gates returned to Beaumont for a meeting at which the Texas Fuel Oil Company became the Texas Company. It was a rush trip for Gates, whose vast interests required his traveling to various parts of the country day after day. When the meeting was over Gates ordered a special train.

He was informed the train could not be ready for about two hours. An active man, old Bet-A-Million walked from the Crosby to the Ogden saloon and up to the second floor where a plush gambling room was in full operation. He started playing faro at $2500 a game, the house limit. His luck was terrible and he finally asked Likens Ogden to raise the limit, but the excited and nervous owner refused. When the two hours were up, Gates had lost $20,000 which he could well afford to do. As he left, he stopped to shake hands with Ogden, who was still discomposed by his winnings.

"Likens, you are a real friend," Gates said, "if you had raised that limit you would be half-owner of a new oil company, and I might be taking a freight out of here tonight instead of a special train."

VIII

On May 1, 1902, it was formally announced that the Texas Company had been chartered for $3,000,000 and would take over the assets of the Texas Fuel Oil Company. Offices were set up in the Exall Building, a frame structure covered with corrugated iron and located on Laurel Street west of the Crosby and north of the S.P. tracks. At the directors' meeting, Cullinan was elected president. Arnold Schlaet was made first vice-president and placed in charge of the New York office in the Maritime Building at 8 Bridge Street. In spite of the necessity for an eastern office, there was a tacit understanding between Cullinan, Gates and Campbell, the Hogg-Swayne man for the board, that the company would never move its main office out of Texas.

This new company brought about an unforeseen incident, however, that threatened its existence. The Independence Oil Company stopped supplying oil under its contract made previously with the Texas Fuel Oil Company for 3 cents a barrel. The Texas Company brought suit and lost. This opened the way for every contract Cullinan had made to be voided if the producers so desired.

Walter Sharp stepped in to save the day. He organized his famous Moonshine Oil Company, with Howard Hughes and Ed Prather and with Cullinan or Texas Company money. Sharp's new company was in possession of a patented process whereby it could inject air into oil wells and make them flow again. The fee was half or more of the oil produced.

The Texas Company's great opportunity came late in 1902 when it was learned that Sour Lake was a definite oil field, probably equal to Spindletop and less than twenty-five miles away. James Roche, the soft-spoken Englishman, had slipped into town and picked up an option on 815 acres, including the old resort hotel.

The option, which Roche again used his credit to obtain, cost $12,000, and the price tag on the land was $900,000. Sharp drilled three wells proving the land before the option was exercised. The first two were controlled and no one knew the result. The gods were with the Texas Company on the third one. Sharp found good oil showings, but delayed testing the well. His opportunity came one night in a blinding rainstorm. It was a tremendous gusher, but by morning all evidence of the oil had washed away. It was realized that if the facts were known, the price of oil would tumble.

Board approval was needed to expend the necessary funds to exercise the option. Gates was informed of the situation and told that an immediate board meeting was necessary.

"Where will we meet?" Gates asked.

"Well," Cullinan replied, "the property includes the resort hotel at Sour Lake. We could meet there."

Gates thought a minute. He recalled Jim Hogg's description of the place. It was a ramshackle frame building located in front of the old Sour Lake now called the "Ponce de Leon Springs" by "Dr. Mud," its quack promoter. The lake was about 200 feet in diameter, had stagnant, dirty water about a foot deep, with gas bubbles gurgling up through the scum-covered waters. The bath house amounted to high boards around a corner of the lake to keep razorback hogs from mingling and wallowing in the gassy mud with the guests who were there to cure the gout, itch, cancer, ringworm, tick bites, or any other normal human annoyances.

"Tell you what, Joe," Gates said, "if you don't mind, let's meet at my suite in the Royal Ponciana at West Palm Beach."

That's where the board met. Gates was so enthusiastic he wanted to put up all of the money and take that much new Texas Company stock. Schlaet, always wary of Gates, said that would not be necessary. All they needed was board approval and the money could be obtained through normal financing channels. Cullinan rushed home and made contracts to sell the oil for 60 cents a barrel. Soon after the well came in Sour Lake's spot oil price dropped to 10 cents, but Cullinan and the Texas Company continued to get 60 cents.

The Texas Company soon took its position in the new world of competition and the star that was born on the hill at

Spindletop began a gradual ascension. Every man who joined Cullinan had made his contribution. None ever lost his respect for Buckskin Joe, or challenged his leadership. The principles and policies that he promulgated in those days were sound and lasting.

Most of the original group stayed with the company to see it through the struggles of the early days. One, however, accomplished his mission early and departed.

James Roche, the handsome, suave, cultured Englishman, got $30,000 for his part in securing option on the Sour Lake land, settled his bill with a grand flourish at the Sabine Hotel, paid his respects to all who had been kind to him, and left to return to his native England, where he later became an earl at the death of his two older brothers. Cullinan pleaded with Roche to take an eighth interest. It would not have been too great a gamble, as the oil was already proven, and it would have made him millions. That was the only trading mistake Roche ever made. The lease is still producing oil.

As the years passed and Gates, Sharp, Hogg, Campbell and the other great individualists died, Buckskin Joe was left with one of his greatest problems. He was determined that the original decision to keep the company headquarters in Texas should be respected. When the stockholders who succeeded Joe's old friends voted to move the offices to New York, Cullinan relinquished the reins of leadership and resigned from the board.

Arnold Schlaet, the German conservative, was largely responsible for the move to New York. Yet within a few years Schlaet himself was forced to resign from the board.

When Cullinan left, the company lost the last of the colorful figures who created the Texaco star out of the storm and strife of the hill, but it would never lose the heritage left it by its sons of Spindletop.

CHAPTER ELEVEN

The Rising Sun

THE day the Lucas gusher came in, Charley Ingals, the self-appointed Paul Revere, rode his cow pony back to the well site after arousing the citizenry of Beaumont to the historic event that had taken place on its outskirts.

As the crowd gathered around the well, he still complained that the monstrosity had ruined his seven-acre farm. He said he had paid $400 for the land, and that he would sell it for a dime.

Two Beaumont businessmen walked over to Charley and offered to buy his farm.

"What'll ya give me?" Charley asked Bruce Greeves and Marion Fletcher.

Fletcher replied that he and Greeves would put up $1000 apiece if Charley would take it immediately.

"I'll sure take it," Ingals boomed, "but we'll have to see what the missus says."

The three men got into the carriage and were joined by Emmett Fletcher, Marion's brother, and C. A. Hageman, the manager of the Crosby House. As they drove off, conservative Beaumonters who had overheard the conversation shook their heads. Some of them mumbled about the foolishness of paying five times the value of a piece of land when no one knew how long the geyser of oil was going to last.

At the Ingals home, Mrs. Ingals told Charley he could take $2,000 if he wanted to, but that she would have to have the same amount. Greeves and Fletcher said they would not pay more than $1,000 each and Mrs. Ingals said the price was $4,000 or nothing. It seemed that an impasse had been reached.

Emmett Fletcher and Hageman, who had been looking out a window toward the gusher, talking quietly between themselves, came into the conversation.

"Marion," Emmett said addressing his brother, "if you and Bruce agree, Hageman and I will put up another $1,000 each and take a quarter interest."

Marion Fletcher and Greeves approved and the deal was made.

It was the first land deal ever made in Jefferson County with full knowledge of the existence of oil. Ingals sold for $4,000 that early afternoon of January 10, 1901, a property which, had he held it another few weeks, could have brought him a thousand times that amount.

II

For almost a month the Beaumonters who purchased Ingals' land were not certain they had made a good buy. Most interest seemed centered in larger acreage, off the hill. In February, however, their doubt resolved itself. Edward G. Schlieder, a prominent businessman from New Orleans, called on Marion Fletcher and made him an offer. It was breathtaking. Schlieder headed a group of men who had conducted the Louisiana lottery until it was declared illegal. They were men with keen promotional sense who saw a great opportunity in Beaumont.

The exact details of the offer Schlieder made to Fletcher were not revealed. The day after, however, Fletcher explained what he knew of the deal and purchased the interests of his three associates for $75,000 each. Later it was learned the Schlieder group planned to form a $2,500,000 corporation with the Ingals tract as the most important property. Greeves and Emmett Fletcher then decided they would like to be in the deal and were permitted to repurchase their interest for $80,000 each. Hageman, content with $75,000 for his $1,000 investment, remained out.

Within a few days the Lone Star and Crescent Oil Company was formed. It was destined to become one of the most fabulous, if short-lived, companies to operate on the hill. Schlieder was president, Marion Fletcher was first vice-president, Greeves was secretary and general manager, and Emmett Fletcher was treasurer. The other New Orleans associates were named to the board of directors.

It was shortly after the Beatty well came in that Lone Star and Crescent spudded its first well, but the company's stock went on sale immediately. Even before the company's first well came in arrangements were made for tankage. On May 3rd, the Lone Star and Crescent No. 1 blew in after two weeks of untold hardship. Virtually every possible mechanical and drilling misfortune befell the drillers. For a short while it was feared that oil might not be found where the company was drilling, although it was only 100 feet north of the Beatty. When the well came in it was, however, one of the most perfect on the hill.

Two weeks later Schlieder made arrangements with H. and L. Kountze, the New York and Omaha bankers promoting Sabine town sites, for 400 feet of frontage on tidewater at Sabine Pass. Before returning to New Orleans, Schlieder let a contract for a six-inch pipeline from the field to the terminal, and another for the construction of five large storage tanks, and pumping facilities. Three of these were to be built in Sabine Pass, one in Spindletop, and another in Beaumont. Arrangements were made to run a smaller pipeline to the storage tank in Beaumont.

For more than a year, Lone Star and Crescent was one of the three great companies on the hill. Its operations were regarded as exemplary. Greeves was a local manufacturer and a man of great imagination. One of his first ideas was to cover the Lone Star well with brick housing to protect it from possible fire dangers. Others copied this idea after the big fires. He tried another plan which did not seem to work. A sixty-foot standpipe was built and the well line turned into it. The idea was that the standpipe could provide sufficient pressure to push oil into Beaumont without pumps, and to serve as additional storage.

In October, when the twenty-two mile pipeline to Sabine was completed, the company was classed with Guffey Petroleum and the Higgins Oil and Fuel as one of the three big oil concerns operating in the field. It was those three that had taken the lead in arranging for transportation and markets for the product of the hill. It was those, newspapers said, that would be there when most of the stock-promotion companies were gone and forgotten.

By far the most important news Beaumont had heard since the great gusher itself was an announcement by Parsons Davis, Lone Star market chief, who returned from England on January 4, 1902, that he had a contract in his pocket for 10,000,000 barrels of Spindletop oil for the Lone Star and Crescent Company. It was cause for great jubilation, but it was probably the reason that Lone Star and Crescent went broke. When Davis went to England oil was selling for 3 cents a barrel. The very day he returned, the price advanced, and within a few months it was 30 cents a barrel. Three months later, the Lone Star and Crescent, stuck with commitments beyond its ability to fulfill in view of the sharp increase in oil prices, went into receivership.

III

Joseph Newton Pew, the son of a farmer, born in western Pennsylvania, was head of one of the small but important independent oil companies of the east. He had entered the industry as a gas producer and marketer, heading the company that supplied the fuel for Pittsburgh to become the first large city in the world to have natural gas for heating, lighting and cooking. He was a conservative, intelligent, brilliant, inventive man with unlimited energy. Ten years before Spindletop he was in the oil business with production in Ohio fields and a small refinery in Toledo. His company, known as the Sun Oil Company, was as successful as any small company not part of Standard. Joe Pew was waiting for an opportunity his intuition told him would come some day.

When the electrifying news of the Lucas gusher reached the Sun office in Toledo on the morning of January 11th, Pew lost no time. He sent his nephew, Robert C. Pew, to Beaumont immediately to see the prospect. Robert stayed a month and came back with fantastic reports. He said some believed the well was a freak that would flow no more, while others, like Cullinan, believed it to be the most important oil discovery in the world's history. Robert Pew was among the optimists. He strongly recommended that further action be taken by Sun.

J. Edgar Pew, Robert's young brother, was then sent to Beaumont. He was only thirty years old, and had started working in his uncle's refinery as a plumber's helper at sixteen. He had been to Texas before to look over Corsicana, and he liked the country. In view of the wild reports of the murders and hijackings, he armed himself with a .41 caliber revolver as he headed for the boom town.

The Beaumont story had not been exaggerated. Edgar Pew stepped off the train into a whirlwind of activity. He saw the stock promoters from Cripple Creek, the unsavory conditions, but most of all he saw the Beatty well come roaring in. He wasn't in Beaumont to go on a lease or land buying spree and he had the restraint that it took to sit and wait. He knew that the time was coming when Sun would take a big part, but he also knew that it would be foolish to plunge in and get head over heels in the production of oil before there was a market or a way to get it out of Texas and refine it.

His reports, after the Beatty well came in, convinced his uncle that the day he had long awaited had finally arrived. To get ready for the big things that to him were certain to happen, Joe Pew bought the eighty-two-acre Lindenthorpe Pleasure Park site, with a 1000-foot front on the Delaware River at Marcus Hook, Pennsylvania, twenty miles from Philadelphia. In November, 1901, still before he had a vestige of interest in the Beaumont field, outside of oil purchases on a small scale, work was started on the refinery that Pew knew he would need. The blue chip his shrewd operations had already won would be put into the game, but he would play his cards close to his vest.

J. Edgar Pew continued to sit patiently around biding his time and watching men plunge into the mad scramble to produce oil which they could not sell. He knew that sooner or later an opening would come. He also knew that when it did come he would need docks and storage from which to ship the crude oil. His first action, after several months of waiting, was to buy two sites at Smith's Bluff totaling forty-two acres. That land wasn't in the oil play, but it was one of the highest and best tracts of land along the Neches River seven miles south of Beaumont and southeast of Spindletop, where barges could pick up oil.

This is a letter head of the Oil Company that I organized in the year 1892. The lithograph represents the business that I aimed to carry on at Gladys City. The business would have been on the ground at this present day 1901, if the Directors of my company had listened to my advice, and Gladys City would have been today the largest manufacturing city in the South.

My Company was chartered under the laws of Texas on the 24th day of August 1892.

PATTILLO HIGGINS.

Pattillo Higgins in 1901 and the letterhead of his original oil company

Captain Anthony F. Lucas

John H. Galey

Gladys City on the Spindletop Mound

A crowd of boomers in front of the Crosby House

Daily scene at Southern Pacific depot during the boom

Hogg-Swayne tract before the fire, 1902

Hogg-Swayne tract after the fire, 1903

The Guffey post office at Spindletop

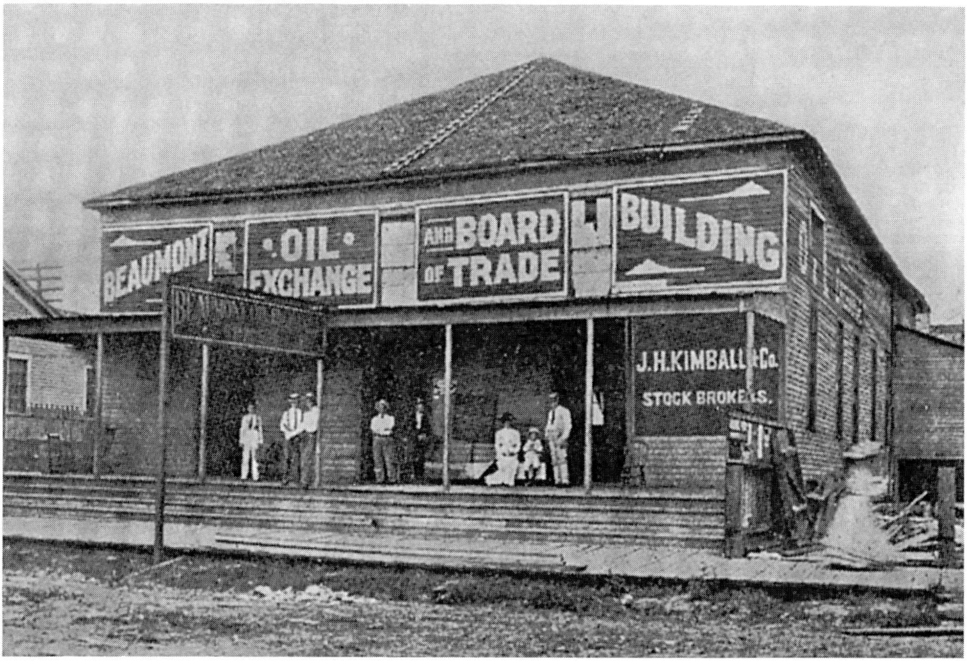

The Beaumont Oil Exchange and Board of Trade

George Washington Carroll, 1900

Daily call, Beaumont Oil Exchange and Board of Trade

Some oil company stock certificates

OIL COMPANIES

CHARTERED SINCE JAN. 10TH, 1901.

TEXAS OIL COMPANIES

American O. Co., Bmt.	$1,000,000
Am. L. & O. Co., Port Arthur	250,000
Alamo City O. Co., San Antonio	25,000
Alamo O. Co., Bmt.	100,000
Acme O. Co., Bmt.	100,000
Anchor O. & Devel. Co., Fort Worth	50,000
Alvin O. & Rice Devel. Co., Alvin	25,000
Acme O. & Fuel Co., Bmt.	60,000
Austin-Bmt. O. Co., Austin	50,000
Aetna O. Co., Fort Worth	200,000
Am. O. & Refin. Co. of Tex., Bmt.	500,000
Brenham-Bmt. O. Co., Brenham	250,000
Bryan Heights O. & P. L. Co., Velasco	500,000
Bmt. Interstate O. Co., Texarkana	500,000
Bunn's Bluff O. & P. L. Co., Bmt.	500,000
Bmt. & El Paso O. Co., Bmt.	1,000,000
Blue Ridge O. & Devel. Co., Houston	400,000
Bay Shore O. Co., La Porte	50,000
Brilliant O. Co., Weatherford	150,000
Bmt. & Brazos Valley O. Co., Bryant	40,000
Black Hawk O. Co., Bmt.	300,000
Chicago-Texas O. Syndicate, Houston	1,000,000
Cincinnati-Bmt. O. Co., Bmt.	250,000
Cacti O. Co., Pecos City	10,000
Dixie Oil Co., Bmt.	100,000
Dallas O. & Fuel Co., Dallas	10,000
Drillers O. Co., Bmt.	150,000
Dallas O. Co., Dallas	150,000
Drummers Oil Co., Bmt.	250,000
Developers O. Co., of Beaumont & Dallas	400,000
Dickinson O. Co., Galveston	250,000
Damon Mound O. & Mining Co., Richmond	100,000
Damon Mound O. Co., Alvin	500,000
Delaware & Texas O. Co. Bmt.	500,000
Denison, Bmt. & Sour Lake O. Co., Denison	200,000
David Crockett O. & Mining Co., Crockett	20,000
Diamond O. Co., Bmt.	100,000
Double Bayou O. Co., Galveston	200,000
Dixie O. & P. L. Co., Marshall	120,000
Saratoga O. & P. L. Co., Bmt.	1,000,000
Spindle Top O. Co., Fort Worth	300,000
Southwestern Refining Co., Houston	100,000
Texas-Kansas O. Co., Bmt.	400,000
Texas and St. Louis O. Co., Beaumont	200,000
Tidewater O. Co. of Texas, Dallas	300,000

PAST

The excellent record of the United States Fuel Oil Company made in the past bespeaks a confidence of greater possibilities for the future than any literature might foretell.

+

PRESENT

Our present operations are well before you now. We are drilling night and day on Spindle Top. We guarantee our stockholders oil and marketing facilities.

+

FUTURE

We make no promise for the future. We propose to develop our High Island, Alvin, Montana and other properties when it can be done safely and advantageously.

Guarantees
STOCK HOLD

FIRST
A Guaranteed C
6-inch producing oil well, av
pacity.

SECOND
Guaranteed Co
for loading and storage purpo

THIRD
Guaranteed Pip
facilities for the transportation

FOURTH
Guarantee
that the title to all propertie
are now held by warranty deed
STATES FUEL OIL COMPANY.

FIFTH
Guarantee
that you shall be entitled to
est your certificate calls for
or contracts held now by the
that may hereafter be acquire
pany.

SIXTH
Guaranteed
that all stock shall be full pa
sable and without personal li

SEVENTH
Guaranteed Inte

List of oil companies chartered from January 10 to August 20, 1901

Miles Frank Yount

Marrs McLean

Howard Hughes, Sr.

Rio Bravo blowout in second boom, 1926

W. E. Lee

Wright Morrow

Harry Phelan

Patillo Higgins and Al Hamill, 1951

The Hamill Brothers — Al, Curt and Jim — at the Lucas Monument, 1941

The Lucas Monument with two old-style derricks in the background

Beaumont, 1952

On this site the Sun Oil Company started construction of four 55,000-barrel tanks, and two tremendous earthen tanks in which more than a million barrels of oil could be stored for shipment. Then a four-inch pipeline was built from the field to this new installation called Sun Station. When the price of oil dropped below 5 cents this storage was filled to await a better day.

Now J. Edgar Pew was ready for whatever might happen, and he knew something would happen. He knew that others were watching for the same opening. His job was to get the first and best property he could find. In more than a year in Beaumont he made thousands of friends in all walks of life. He was as much at home with the men in the blue denims in the field as he was with senators, governors and millionaires in the Crosby dining room. Two of his best friends in the field were Pattillo Higgins and Al Hamill. Edgar Pew was one Yankee who had ready acceptance in Texas. From almost the first day he set foot on the station platform in Beaumont, he was an adopted Texan. What he didn't know about the oil business when he arrived in Beaumont he learned very shortly. The hill always fascinated him and it was a common sight to see him playing horseshoes with Hardy Roberts, one of his employees, and some of the other men. He studied the tools of the trade and observed the waste brought about by the multiple types of equipment. It was this that later caused him to head a movement for uniformity and standardization of pipe and other equipment that eliminated millions of dollars in waste.

IV

On May 30, 1902, hardly a year and a half after Lone Star and Crescent was formed, Sheriff Ras Landry conducted the public auction of the big company's properties, including thirty-two miles of pipeline, the wharf facilities at Sabine, a half-dozen 37,500-barrel storage tanks, pumping stations, loading facilities on the railroad, the wells on Charley Ingals' old farm, and the land itself. The property was conservatively valued at $1,000,000.

Fate had dealt Lone Star and Crescent a cruel blow. It was only a matter of months since Parsons Davis had announced the sale of 10,000,000 barrels of oil. Now, however, every well on the company's property had ceased to flow. One of them had turned to salt water. The company was forced into bankruptcy.

It was the same story everywhere. Men who knew nothing about the oil business were not able to fathom its mysteries. Its backers were men who knew promotion, but their talents ended there. They learned too late that the oil business is not a promotion, a fact that would continue to confound others for years to come.

That Decoration Day of 1902, J. Edgar Pew knew that the thing he had been expecting was at hand. He told his Uncle Joe about the public auction and received his instructions. As soon as the bidding opened, J. Edgar Pew bid $100,000. That bid was the first and the last.

Much to Edgar Pew's relief others who could use the properties and could pay for them did not top his bid. He had opened the pot with a blue chip. They were startled, apparently, at the large first bid and were not immediately prepared to go higher. Ras Landry's hammer pounded, once, twice and then another time, and he announced: "Sold to Sun Oil Company for $100,000."

It was the windfall that caused the rise of Sun Oil to prominence in the new world of petroleum competition. Joe Pew's patience had paid off.

"You know, of course," Ras Landry told Pew when the bidding was over, "that you must have a fourth of the money here by four o'clock this afternoon."

"Yes, Ras, I'll go to the bank now and get the money. I'll be back in an hour," Pew said.

Going first to the Beaumont National, and then to the First National, Pew found them and even the smaller banks closed. The signs on the doors said it was Decoration Day. Beaumont banks were the only ones in the state observing the holiday.

As he realized the seriousness of the situation, Edgar Pew's pulse jumped a few beats. He knew that he had made one of the most phenomenal buys in the history of the industry and that should he fail to make the necessary deposit the bid would be void. The next day, he knew, he would have more competition. He thought of Cullinan and Mellon and even Standard Oil men who were now in Beaumont. There were others, too. The boom in Beaumont was not over. Although the wells were not gushing as they had before, there was still more oil on the hill than anyone could use for many years to come.

At a loss as to how to get the money he needed, Edgar Pew walked the streets in deep thought, puzzled, seeking a solution to his problem. As he walked he came to a gang of men feverishly at work remodeling an old dwelling that had recently housed his barber shop. In his typical friendly manner, he asked the gang pusher what was happening. "We're getting this ready for a bank that opens tomorrow," the pusher said, "Old Zeke, the barber, got $8,000 for the four months his lease had to run, and. . . ."

But Edgar Pew was rushing to the door of the building and the gang pusher didn't get to finish his sentence. Pew had seen someone inside the building and was banging on the door. The man inside, a pleasant, stout gentleman in his early thirties, walked calmly to the door and opened it.

"I'm J. Edgar Pew of the Sun Oil Company," Pew said introducing himself, "and I would like to do a little business with your new bank."

I'm glad to know you, Mr. Pew. I'm A. L. Williams and this is the Gulf National Bank. That is, it will be tomorrow," the man said. "We are not open today but if you can come around the first thing in the morning I will be glad to accommodate you."

"Mr. Williams," Pew said, "my business is more urgent than that. I need a bank today. Right now, in fact. I need $25,000."

Williams didn't bother to ask why he needed the money; he merely asked how he would like to have it. Pew said a cashier's check would be fine. Williams assured him that he could have it and promptly made one out.

"What will I sign, or how can I provide collateral?" Pew asked recalling that the two men were strangers as far as he was concerned.

"That's all right, Mr. Pew," Williams said. "I know you and you can come around at your convenience tomorrow and fix it up any way you wish."

Pew was flabbergasted, but he was also a very happy and relieved man. He went to the courthouse and paid the deposit.

Al Williams was cashier of the Gulf National. He had come from Shreveport several months before and had spent his time promoting a bank. Finally his efforts had succeeded, when S. G. Bayne, president of the Seaboard National of New York, had financed the project. Bayne, an agent of a group of men since recognized as Standard Oil people, was in Beaumont to organize a refining company. Being a banker, he believed it wise to have a bank that could handle his business without gossipers knowing too much about it. It was ironic that a Standard-backed bank should have provided funds with which the Pews purchased the distress properties they would use to build a foundation for new competition for Standard.

As the years went by, the Sun Oil Company was one of Al Williams' most important customers. Standard-backed or not, the bank never lost the respect J. Edgar Pew had for it and the official who had saved the day for him. Had it not been for the incident that brought Pew and Williams together, the Sun's day might never have dawned.

V

J. Edgar Pew, as far as Spindletop and the rest of Texas was concerned, was the Sun Oil Company. He established his home in Beaumont and it was there that his son, who today holds his old position as vice-president in charge of production for Sun, was born and attended school.

It was prior to the Lone Star and Crescent failure that J. Edgar Pew started buying Beaumont oil. Nine days before the purchase Sun's first tanker, the *S.S. Paraguay,* converted from a Great Lakes iron carrier, picked up 18,000 barrels of Beaumont oil at Sabine Pass. Later in 1902, the *S.S. Toledo,* a 22,000-barrel tanker, was added to the fleet. Partly due to the acquisition of the Sabine property, and partly because of the long delay in developing a channel in the Neches River, it was 1915 before oil was shipped from Smith's Bluff, where Pew made the first land purchase as protection. In 1917 one of the large earthen tanks of original Spindletop oil went to the United States war effort. In 1937 the last of the original oil was drained from the old tanks.

The history of Sun has been written since the day of J. Edgar Pew's arrival in Beaumont. By 1903 the company had ten wells on the old Ingals tract. In 1950 the company produced 33,000,000 barrels of oil, mostly in Texas, and purchased more than twice that much.

Old Joe Pew's Marcus Hook refinery by the end of the Second World War was producing more one hundred-octane gasoline than any other plant in the world. Today Sun operates oil properties on more than 350,000 acres, mostly on the Gulf Coast. And from a little company with thirty-seven employees in Toledo and 200 in the Ohio oil fields, it has grown in personnel to 14,000 workers. Its oil discoveries stand out among the most important in the world, with credit for such finds as Sea Breeze, Oyster Bayou, Willough Slough, Fig Ridge, Midfields, Caplen and LaBelle. Its fleet of tankers sail the seven seas.

J. Edgar Pew, the adopted Texan, saw the problem of Spindletop clearly and was among the first to put his mind to the task of breaking the great bottleneck of the field, transportation. And after all other oil companies born in Beaumont had virtually deserted it, the Sun was one major outfit that filled a skyscraper with its division offices there.

CHAPTER TWELVE

Standard Steps In

CALVIN PAYNE watched in silent awe as the Higgins well spouted a six-inch column of oil 200 feet into the air. The heavy green fluid spread into a wide plume above the crown block and disintegrated into a fine spray.

"Joe," he said, turning to Cullinan, "I believe you brought me here to share the embarrassment you must have suffered back in January when you first saw the Lucas well."

Joe Cullinan smiled at the accusation.

"No, Cal, but I wanted you to see this hill," he said, "so you could realize how wrong experts can be. But don't feel bad. You are surrounded by fellow sufferers. There isn't a Beaumonter in this crowd who didn't have a better chance than we had to help Pattillo Higgins and Captain Lucas. At least we didn't scorn and pity the men or call them crazy."

It was mid-April of 1901 and Payne had spent the morning with a party of other Standard Oil Company officials and leading Beaumonters looking over Guffey's refinery site in Port Arthur, the proposed pipeline route, pumping facilities at El Vista and the giant storage tanks that had been erected at Gladys City. The party was in Beaumont at the invitation of the Oil Producers Association to observe and then advise on pipeline problems. The Beaumont men welcomed the opportunity to get whatever advice the Standard visitors would give them.

At dinner that night Payne called Spindletop the greatest oil field in the world, but advised the men and companies to begin figuring on how they were going to get returns on the money they were putting into the ground. He spoke of the dire consequences of overproduction and the need for a controlled drilling program and more refineries.

"I fear this field will prove a great problem," he said. "If the production could be confined to the hill it might be a simple matter. The trouble is that the oil land may extend ten miles in every direction with deeper sands like Baku in Russia."

He then said that Standard did not have a cent invested in Spindletop and probably would confine its interest to the purchase of oil at Sabine Pass. Texas' antitrust laws, Payne said, would keep the Rockefeller interests out of the state, but he expressed the belief that if the people of Texas could vote on the subject, they would approve of trusts.

II

The Standard Oil Company was anathema in Texas. It was a monopoly and if the politicians and the press were to have their way, the company could do its monopolizing beyond the borders of the Lone Star State. Already the antitrust laws of 1899 had ousted the Waters-Pierce Company, Standard affiliate, on the charge of monopolizing distribution when the very existence of Texas' only oil field at Corsicana depended on the company for an outlet. Had the trust-busters realized that Cullinan, the man invited by Governor Culberson and Mayor Whiteselle to organize the industry in Corsicana, was backed by Standard dollars through Folger and Payne, they would have been horrified. Cullinan had been forced to resort to the Standard men for financial aid when his promised backers reneged after reading a geological report that said the peculiar subsurface soil of Texas would never produce oil in paying quantities.

It would have been most embarrassing to some segments of the press and the state government to know that Texas' newest and most promising industry could not have come into existence successfully without octopus money and know-how. Guffey and Galey had pulled up stakes at Corsicana before Cullinan took over. Cullinan would not have sought Payne's help if he hadn't been stuck with a contract.

Texas owed an unknown debt to Standard. Corsicana, financed by Standard, was the training ground for the Hamills, Sharps, Sturms and other rotary pioneers without whom Spindletop might have remained an enigma. But Texas leaders would never accept the trust. They wanted their wealth kept at home instead of being siphoned off to Wall Street and particularly into the bulging pockets of Mr. John Davidson Rockefeller. Spindletop's superabundance of fuel for industrial development had bolstered that determination.

The oil monopoly had both virtues and vices. In its favor were the elimination of the ills of instability, and the establishment of an orderly, sound, dependable plan of operation. Without its effective scheme of organization it is possible the oil business might have died of self-inflicted wounds. When Standard took charge consumers received a better product at a lower price, operators gained a steady market and a reasonable return on their money, and stockholders realized a return on their investments. But to maintain their monopoly Rockefeller and his "trustees" employed ruthless and sometimes contemptible practices which they justified under the law of the survival of the fittest. They controlled prices through covenants with the railroads and pipeline systems which called for rebates and drawbacks. So-called independents were regimented and permitted to exist by sufferance of Standard. Those who became recalcitrant found there was no market, or that prices in their area were extremely unprofitable. Those with the will and the means to outlast the trust's onslaught, such as the Mellons, were bought out after the normal means of elimination failed.

Bold enterprise was regarded as sheer folly, when it meant bucking the monopoly. John Galey was the last of the intrepid wildcatters. Few others were finding new oil and the nation's supply was rapidly dwindling. Russia had already overtaken America's production leadership. It was to get out of the Standard sphere of influence that Galey had turned to Texas, California and Kansas. Conservatism was threatening the dynamic, pioneering, progressive spirit of a nation. Standard man Archbold said he would drink every drop of oil found west of the Mississippi. Then Payne turned down the greatest bonanza in petroleum's history because there was no precedent for Lucas' nascent-dome theory. Precedents were necessary. Venture was taboo. As bright as his future was with the Standard, a man like Joe Cullinan could never conform to the company's pattern of complacency.

III

The impact of Spindletop did not immediately move the occupants of Standard's inner sanctums to action. They were prone to believe the calumniators. It was a crevice well, a freak, they reasoned. Yet when the Beatty, Higgins, and Lone Star and Crescent wells came in, they were quick to accept the invitation to inspect the field and advise the operators. What the Standard men saw on the hill was alarming to them. It wasn't simply the apparently inexhaustible supply of oil, but the new and increasing optimism of the thousands of people swarming Beaumont's streets that spelled out the end of monopoly. Men who had been born and bred to believe in security had lost all reason. Bankers who counted dollars as if they weighed a ton apiece were there squandering them as if they were chips of ice with ephemeral value. Smug sons of puritan families who wouldn't permit a deck of cards or a pair of dice in their homes were gambling thousands and hundreds of thousands of dollars in the biggest gamble of them all—the oil business.

Standard was barred from Texas. Yet some way had to be found to control this situation. Standard either had to get a foothold somewhere on the hill or its golden age of domination was over. Therefore when Payne said that his company was not interested, he failed to convince anyone. Newcomers were viewed as possible agents of the octopus until they proved themselves otherwise. The cloud of suspicion covered even the noblest of Spindletop's pioneers from time to time. The activities of J. Edgar Pew, Galey, Mellon, Gates, Heywood, Beatty and Sharp came under scrutiny. Jim Hogg puffed up and exploded with righteous indignation when rumors connected him with Rockefeller. Cullinan barely withstood the jeers that met his declaration, honest though it was, that he had parted company with Standard forever.

Every man in the maelstrom of the boom was a self-appointed counter-intelligence agent seeking out bits of information regarding Standard's plans for invasion by infiltration. The trust had to slip in, they believed, because the legal ramparts could resist frontal attack. Whatever method Standard adopted to get into Beaumont would have to be clever. Its enemies included the demagogues who made political hay by posing as champions of the little people, promoters who knew that any day Standard stepped in their racket would be ended, landowners who realized that inflated values would be punctured, rival companies that based their hopes on an uncontrolled operation, and the sincere opponents of a system regarded as one of organized greed.

The listening posts were continually sending back reports and warnings of signs of the enemy. For example the Oil Exchange bulletin board was plastered one day with an unconfirmed report that Standard men had purchased 20,000 acres of waterfront covering every foot from Sabine Pass to Port Arthur. The same day there was a rumor that Cullinan had purchased the 33,000 acres nearest Gates's new ship channel in Port Arthur. Guffey's 4,500,000-barrel deal with Shell Trade and Transport Company had been well broadcast by the colorful Colonel from Pittsburgh. Therefore, Beaumont was in a state of confusion when a newspaper article with a New York dateline reported that Rockefeller had purchased the Shell Company. Walter Sharp's Producers Oil Company, the newspaper reports stated in bold headlines, was also Standard controlled. And of course, there was no doubt that Cullinan's Texas Fuel Oil Company was the same old Corsicana crowd.

Rumor followed rumor, yet no one could trace anything directly to Standard. It wasn't natural. It didn't make sense. Rockefeller wasn't crazy. He was somewhere in Beaumont and had been all along. But where?

As the months passed it became obvious that Payne's fear that oil land would extend ten miles in every direction and that additional producing sand would be found was wrong, or at least premature. But what did happen was worse. Not even Payne anticipated that the Hogg-Swayne Syndicate would open the hill to every swindler and promoter in the country with doormat land sales. But Hogg did and the dizzy days were on. The landowners on the hill were getting rich, but the operators still had no prospect of getting their money out of the ground. The shyster promoters didn't care about anything except selling stock. The legitimate but inexperienced oil producers were facing a problem that seemed to have no solution: the market for fuel oil was growing every day and yet prices were falling in the flood of oil that overwhelmed the demand.

The hill was a jungle of derricks, a tidal wave of oil, and the scene of wild disorder and reckless abandon. Fires, blowouts and explosions were destroying one property after another. The safety committee was unable to cope with the conditions. Investors in bogus stocks were beginning to demand an accounting. This brought about a few open suggestions that it might not be too bad if Standard did come in. Monopoly was better than nothing. Was it possible that Calvin Payne was right? Would the voters favor the trust if given a chance? Was old John D. waiting for another call to bring order out of confusion and step off with control as his reward?

IV

It was into this atmosphere that a bluff and blustering gentleman with a swagger like a South American general stepped onto the Beaumont scene in November, 1901. He was Colonel George A. Burt, a former railroad executive who had once been associated with the abortive attempt by Ferdinand de Lesseps to build the French Panama Canal. He was a fabulous figure who could gamble and drink with the boomers and match Jim Hogg as a storyteller. Burt could be a man's man or he could take his place as a suave member of the social set, depending upon the demands of the occasion. One of his first friends in town was John Gilbert, president of the Higgins company. He purchased a home across the street from the Gilberts in spite of the impossible housing shortage, and was immediately welcomed with open arms by the first families of Beaumont—either feat was a miracle in itself.

Where the Colonel got his background and introduction, when governors, generals, senators and princes were finding the going rough, was never adequately explained. His only comment, as he settled his family into their new and hectic home, was that he was interested in the possibilities Beaumont offered. Not for one moment did he seem out of place in the whirl of activity. In late December he mentioned over cocktails between friends that he had purchased the eighty-nine-acre Caswell tract at the bend of the Neches for $89,000. The Colonel said he intended to back a company which he would call George A. Burt and Company, and would let a few of his closest friends have a few shares of stock. Anyone else doing the same thing might have been regarded as a colossal stock salesman, but Burt found a ready market for the limited number of shares he judiciously placed.

On January 4th, the *Beaumont Enterprise* announced with a scoop and a flourish that Burt would build the world's largest refinery on the Caswell tract at a cost of more than $5,000,000. The location, ideal for its purposes, was described as being two miles from Beaumont, three miles from Spindletop, and less than a mile from John W. Gates's new Kansas City Southern Railroad tracks. Other incorporators with Burt in the company were said to be S. G. Bayne of the Seaboard National Bank in New York and Colonel Fred W. Weller, outstanding refinery builder and designer of the day. Never had Beaumont been more honored than with the name value of the incorporators of this company. Yet there was not the slightest suspicion of anything that smacked of Standard.

A most appropriate date, January 10th, the first anniversary of the Lucas gusher, was chosen by Colonel Weller to break ground for the project. Dan Weller, the Colonels brother, was named his first assistant. Within a few days tons of machinery had been ordered and it was evident that work was going forward without delay on the Beaumont refinery. This was in contrast with the previous big talk and no action on a dozen or more refineries for the home city of the great oil field. It was the first step anyone had taken in the refinery field, as a matter of fact, except Guffey at Port Arthur.

Things that were hard seemed to come easily to Burt. On the date that he announced he would build terminals at Sabine Pass and four product lines to them from Beaumont, he stated, in a way that seemed naïve enough, that this method of disposing of the oil would be utilized until the Neches became a navigable stream—a realization that he anticipated would not be too long coming. Reference to deep water for the Neches was an inspired pronouncement. For years the Carrolls, McFaddins, Keiths, Gilberts, Wiesses, Greers and Congressman Bronson Cooper had importuned Washington for a channel to the sea. It was the pet project of the board of trade and the local press. In the days of the boom the river had been almost forgotten, but now Burt had revived interest in it and none doubted but that he would do something about it. Colonel Burt was definitely in. Even the previously skeptical *Beaumont Journal* eulogized him in an editorial.

Burt let everyone know that he was determined to keep the progress of his plant, its technical design and other facts completely to himself until he was ready to announce its opening. He impressed his rule of secrecy with an eight-foot board fence completely around the building site. He imported German and Pennsylvania Dutch superintendents and foremen for the job and Mexican laborers who spoke no English and who couldn't tell a cross still from a hot tamale. There was no welcome sign out for newspaper reporters on the construction job and Burt made only such announcements as he wanted to make and when he wanted to make them.

The torrential rains of 1902, which fell unabated for sixty-three consecutive days, an epidemic of smallpox, which broke out among his Mexican laborers in their "lower woods" housing area, three feet of mud, which normally covered the entire construction site, a road for material hauling which became a winding quagmire were among problems Burt and Weller had to overcome.

In May Burt permitted the *Enterprise* to report that 10,000,000 barrels of earthen storage was part of the building going on behind the high board fences. The implication was that the heavy green oil spouting out of Spindletop hill in every direction would be purchased to fill the storage. That was only a few weeks before the gushers became pumpers and the hope of disposing of the hill's surplus put Colonel Burt in a hero's toga as far as the bewildered oil men were concerned.

V

Then came the day in 1903 when the Burt refinery was a completed project. The announcement that accompanied the news of the completion was startling to everyone in Texas. It was that Burt was no longer a part of the company that would operate the plant. Bayne, the banker, was to head the new company that was chartered under Texas law. Colonel Fred Weller was the vice-president, and a lovable, eccentric Irish Ulsterman, Courtenay Marshall, Bayne's relative, was to be secretary and treasurer.

It might have been as a gentle hint of the Rockefeller philosophy of the oil regions as contrasted with the turbulent, truculent, brash activities of this new oil world that centered around the hill that inspired the name of the new company. They called it the Security Oil Company.

Within a few days everything was in readiness for operations to begin. A half-dozen expert stillmen stepped off the Southern Pacific onto a street knee-deep in mud in Beaumont. Among them was Fred Driehs, a towering German with a Hohenzollern moustache, a barrel chest and broad shoulders. Driehs was the kind of self-made stillman that Eastern refineries developed in the early days. He needed no test tubes or chemists. By tasting, smelling or feeling the product of a batch of oil he could tell what he wanted to know about it. Not only that, but he could rule the yards in the manner designed to get the best results for the company. He had a capacity for his job and for keeping peace among the workers. And keeping peace was no easy assignment. The imported refiners were a mixture of Pennsylvania Dutch and New Yorkers who didn't get along with a third element from West Virginia. Inside the plant Driehs demanded, and got, peace. Outside all hell would break loose. The narrow boardwalks leading to the plant were ideal for "accidents" which resulted in mud dunkings. But the bloody and battered men always made their way to the plant on time for work.

For some reason Beaumont never seemed to accept the name Security. Even the men in the plant called it the Burt Refinery. The Colonel's personality was one that could not be submerged by a set of notarized instruments from the Secretary of State's office. To the wild boom town of the Neches, Burt meant something, while Security seemed a word out of the dim past.

The refinery did a phenomenal business. Fred Weller's genius had assembled the latest in processes. Products were being made that the hill knockers had said could never be made from Spindletop crude. The local dollars invested in the Burt stock multiplied many times, and as the hill lost its excitement and glamour, the Burt refinery took up the slack in employment. More and more local men became refinery workers. Many of the imported workers became adopted Texans, particularly Fred Driehs, whose importance in the plant increased with each passing day.

In the meantime most people had forgotten about Standard coming to Beaumont. They reasoned that the antitrust laws, after all, had been too rigid even for Mr. Rockefeller. But when Fred Weller left Beaumont to become a member of the board of directors of Standard, a light began to clear up the picture of what had really happened. In its own inimitable manner, Standard had stepped in.

There was no local outcry as the fact became more apparent. Beaumonters had come to depend on their refinery and, as far as they were concerned, if this plant was owned by the Standard Oil Company, they had no objections. On reflection, those who felt they knew now what had happened talked about the cleverness of the plan of invasion. They thought back to Burt's approach, his secrecy, the timing of his statements, and the winning of the unstinted support of a city. Now they could see that Bayne had opened the Gulf National Bank in Beaumont largely for the purpose of handling his company's business without letting important facts become known to other local bankers who might not be as interested in secrecy as he was.

However, the small talk and unconfirmed speculation eventually led to a low rumble of protest against the trust and its refinery operations. A state investigator turned up the evidence that Folger and Payne had been financially interested in the Beaumont refinery since its inception. Finally, the rumble became a roar and the politicians, rivals and righteously indignant made things difficult along the Neches.

Then came an announcement that Standard was building a great refinery at Baton Rouge. Dan Weller, who had been with the plant since the construction job started, left and took over the Baton Rouge project. Many of his best men followed him and the activity at the Beaumont plant dropped off to the point where there were less than one hundred men employed there for a while. A large tract of land which J. Edgar Pew had bought and then turned over to the Security Company next to the Caswell tract was left a large, vacant space. The talk was that before the state started its attack on Security and on Navarro, the old Cullinan company in Corsicana, plans were under consideration to place the Baton Rouge project in Beaumont.

In 1906 the Security and Navarro oil companies were charged with violating the state's antitrust laws, and a half-million dollar fine assessed. The plants were in temporary receivership while the fines were paid out of receipts. In 1907, after the fine had been paid off, the attorney-general sued the two companies again, this time calling for their ouster from the state. The case was bitterly fought, but the companies lost and the plants became the property of the state.

Then E. R. Brown, the man Folger had sent to help Cullinan in Corsicana in 1898, went to work to save the situation. He turned to John Sealy of Galveston for aid. Sealy was one of Texas' most prominent citizens. He had been the most important figure in the rehabilitation of Galveston after the great storm of 1900. He had built hospitals, churches, libraries and orphanages and his name was enshrined in the hearts of his fellow Texans. Sealy had dabbled in oil at both Corsicana and Spindletop and was interested in the two refineries getting back into private hands. Brown proposed financial aid if Sealy would purchase the plants at a public auction.

On December 9, 1909, Sealy bid $875,000 for the properties, which were worth many millions, and bought them. The sale price amounted to little more than another harassing fine against Standard, because there was no particular effort to conceal the fact that Folger, Payne and other members of the trust were financially interested in Sealy's purchase. At first the new company was titled simply John Sealy—Refiner of Petroleum. After a few months it became John Sealy and Company. Sealy seldom visited the plants and paid little attention to them. Brown and others ran the companies. In 1911 the Magnolia Petroleum Company was formed as a joint stock association out of the properties bearing Sealy's name. Sealy remained as president until fourteen years later, when he became chairman of the board, where he served until his death.

Magnolia became a great refining company and one of the Southwest's leading oil producers. It also became Beaumont's most important tangible asset salvaged from the storm that Pattillo Higgins blew up on the hill known as Spindletop.

CHAPTER THIRTEEN

Humble Beginnings

LEE BLAFFER couldn't believe what he heard.

"The Southern Pacific is going to quit using coal altogether?" he asked Charles Markham, the road's division chief.

"That's right, Lee," Markham replied to the young man, "but I believe we have something for you, if you are interested."

Certainly, Blaffer was interested. Without the S.P. account, his coal business was doomed.

"Go to Beaumont and buy oil for us."

That was Markham's proposition, and it appealed to Robert Lee Blaffer, son of an aristocratic New Orleans family and manager of his father's Monongahela Coal and Coke distributorship. He quickly thought over his present plight.

The Beaumont oil boom had already put a crimp in the coal business. Dealers were dropping off every day. Ice plants, power plants, shops, sugar mills and other industries were turning to Beaumont oil. The Heywood brothers and the Waters-Pierce Oil Company were flooding the country with smelly oil-burning heaters and cook stoves. The Southern Pacific account was all that kept Blaffer in business, and now that was gone.

Lee Blaffer didn't wait long to reply. He caught his breath, swallowed nervously, turned the offer over in his mind for a few minutes, and accepted with a vigorous handshake. He conditioned his acceptance, of course, upon the approval of his father. At home the senior Blaffer, a veteran of the Army of Virginia who had named his son for the South's immortal leader, agreed. Within a few days Lee Blaffer departed the beauty, serene comfort, culture and social attractions of his beloved New Orleans. He said goodbye to his family and his old Tulane classmates and headed for the great oil boom less than 300 miles west.

His first days in Beaumont were exciting and challenging. Before long the pungent air of the boom town captured him and oil seeped into his blood. The S.P. assignment provided no particular problem. Buyers were being pleaded with to take oil, and the railroad had a corner on Union tank cars. Soon Lee Blaffer was looking for some way to exploit the opportunity that was everywhere before him. One of his first outside jobs was cleaning tanks on a contract basis with J. W. Kinnear, a schoolteacher who had been secretary of seven oil companies for J. B. Treadwell, another S.P. man. Occasionally Blaffer would take a lease and turn it.

Walking down Pearl Street one day he accidentally bumped into a stranger. The two stopped in the mad melée long enough to apologize to each other. Such apologies were unusual, and they laughed about it. One word of courtesy led to another and the stranger introduced himself as William S. Farish, lawyer, from Natchez, Mississippi. Lee Blaffer was glad to see another single man about his own age from the banks of the Mississippi, and the two discovered they had several mutual friends.

Shortly, Lee Blaffer and Bill Farish found themselves living together in the Ervin boarding house across the street from Captain William Wiess' home on Calder Avenue. And it wasn't too long after that that Farish said he had completed his business for a client, but had decided to stay in Beaumont and get into the oil business. This decision impressed Blaffer. He congratulated Farish and admitted that he was thinking of stepping out on his own, also. That night they decided to make Blaffer and Farish a partnership.

The Ervin boarding house was more than a place to sleep and eat. It was in the center of the neighborhood of Beaumont's first families and both Lee and Bill were young bachelors in their early twenties. More than that, they were living with some of the most colorful oil men, including Frank Ireland, Ed Prather and Ed Simms. These three introduced them to others. Captain Wiess, a lumberman, was also in the oil business, and he frequently dealt with the new partnership which dwelled conveniently across the street. He liked the two young men because they took an unusual interest in his son, Harry, who was in his middle teens.

Through Wiess, also, Blaffer and Farish met L. A. Carlton, known to the youngsters in the town as Uncle Lobe. He was Wiess's legal adviser and sometimes partner, and he had the reputation for being one of the best poker players along the Neches River.

Ed Prather was one of the most interesting of the men around the boarding house. Prather arrived in Beaumont with Walter Sharp the morning after the Lucas gusher came in. The two then leased everything they could get between Spindletop and Sour Lake on the theory that the whole area was underlaid with an oil lake. It wasn't, of course, but they made a lot of money selling leases on the land.

It seemed that Prather knew everyone. He intrigued his young listeners with the story of Cullinan. He said that when Cullinan saw the gusher he was afraid it was a freak, which is the reason he didn't stay in Beaumont after the well was controlled. Cullinan had told Prather of a well he drilled in Indiana several years before that looked a great deal like the Lucas gusher. He had built tanks and a pipeline to it and then it had stopped flowing. He drilled four more wells around the dead gusher and they were all dry. That, Cullinan said, caused him to have little faith in the Lucas well at first.

J. Cooke Wilson, another Mississippian, joined the group later, and was a charming addition to the circle. He was a wise investor and a good manager. Jesse Jones, a rising young lumberman from Houston, frequently visited with Blaffer and Farish, as did Ross Sterling, who operated a chain of feed stores from his base in Anahuac, west of Beaumont.

But one of the most fascinating of all the men encountered in everyday activities was Walter W. Fondren. He had built a drilling company from nothing and was a genius at the application of new techniques. Fondren started work in a sawmill in Arkansas as a boy. He drifted to Corsicana and learned how to operate a rotary rig when the contraption was first introduced. When Spindletop came in, Fondren happened to be drilling a water well within a few miles of Beaumont. He took a job as a driller and soon saved enough money to buy a rig of his own and start in the contract business. By the time he met Blaffer and Farish he was fairly well established and worked with them on several deals.

Probably one of the most interesting men among the boarders at Ervin House was young Holland S. Reavis, a reporter who had been sent to Beaumont to cover the boom for a St. Louis newspaper. Reavis started the *Oil Investors' Journal,* which became the nemesis of fraud and the champion of legitimate oil men. His publication survived the years to become one of petroleum's most important organs—*The Oil and Gas Journal.*

II

Beaumont was never short of excitement. The Hamills started a fad on the hill by guaranteeing gushers for promotional companies. They got contracts for $10 a foot. If there was no gusher, the Hamills would take the drill site and whatever type of well they found as pay.

D. O. Lively, who had a significant name, promoted a well east of the flats and across the T. & N. O. tracks for a deep test. The land was Federal Crude Oil's and the equipment was Buffalo Oil Company's which had adjacent acreage. At 2039 feet Lively reported the same sands he found on the hill at 730 feet. His equipment was good for another hundred or so feet, but he was forced to abandon the hole. Had he been able to continue another 300 feet, Spindletop would not have had to wait twenty-four years for a second boom.

Frequently there was discussion of how unfortunate it had been that J. A. Paulhamus had not joined forces with Pattillo Higgins. Paulhamus had gone to Beaumont in 1898 to represent the Forward Reduction Company. C. B. Forward had invented a process for making lubricating oil out of waste oil. Standard had a $50,000 offer for such a process, but Forward had refused that and also a final offer of $150,000. Cleveland interests backed him and he sent Paulhamus south to look for oil along the Gulf. Beaumonters steered Paulhamus away from Higgins, telling him the man was obsessed with wild visionary ideas. Paulhamus had then gone into other parts of the county to look for oil with no success.

By late 1901 Charles Markham, Blaffer's old coal client from New Orleans, had succumbed to the oil business and was with Guffey. The Guffey Company had sent shivers up the Standard Oil Company's back with the announcement that a process for producing illuminating oil from Spindletop crude had been found in its Port Arthur refinery. The Hardy Oil Company was drilling a secret well, surrounded by a quarter-mile-square fence, a mile northwest of the Lucas gusher in an area where a third boom would start in 1951. The Drillers Oil Company was suing Harry Decker to force him to take 300,000 barrels of oil at 3 cents a barrel. The suit was lost. Oil City was a new promotional development a few miles west of Spindletop. It was advertised as being in the center of a triangle that had Spindletop, Sour Lake and an oil pond off McFaddin's Beach in the Gulf as its points. Promoted by a group of politicians and newspapermen, the project failed.

Walter Sharp, Ed Prather and Howard Hughes formed the Moonshine Oil Company and were cleaning up with wells that were going dead. They would simply insert a two-inch line down to the oil sand and kick it with compressed air. Their fee was 50 per cent of the recovery.

The liveliest place in town was the Oaks, where Jim Hogg usually held forth when he wasn't in the Crosby lobby. Hogg and his friend Jim Roche were super attractions with the ladies of the Oaks. Hogg called the oil wives his gossip club. Roche, tall, handsome, charmed them with the story of how he placed a wreath on his own grave before going to Texas. His North Dakota ranch had been raided by Indians and several men were killed. One of them was identified as Roche and he found out about it when he visited the cemetery where his friends were buried. He saw his own name on one of the headstones and placed a wreath on it and departed. That was the incident that led him to Texas and a fortune.

Beaumont by mid-1902 was beginning to look like a real city. The Wiess, Gilbert, Keith and other buildings represented the benefits of oil wealth. Wes Kyle had built a magnificent opera house that was heralded as the finest in the South. H. A. Perlstein, the town's blacksmith, who had brought in oil where Lucas first drilled for it, planned a tremendous skyscraper of six stories. Jim Weed and others were building the famous Alamo block of buildings. Trolley lines had been built and the city had more paved streets, sewage and street lighting than any other city of its population in the country. Out in Calder the magnificent Frank Keith mansion was being completed as the showplace of Texas. Other oil millionaires were also lining the famous old street with large and handsome mansions.

George W. Carroll, who had become Beaumont's wealthiest man by 1903, provided the town with its most hilarious episode of the year. Unrelenting in his attacks on corruption, booze and gambling, Carroll had taken on an all-out battle against the dice tables. The police chief, who seemed to see little sin in gambling in a community that was becoming famous all over the world for its bogus stock gambling, tried to convince Carroll there was no big betting going on in Beaumont. Of course, that was ridiculous; the gambling was going as strong, if not as open, as ever. In dozens of plush and plain rooms over and behind saloons highly polished silver dollars were stacked high on roulette, faro, poker and dice tables.

Carroll was thoroughly convinced that Hickory Tom and Jack were going strong over the Ogden saloon. He insisted on that fancy den being stopped first, but the authorities discouraged him and he couldn't get in to see for himself. One night he conceived a plan and related it to his friend "Bunnie" Moore, a football great from Carroll's beloved Baylor University, a good Baptist himself, and a successful oil operator. Carroll had decided to shave off his heavy beard of some fifteen years' growth, put on a fancy sports cap, and one of his son's youthful suits, and gain admittance to the Ogden gambling emporium. The idea convulsed Moore, who said he would go along for the fun. The fact is that Moore was afraid Carroll, a relatively slight man, might be endangering his life and he wanted to go along to protect him.

The two men got by the guard at the door, as anyone could do except Carroll or some other reformer. Moore shot a few rounds of dice while Carroll watched. Finally, with all of the evidence he needed, the multimillionaire mounted a table and announced that the place was raided and everyone was under arrest. For a moment the players and house men alike thought he was some innocuous little inebriate and started to pull him down.

Then Sam, one of the waiters from the café below, recognized Carroll and shouted, "Lawd help us, ef it ain't Mister Gawge Ca'll hisself."

There was a moment of stunned silence and then out every door, window and transom, as if drawn by giant magnets, men scurried until the place was completely emptied. For a few weeks there was little gambling in town.

Jack Ennis was probably the most notorious character on Spindletop Hill. He bossed Texas Fuel Company's rugged pipeliners before getting into the oil play himself. He was a powerful man and as rough as anyone in Beaumont. Ennis made two fortunes and lost both of them. He was one of the boom's fabulous characters. One of his stunts was to bet all comers that he could drive from Johnny Callaghan's Hamilton Hotel Bar to Spindletop in fifteen minutes, rain or shine. He would hitch a team of ponies to a buckboard, strip the horses down to collar and traces, and take off like a jet plane. Out Orleans Street, across the old double bridge behind George O'Brien's home, past the Carroll home on Park, and on out Highland Avenue he would fly. Usually the man he bet with would make the ride also. The thrill was sufficient for one lifetime, but Jack always made it. The one time on the record that he failed was when he lost a wheel and almost lost his witness's life. He paid off the bet with a half-interest in a gusher.

Jack Ennis was completely disconcerted by Carroll's reform movement. He foresaw Beaumont becoming a dude town run by preachers and prohibitionists and that was a fate he didn't care to participate in. He walked into the Hamilton Saloon one day and told Callaghan that he was fed up with the reform wave, which was then a day old, and was going to Saratoga or Batson where a man could do something besides go to prayer meeting or a gathering of the Anti-Saloon League.

"Johnny," he said to Callaghan, "You can have my Nancy Davis lease. There are ten wells out there and enough oil left to make you rich."

Callaghan was not impressed. He knew Ennis and he wanted to know if he had to assume the liabilities, also. Ennis said he would get everything—including the liabilities. Callaghan politely declined and Ennis left. He went around the corner to Harry Heilborn's jewelry store, gave Heilborn the lease for a hatful of assorted diamonds and other baubles, and went back to offer Callaghan his pick for past favors, but Callaghan was out.

Ennis then went to almost every house on Deep Crockett and distributed the gems to the ladies of the demi-monde out of sympathy for their plight. He believed Carroll would disperse them next. That was the last Beaumont ever saw of one of the most dashing sons of Spindletop.

III

Blaffer and Farish and their friends enjoyed this exciting panorama of everyday life in Beaumont, but they were equally intrigued by production problems and the opinions of the experts.

For instance, they learned, among other things, that no two oil wells are alike. Mat McAlister drilled a well fifty feet southeast of the Lucas gusher and didn't even find the sand. Had Galey chosen that spot for the Lucas well there might have been no Spindletop boom. But even the flowing wells had their individual personalities, temperaments and illnesses. The Lucas gusher, for instance, baffled its operators continually, and never paid for itself. Another well came so fast that Guffey left it to itself too long. When it was opened again months later, it proved too troublesome to bother with, and was so completely abandoned that its own operators even forgot precisely where it was located.

The classic remark of the boom was made by William Kennedy, the expert who condemned Pattillo Higgins' prospect on the hill. It was a few weeks after the Lucas, the Beatty, and the Higgins wells came in. Kennedy was walking down the street when he ran flush into Higgins. He turned a little crimson, ducked his head slightly, but greeted the man whose hopes be had punctured with his published opinion a few years before.

"Well, Mr. Higgins," he said, "I guess I was surely wrong about Spindletop."

Higgins smiled a little and replied, "Yes, Mr. Kennedy, I guess you shore were."

What Higgins didn't know was that Kennedy was in town as an expert for the United States Geological Survey with the title of "reviewer" for the field. Not only that but he was working for C. Willard Hayes, the man who had condemned the same prospect for Lucas.

Hayes was voluble in his praise of the field and his expectations for Texas' future power and prosperity. He immediately proclaimed the supply of oil inexhaustible, a completely different tune from the one he sang for Lucas less than a year before.

David Day of the U.S.G.S. didn't exactly take credit for the development, but he didn't use as much authority as he might have in suppressing a release from his Washington office that gave him more credit than he was entitled to. Day did say that the surface had only been scratched, but even then he was echoing the words of Pattillo Higgins and Captain Lucas.

C. Z. Carachristi, C.E.E.M., became somewhat of a self-appointed authority among the ranks of the non-government experts and claimed to have advised European clients to drill on the Texas coast years before. He said his clients took the matter up with Standard experts and were discouraged. Carachristi also boldly accused the U.S.G.S. of being controlled by Standard. In 1902 Carachristi took issue with Lee Hager, an oil man of considerable stature who had estimated the ultimate Spindletop production at 26,000,000 barrels. At 20 cents a barrel, that would mean less than $6,000,000. Carachristi called that ridiculous in face of the fact that some $80,000,000 had already been invested in the field. He said a better estimate would be 10,000,000 barrels a month for several years. Both were wrong. The first boom produced and sold some 50,000,000 barrels, which was far short of paying off the investment, even at 50 cents a barrel, which might have been the ultimate average price.

In the first two years of production more oil was burned every day in Taylor's Bayou than was disposed of at any price. There is no way of estimating how much was lost in other ways.

Once there was an announcement that Guffey would drill a chain of wells every mile from Beaumont to Brownsville and possibly on into Mexico. That didn't happen, but within a period of thirty years there was proof that it would have been profitable.

T. C. Stribling, who quit one test on the banks of the Neches because of mosquitoes and became wealthy through the sale of a well to General Crude Oil Company a few days before the gusher went dead, added to the nervous tension of Beaumont's skeptics and the superstitious with an interview in the *Houston Post.*

> This celebrated hill is nothing more than the neck of the great fuel volcanoes of Mexico which have been burning for hundreds of years. Some of these days there will be the greatest volcanic eruption at Spindletop that the world ever saw. The gas that supplies the pressure which shoots the oil 200 feet above the derricks circulates fully

> 2000 miles under the surface of the earth, coming under the Gulf from its volcanic origin—in Trinidad. This field is the only thing in the world that really exceeds the wildest flights of imagination. Hope, the fawning traitor of the mind, never conceived such an air castle.

Jim Swayne, the energetic partner of Jim Hogg, Campbell and others, was chided by the *Beaumont Journal* for appropriating the DeLong Hook and Eye company's slogan. Swayne, the *Journal* said, was flitting from one mound to another along the Gulf with prospective investors, pointing and exclaiming, "See that hump." Almost every hump he saw soon turned out to be an oil field. On almost every one of them a graveyard was located because, in most cases, it was the only high ground for miles around. Frequently, there was a church nearby which was to become endowed with the benefits of the earth's bounty.

But even with all of this going on, with the country overrun with experts, formation men and government geologists who knew considerably less than nothing about oil, there was no undue excitement over a story that appeared in the *Galveston News* on January 28, 1902.

Under a Houston dateline the story told of Harris County farmers utilizing gas in saving their cabbage crops.

> By sinking hollow pipes into the ground from eight to ten feet the farmers around Humble have succeeded in striking gas and utilizing the heat generated in saving their cabbage crop from destruction by frost. While erecting an improvised fence the phenomenon was discovered. A hollow post was driven into the earth a few feet, and something whizzed at the top. A match settled the question. Natural gas was pouring out in a continuous pressure.

> The idea of thus protecting the cabbages by utilizing this product was conceived, and now all through the cabbagefields of this section of the country hundreds of pipes have been sunk, with valves fitted to them, and the approach of a norther is hailed by counteracting fires. The entire country is alight during cold weather. . . .

With all of the genius loose and expounding one theory after another in the press, not one picked up that item and it was three years later before Dave R. Beatty, the Galvestonian who had moved to Houston, drilled a well where the cabbage patch would give birth to the fortunes of future oil kings.

IV

Harry Carothers Wiess grew into young manhood in the midst of the greatest excitement and the most interesting era of his age. He was the son of a man who was wealthy and successful long before Spindletop, but who owed most of the vast fortune he later controlled to the perseverance and determination of Pattillo Higgins. Harry was energetic, smart and daring. When the age of the horseless carriage got under way, he took to racing cars in the old Spindletop Park near the oil field. When his souped up Marion Wildcat bolted through a fence and almost killed Harry and several patrons of the track, the young man's racing days came to an abrupt halt.

He watched the oil bloom that blossomed at Spindletop grow into a mighty tree like the giant magnolias in his front yard. Like the large white flowers that dotted the bright green of the trees, the new fields popped out all along the Gulf Coast.

First the Heywoods moved to Jennings. Then his neighbors, the Gilberts, brought in flush production at Sour Lake. At Lucas' behest, Guffey moved to Anse LaButte and opened a new field. Welch in Louisiana and the wild, untamed Saratoga country west of Sour Lake followed. Then came discoveries at

Batson, Humble and North Dayton, all by 1905. That was about the time Harry went off to Princeton. When he returned, the march of the salt domes was continuing. Goose Creek, Edgerly, Vinton and Orange were the next in line.

The Great Davis Hill, the highest salt-dome structure in the Gulf Coast Country, rising 170 feet above the surrounding plains, and Damon Mound, the second highest, which punched the surface of the earth up eighty feet above the level prairie, had been explored, but had failed to produce. High Island, Bryan Mound, the Big Hills in both Jefferson and Matagorda Counties, and Pattillo Higgins' promising prospects at Barbers Hill, Pierce junction and Hockley, were still stubbornly resisting successful exploration.

Even before he left for college, however, Harry Wiess had heard the lore of Sour Lake, Saratoga and Batson. Batson and Saratoga, nestled in the heart of the big thicket, were the roughest and bloodiest oil boom towns in history.

Howard Hughes was closely associated with Walter Sharp, himself an inventive genius and a mechanical wizard, and Ed Prather. Sharp was a practical man as well as a genius, so he sometimes despaired of his partner, Hughes. Hughes took a lease in Sour Lake but didn't get enough time. Homer Chambers was moving a boiler, which he had purchased for $525 in Beaumont, onto the Gilbert lease. Hughes, whose lease was about to expire, had everything he needed but a boiler. He offered Chambers $3000 for his, but to no avail. That boiler was the one used to drill the 17,000-barrel gusher that brought in the field at 716 feet.

Then there was the story of Hughes needing oil for fuel for a later operation he and Sharp were drilling together. Hughes was almost out of money when he paid Chambers for the first supply. He went back a second time and put up a diamond stick pin for more fuel oil, and on a third occasion he put up his watch. Sharp, who could have helped his partner more, wanted to teach him a lesson and told Chambers to take everything he had. But one day Hughes came running to Chambers with a piece of sand wrapped in a $10 bill he had borrowed from Prather. It was pure oil sand and Hughes's troubles were over—temporarily.

Chambers, who finally drilled more than 300 wells in Sour Lake, was with Hughes the day he got his first idea for the famous rock bit which later revolutionized rotary drilling. The two were in a machine shop when Hughes saw a three-wheeled emery wheel with the outer wheels going in one direction and the inner wheel moving in the opposite direction.

"Homer," he said excitedly, "there is an idea that the oil business can use. If we could develop a drilling bit that operated like that wheel, most of our drilling problems would be over."

From that day on Hughes worked and experimented until he developed the tool that built one of the greatest oil-tool industries in the world.

Hughes was the kind of man who could both inspire confidence and drive his friends to the point of exasperation. The first time Ed Prather saw him he lent Hughes $200 to close a deal. Later, Hughes gave Prather half of the stock in his company for practically nothing, and Prather sold out to others because Hughes's business methods were driving him to distraction. These were the stories that Harry Wiess took to Princeton.

When he came back to Beaumont, Harry fell in love with beautiful Olga Keith, the daughter of J. Frank Keith, prominent lumberman and another beneficiary of the great treasure of Spindletop. It was his land, which he had divided with a relative, John C. Ward, that formed the famous Keith-Ward tract on the hill. Keith was not too enthusiastic over Olga's love affair. He knew Harry's two older half-brothers and believed that if Harry followed their footsteps he might not be the kind of provider he wanted for his daughter. To offset this objection Harry Wiess went into the printing business with the finest quality materials and the best workmen obtainable. The innovation of quality printing work soon made his business a tremendous success. Captain Wiess was as interested in Harry's performance as Frank Keith was. And Harry, realizing the test he was being put to, absorbed the principles of business in little more than a year or two.

His performance won for Harry Wiess the supreme prize of his life, the hand of Olga Keith. It also won him a partnership in his father's business—that of running the oil properties. Like Keith, Captain Wiess always felt devoted to the lumber business, which, incidentally, had enjoyed an astounding prosperity as a result of the building of derricks, board roads, buildings at Spindletop, and thousands of new homes in Beaumont. Harry Wiess's success during his father's lifetime resulted in the entire Wiess Estate being left in his hands. And time would prove that it could not have been left in better hands.

V

For the most part, all of Harry Wiess's friends, including Blaffer and Farish, had remained in and around Beaumont. The firm of Blaffer and Farish had become most prominent and the two men were also interested in other companies. That was a far cry from the day when their spirits were at the lowest point after Spindletop.

They had gone into other areas and had ups and downs in fortune. In the early days of Humble they followed a confusing freak well which came in twelve miles from where the field was ultimately found. The well, drilled by a man who knew nothing of the oil business, was a beautiful gusher. Immediately others started digging holes in every direction. Hundreds of thousands of dollars were spent, many operators went broke or bankrupt and yet another producing oil well was never found in the vicinity.

It was at that time that Lee Blaffer and Bill Farish were suffering financially. They owed many thousands of dollars. One day they were sitting around a shack they had rented on the outskirts of Humble discussing ways and means of paying off their debts. As they talked a native approached the house with a fine-looking bird dog. Farish excused himself and went to the gate to see the dog. After a few minutes he returned, leading the animal as the stranger departed.

"What are you doing with that dog?" Blaffer inquired.

"I bought him," smiled Farish, a bit sheepishly.

"You did? For how much?" asked Blaffer.

"Only $50," Farish admitted after a slight pause.

Blaffer looked for a moment as if he were going to explode. Finally he shook his head in disgust and asked Farish how he could think of paying $50 for a bird dog when they were so heavily in debt.

In later years Blaffer, who was the watchdog of Humble's treasury, maintained his reputation for frugality. It even followed him into the field. His own company's geologists honored him by naming an oil sand after him. He chuckled when he read the description of the stratum's characteristics. "It is a rich, but a tight and unyielding reservoir," the report said.

While the "Beaumont Group" was progressing and accumulating leases and oil properties in various companies, the Sterlings were moving forward. Their chain of feed stores, forerunners in a sense of their gasoline service stations of the future, expanded in number. Later, the family, headed by the energetic, affable and brilliant Ross Sterling, went into the banking business. Between the two businesses they had several unwanted oil properties wished off on them. Through those properties and others they invested in themselves, they decided to enter the oil business. In 1911 they formed the Humble Oil Company, named after the little town they had moved to and the oil field nearby which also bore the name of the hamlet. Starting small, the Humble Company, which itself had no direct Spindletop connection, was capitalized for $150,000. Five years later the capital stock was increased to $300,000. This company was the key to a great enterprise that was worked out between the Sterlings and the "Beaumont Group." Neither the Humble nor the other companies alone had sufficient production to assure any large purchaser of a guaranteed supply of oil. Bill Farish had gone East to try to interest Atlantic Oil and Refining Company and others in oil, but the answer always resolved itself down to the amount he could guarantee on a steady basis. His first action on returning was to form the Independent Oil Producers Association, which helped some. But the eastern buyers preferred doing business with a corporation instead of an association of independents.

On March 1, 1917, the Humble Oil and Refining Company was formed and applied for a charter. It included the partnership of BIaffer and Farish; the Schultz Oil Company, owned by Blaffer, Farish, Prather, Carlton and Bert Broday; the Globe Oil and Refining Company, which was owned by Blaffer and William and Steve Farish, and which was the first oil company to sell products at a service station; the partnership of Farish and Ireland, which included Bill Farish, Frank Ireland, Jesse Jones, Carlton and Prather; W. W. Fondren's drilling company, which was regarded as the best operation of its kind in the state at the time; properties owned by J. Cooke Wilson and C. B. Goddard and important properties out of three companies in the Wiess Estate, the Reliance, the Paraffine and the Ardmore Oil Companies. These were most of the Independent Oil Producers Association companies.

The new company was incorporated for $4,000,000. When the secretary of state learned that it was the intention of the group to produce, transport, refine, purchase and market oil, he refused to issue a charter. For four months the tremendously valuable properties of the group were held together without a scratch of a pen in any kind of an agreement beyond the oral understanding between the partners. The legislature finally changed Texas laws to permit an integrated company, and the charter was issued on June 21, 1917.

Ross Sterling was the first president, Farish was vice-president, and Blaffer, of course, was treasurer. Two years later the capital stock of the company was doubled.

During World War I Farish served conspicuously on the War Service Petroleum Board under A. C. Bedford, chairman, of Standard Oil of New Jersey. His work threw him into daily contact, also, with W. C. Teagle of the same company. The three men became devoted friends. After the war, the Humble company wanted to build a large refinery and a pipeline system. The board of directors realized that to become a major company such a move was necessary. Investment bankers were interested, but wanted more interest than Blaffer and the others were willing to pay. The local bankers were interested, but the amount needed was far beyond their limits.

Finally Farish was authorized to make some kind of deal with his Standard friends. After two very brief valuation inspections, Standard agreed to put $17,000,000 into the company for half interest. This not only enabled the stockholders to get the value of most of their original investments, it provided the money for the desired improvements. The Bonner Oil Company of Houston and the Dixie Oil Company of San Antonio were acquired as a marketing nucleus. John Bonner and Ben H. Brown came into the company. Maston Nixon preferred cash to stock for his Dixie Company. A few years later the stock he would have received doubled and quadrupled in value.

In 1921 Farish succeeded Sterling as president, and in 1922 the Humble Oil and Refining Company's capital stock was increased to $43,000,000. Still under the Farish régime, in 1926, the company became a $75,000,000 corporation. In 1932 Farish left Humble to become president of Standard of New Jersey and his old friend, Lee Blaffer, took over the presidency. In 1934 Blaffer was at the helm of a $175,000,000 oak tree that had grown from oil talk around a boarding house at Spindletop during the boom days.

It was in 1936 that Harry Wiess, the kid in knee britches of Spindletop days, ascended to the presidency of the Humble Company. In 1946 he found himself the head of a $300,000,000 corporation.

From the humblest of beginnings the greatest oil-producing company in the nation had been born with the men and ideas that came out of Spindletop.

CHAPTER FOURTEEN

The Second Prophet

IN 1908 Spindletop was in the doldrums. Only a few years before, a 10,000-barrel well was shut in as a nuisance, and now the whole field was flowing less than 5,000 barrels a day. The play had been taken away by other domes along the coast of Texas and Louisiana. But men were still curious about the hill, and Marrs McLean had taken a small interest in a syndicate operating in the oil-soaked, boggy flats. He left his business in town several times a week to watch the drill bite into the tricky sands. The promoter of the project was L. J. Benckenstein, a Yankee who had come in during the height of the boom with a load of cash he had made raffling off diamonds in the north. Benckenstein had a flair for promotion, and in that regard he was kin to McLean. They were looking for a bonanza, but had to be satisfied finally with two or three small pumping wells that tapped the shallow, thin pay sands above the caprock.

Marrs McLean had much in common with Pattillo Higgins. He was stubborn, determined, aggressive and mechanically inclined. Adversity was his frequent companion, but he thrived on it and seemed to turn most setbacks to his advantage. He was a tall, rugged, raw-boned young Texan who, in later years, could have doubled for Walter Huston.

Had he chosen to do so, McLean might have become a successful attorney. He completed a law course at Texas University in 1904, but he was not sufficiently interested in the profession to take the bar examination. He was restless and ambitious but confident in his own ability and decisions. Fresh out of law school he went to Bolivar Peninsula, a long, narrow strip of land that juts westward toward Galveston Island between the Gulf and East Bay on the Texas coast. High Island is about where the peninsula joins the mainland. It is a hamlet built around a giant uplift that seems to rise out of the sea. Lucas had gone there after he left Spindletop, spent some of his new fortune, and turned down a million-dollar offer for the lease before he gave up without a solution to the mystery of the great mound. Marrs made High Island his headquarters, but he was not there for oil. He was there to grow cabbages and watermelons in the sandy loam of the coastal plain, where he could deliver products directly to steamers in Galveston for shipment to the east coast. The plan had merit and it worked for a while. With the idle time he had between crops he promoted a small, unpretentious hotel with B. E. Quinn. They bought salvage lumber from an abandoned sawmill at Hyatt to build the shabby beach resort.

Things were too slow for Marrs along the beach, so he gave up his interest in agriculture and bought Quinn's share of the hotel, which he leased out during the summers. In 1907 he went to Beaumont with a new idea. The old boom town was beginning to regain some of its mellow magnolia composure and there was an expansion in cultural interest to replace its former activity. Marrs promoted a theater and a dramatic stock company, as well as promoting himself into the management of the venture. As a profitable sideline, he obtained advertising rights on show curtains and in programs in all of Beaumont's theaters. As a combination hotel, theater and advertising impresario, he was doing fairly well for a young man.

II

It was about this time that he became interested in the hill. There he met with moderate success and the madness that old boomers called petrofobia gripped Marrs McLean for the first time. He went to Vinton in Louisiana, where prospectors had been trying to make an old salt dome pay off since 1901. Unlike the Spindletop dome, the Vinton caprock was barren. McLean's group, however, found some oil off the dome. The money Marrs made there enabled him to sell his theater and advertising business and devote himself entirely to oil.

He moved over to North Edgerly in the same Louisiana area and put his promotional talents to work to raise the money for a wildcat test. His fund-raising venture was successful, but the well produced so little oil that it was abandoned.

With a little income from Spindletop and Vinton as a backlog, McLean decided to learn the practical side of the business. He bought into an operation with the Higgins Oil and Fuel Company near Eagle Pass on the Rio Grande. He bought the interest with the understanding that he could have a job as a combination tool dresser and junk hustler. His job was to assemble supplies, materials, fuel and lumber and keep the drilling tools in good shape. He cut and collected all of the mesquite wood in the desert country to fire the boilers. When he ran out of trees, he made arrangements with one of Texas' vanishing coal mines for lignite for fuel. Further opportunity to apply his natural resourcefulness and lessons in oil-production methods were worth all of the time he spent on a hole that produced nothing but expense.

His next venture was to raise the money for a wildcat on Mitchell Lake south of San Antonio. Again his success at promoting money exceeded his good fortune in seeking oil. The hole was dry. But by 1913 he had learned enough about the oil business to test an idea on Vinton's flank. For some years men had bored into the caprock only to find trouble and expense as a reward for their curiosity. Marrs was convinced they had done the job wrong. He had a new plan. Against the advice of Benckenstein, who urged him, as a friend, to refrain from throwing his money away drilling the caprock on Vinton dome, McLean went ahead. His plan was simple. He would drill to the top of the rock on the edge of the dome and set his casing. Then, instead of using mud to get returns in which he had no interest, he would drill with an open hole through the rock. It worked, and he found that an overhanging ledge of caprock covered a fair oil sand. He used dry sawdust instead of mud to fill the caprock crevices. The idea revolutionized practices in the field. But this wasn't the thing that was tugging at his interest, so he sold out in a deal whereby he kept an overriding royalty interest in his holdings.

III

McLean was interested in a small producer on the southwest flank of Sour Lake dome. Then he took a block of acreage on the north flank. A small trickle of oil came forth as his reward, but this was still not what he was seeking.

By early 1915 Marrs McLean had studied maps, geological reports, stratographic sketches of domes, and he had done a great deal of thinking. He had seen oil produced from the offsides of Sour Lake, Vinton, Hull and Saratoga domes. In spite of Vinton's barren caprock, oil was found on the flanks.

In his mind McLean pictured the great salt column pushing itself up through the subsurface strata over the centuries, ages and eons. This phenomenon, he reasoned, caused an upthrust of the sands and shales, pulling them from their natural levels and, frequently, out of contact with the crust that formed the caprock. This, McLean imagined, caused the oil-bearing sands and shales to tilt at all degrees between horizontal and perpendicular, forming perfect traps for migrating water, oil, or gas. He reasoned that if the caprock was productive it was either because it was in contact with these off-side sands, or had been fed by them in the dim ages of the past. Barren-top domes were the result of contact being broken with the offside sands. Marrs McLean became definitely committed to the theory and thereafter nothing could shake his conviction.

With this idea in mind he leased and bought land at bargain prices around all of the Gulf Coast domes wherever he could find it. Then he started on a program of trying to sell his idea to major companies. All of the large operators except the Gulf Oil Company turned him down. Some would listen, discuss the proposition with their experts, and then shake their heads in the negative. L. P. Garrett of Gulf took some of the prospects, reserving 10 per cent of the profits for McLean, but seldom recommending action. The others were completely adamant, but their attitude failed to budge McLean from his belief.

IV

It was the great hurricane of 1915 that destroyed the beach hotel and took Marrs McLean back to High Island. The town was leveled, but the topographical structure stood out more prominently than ever. It was a fascinating sight, which he viewed not only in the light of his experience with oil fields, but also in the light of his newly adopted theory. He leased almost the entire hill and its periphery and for three years he punched holes along the sides of the dome. The natives watched with some of the same misgivings that the old nesters of Beaumont had regarded Higgins and Lucas, but they were glad to have the free-spending oil crews in their midst. The drilling operations were terrific and the expense was enormous. Heaving shale, gas pressures, gumbo and all of the other miseries of Spindletop were here in multiplied abundance—but no oil.

One night in 1919, as he rode with young Joe Pew of the Sun Company on a train between Beaumont and Houston, Marrs McLean talked about his theory and about High Island. Pew was intrigued and made arrangements to take over McLean's High Island leases for a small bonus and an overriding royalty. Actually, McLean probably introduced the overriding royalty idea to the coast, where it is found today more than anywhere else. It means that the broker or promoter turns his leases and retains an agreed upon royalty share of any mineral production out of the operator's seven-eighths interest in the oil or gas produced. It relieves the broker of the responsibility for land taxes, rentals, or other expenses, while permitting him to retain a royalty interest for his ideas and efforts.

It was eight years and more than $2,000,000 later that Sun, one day in 1927, turned the High Island leases back to McLean, admitting that the old hill was more than they could conquer. McLean then took over the operation again.

V

In 1920 Marrs McLean went back to Spindletop after an absence of more than eleven years. The hill had been constantly on his mind and now he felt that he had the answer to his part of its riddle.

Gulf held most of the Gladys City and McFaddin acreage on all sides of the mound. Under the original Lucas leases that expired in June of 1920, the company took a parting shot with a hole on the south. The hole bottomed on salt at 1,775 feet 300 feet south of the old Lucas gusher. When the lease came up for renewal, the company retained only 200 acres it held on top of the hill. Everything on the flanks was turned back to the original owners, because only dry holes had been drilled on them.

McLean took an interest in a test 200 feet west of the old Gladys City depot, but the hole was dry and abandoned at about 2,000 feet. Then he purchased a lease from S. G. Burnett, A. L. Kiber, John I. Pittman and John W. Henderson, covering one hundred acres that started at the tracks and extended west nine blocks and south five blocks. He paid $5,000 cash, $5,000 out of a tenth of any oil produced, and a twenty-fourth overriding royalty. Thirty days later he bought the override for $1,600, paying $800 cash and $800 in oil if produced. Around the first of the year he staked a location in Gladys City Square No. 12, one of Pattillo Higgins' designated industrial tracts.

When McLean went out to the field to supervise the construction of the derrick, he found that the haulers had erroneously offloaded the lumber and machinery at a spot directly between lots 100 and 101. At first he ordered the materials moved, but when he was informed it would take several days and more money to get the location set up 300 feet east, he decided that the location was a matter of sheer guesswork anyway, and let the materials remain. The well was spudded there. After drilling down more than 3,700 feet and finding no evidence of oil, the derrick, stacked full of drillpipe, was hit by another coastal hurricane and completely demolished. That ended the test. The pipe was a bent and twisted mass of junk. All he had for his efforts was a sample of drill cuttings of sand with an oil smell. Future events, however, would prove two facts. First, that McLean would have never found oil where he was drilling and second, that he would have found it at around 2,500 feet where he first intended to drill. But that is another story.

This failure, assisted by the elements, did not weaken McLean's faith. He stretched his resources and credit to lease every Spindletop flank acre he could get. His idea was to control enough acreage to keep anyone else from being interested. If he could have, he would have leased everything, but his credit limitations would not permit that.

Then he started his rounds to the oil companies. L. P. Garrett, the Gulf man who occasionally took one of McLean's flank leases elsewhere, summed it up.

"Marrs," Garrett said, "Spindletop is a graveyard, and we are through digging graves."

Marrs McLean went over his theory day after day with one executive after another, showing each the oil sand. None was interested. Finally, the Amerada Petroleum Company, headed by E. DeGolyer, one of the outstanding geologists on the coast, listened to his story. Adrian Moore, the Amerada manager, asked for time to talk the matter over with DeGolyer, and a few days later decided to take over the leases. The company went further. It expanded the lease holding to virtually encircle the hill. Three dry holes were drilled before Moore went to McLean one day, several months later, and said that Amerada had enough. The contract called for three tests, they had made them, and they were all failures.

Marrs McLean was stunned by the news. He sat down with Moore once again and expounded his idea.

"Adrian," he said, "you have not drilled south of the Gulf well. The slowly dropping salt line there indicates a favorable condition. I'll make you a proposition. If you will try a well there, I'll stand half of the expense."

Moore looked at sketches McLean had drawn and pondered the problem. He had orders to pull out of Spindletop, but was reluctant to do so. He agreed to take the matter up with DeGolyer and other officials. The geological department had made three locations, and Moore understood he had the right to make one of his own choosing. He said he would recommend the south flank location. For a few days McLean had hopes that his south test would be drilled, but Moore came back, apparently disappointed, with a negative reply to the proposition. Amerada dropped its leases.

VI

Amerada's decision did not deter McLean. He not only reinstated most of the Amerada leases in his own name, he picked up a half-dozen small tracts in fee, including one five-acre triangle in the Pelham Humphries survey.

He went back to Vinton one weekend to look over the wells there in which he still had an interest. Production was down, but the wells were still pumping. As he boarded the train to return to Beaumont he met Alexander Duessen, who had recently taken over production matters for Marland Oil Company. The men greeted each other and started talking oil. Duessen, one of the most highly regarded geologists and geophysicists in the world, told McLean he needed production and was looking for wildcat prospects.

McLean almost leapt from his seat.

"Why man, I've got exactly what you want," McLean said. "It's on the flanks of Spindletop. There is no doubt about oil being there, probably more than was ever found in the caprock.

Duessen listened respectfully for a while. Then, as if overcoming a temptation, he declined.

In spite of the fact that two of the most eminent geologists and geophysicists in the petroleum industry had condemned his prospect by implication, one by abandoning his leases and the other by declining them, McLean's faith remained as firm as ever. Possibly he didn't realize that Higgins had received the same treatment from Kennedy, and Lucas had heard his prospect condemned by Hayes and Payne, but he was having the identical experience with the experts that his forerunners had encountered. And oddly, the opinion of the experts was having about the same influence on the thinking of McLean as it had on Higgins and Lucas. The only difference was that McLean had neither the bitterness of Higgins nor the disappointment of Lucas. All he felt was a deep determination to prove that he was right.

Again he started knocking on oil-company doors and again they were figuratively banged in his face. Like Higgins, he was becoming known as a nuisance about the hill. He was forced to the decision to drill the prospect himself. McLean's finances might enable him to drill a well of his own, but it would mean risking every dollar he had. Yet, when he decided that that was his only course of action, he prepared to stake a location. If the hole was dry, he knew that he would be back in debt, but the experience would not be new.

McLean spent a morning in mid-April making arrangements to move in equipment to drill his well south of the dome. At noon he decided to walk home for lunch. On the elevator in the San Jacinto building he was greeted by Frank Yount, his next-door neighbor, who was also walking home that bright spring day.

Yount was president of the successful but unheralded Yount-Lee Oil Company. He had brought in deep flank production in both Sour Lake and Hull. Knowing Yount's background in such activities, McLean started talking of his plans to drill in Spindletop.

Yount listened eagerly to McLean and plied him with questions. The routine promotional sales talk he had given every major oil-company land man and geologist in Texas flowed freely from McLean's lips all the way to his front gate on Calder Avenue where the men stopped for a few minutes.

Frank Yount learned that McLean was going to drill for himself as a last resort and that he had pleaded with at least a half-dozen others to take over his leases.

"That is very interesting," Yount said, as he excused himself in departing. "I hope you have good luck."

It was early in the afternoon that Yount came into McLean's office.

"Marrs," he said, "I was wondering why you had not offered your Spindletop leases to me."

McLean was startled by the approach. He was without an answer. Here was his next-door neighbor who had offices in the same building and it had never occurred to him that Yount would be interested. He had spent more than two years talking and drawing sketches and flattening maps out before big company executives, but he had never approached the one man closest to him and the one man in the country who had been successful in flank production. Was it possible that the help he sought could have been one house away or one floor above all of that time?

"Why, Frank," McLean said, "I really don't know. I guess I thought it would take a major company to handle this deal. Would you be interested?"

"I certainly might be under the right conditions," Yount said.

"Well, man, I'll make the conditions right. If the leases need revamping or if you want me to help fill in some of the blank spaces, besides the few acres I own myself, in the circle around the dome, I'll do it," McLean said, still in a state of considerable surprise. "There's only one condition, however, and that is your promise that you will drill your first well south of Gulf's abandoned hole on the McFaddin tract—and if that fails, to move out some 300 feet and drill a second well. I promise you that if the first doesn't hit, the second one will."

Yount said he would do that. The two men spent the next two weeks clearing up details. McLean's leases were assigned to the Yount-Lee Company on May 11th. McLean was given a 3 per cent overriding royalty interest in all of the Gladys City and McFadden leases.

The second prophet, unlike the first, sought his help abroad and then found it at home.

CHAPTER FIFTEEN

Master of the Mound

By 1925 Spindletop was like a desolate and decaying battleground around the old Log Cabin saloon. A few houses and rundown stores were standing in the Gladys City area. A dozen squatty derricks, survivors of the 1915 storm, dotted the landscape. Such relics of the former feverish activity as black and oily wooden storage tanks, junked rigs and joints of rusted pipe were all around. There was the overwhelming odor of sulphur gas and waste oil, and the creaking, grinding noise of pump jacks and sucker rods as they siphoned off the last remnants of oil from the honeycombs of the old caprock.

The storm that the boom swept up had moved on to other salt domes. Virtually forgotten were the exciting days of less than a quarter-century before. Because of this hill a new age had been born. Automobiles were commonplace. The airplane was coming into general use. Highways connected every village, hamlet, town and city, and most farmers were within T-model driving range of their markets and sources of supply. Factories and plants, born of Beaumont oil, were humming out a new symphony of mass production. Yet on this scarred old hill grass was beginning to grow where excursionists once milled, men worked, fought and died, fortunes were made and lost and holes were punched down like perforations in the top of a giant salt shaker.

Old Spindletop was said to have petered out and to be on its last legs. The only hope was that voiced by an occasional veteran manning the pumps and gauges of marginal wells still producing. Once in a while one of them would be heard to say that only God knows what might be found if they drilled deeper.

No one knew who held the leases on the flanks. If Frank Yount had taken them over from Marrs McLean, it was all right. But who was Frank Yount? Was he another misdirected wildcatter who would pour money down a rathole to get a dose of salt water, a puff of gas, or a gurgle of oil too weak to hold back the quicksand that choked up the ephemeral wells on the flanks?

The old hill had shadow-boxed, feinted and flirted with one intrepid wildcatter after another as they punched holes around its outskirts. Every now and then another would come along with new hope and a new idea to probe until he lost his last earthly dollar. It was said that more money had been spent looking for oil on the hill's flanks than had been made out of the 60,000,000 barrels of oil produced on the crest of the dome. When things slowed down anywhere else, the magnet seemed to pull the sons of the hill back to its unfathomed flanks for the treasure they thought was there. Lucas and Higgins both said it was there, and so did John Galey. Those old masters knew something, so men kept returning, and just as frequently they went broke.

II

There were only a handful of people around Beaumont who had ever heard of Miles Frank Yount or his Yount-Lee Oil Company when he started drilling on the south flank at the location where he had promised Marrs McLean he would put down his first hole. And when the hole was dry there wasn't a scout from a single major company interested enough to learn that he had topped the salt some 700 feet lower than it had been found in the previous south outpost. The only surprise was the one his partners got when this man, almost as inscrutable as the hill he was destined to master, told them that finding oil on the flanks was now assured. By a dry hole? they asked themselves.

It wasn't easy to understand Frank Yount, but those he had led to wealth beyond their dreams in the last ten years were willing to believe him. He was the boss of his company and acted with a freedom seldom exercised by the chief executive of even a closed corporation such as his own. What Yount said and did was the way the company moved. He was surrounded by balance wheels, but he steered a free course and a daring one. For all intents and purposes the Yount-Lee Oil Company was Miles Frank Yount. He was the independent head of one of the best independent oil companies on the Gulf Coast.

Yount's journey to the position he now held was a hard and perilous one. What he knew, he had learned by his own methods. Forced out of school at the age of nine when his father died on the family farm in Monticello, Arkansas, Frank soon learned to accept the responsibilities of life.

Four years before the Lucas gusher came in he was a laborer on an irrigation ditch being dug through the very McFaddin land he was today drilling on. By the time the great gusher burst out of the knoll south of Beaumont, Yount was in his twenty-first year and was working in the rice fields as a contract thresher and harvester. The great boom fascinated him, but it didn't pull him away from the rice fields. He still had responsibilities and was unable to gamble.

He was a quiet, amiable, dignified man with an almost saintly face and gentle manner. His days of hard work had endowed him with a trim, wiry figure that gave others the impression he was unusually tall when actually he was an inch or two less than six feet. Yount was known as a man of impeccable character with a reputation for honesty and fair play.

When he went to Beaumont in 1923, and moved the main office of his company into the San Jacinto building, he was head of a $2,000,000 corporation. His company had reached that high level of success through a strange and interesting background of struggle and good fortune, both participated in and inspired by its founder.

Yount's first interest in drilling was as a water-well contractor for the rice farmers, who had been practically deserted by drillers since the Beaumont oil boom. He became highly proficient and then succumbed to the siren call of black gold himself. His early oil days were spent around Sour Lake, where he made solid and lasting friends and very little money.

One of these friends was Peter Cannon, a one-time itinerant Irish peddler, who made a modest fortune in the Sour Lake boom. Peter Cannon was the man who introduced Frank Yount to Harry Phelan, a young grocery salesman who had been attracted to Beaumont by a traveling job that paid $175 a month. Sour Lake was on Phelan's route of small towns around Beaumont. There he and Yount lunched together almost every week, and became fast friends.

The first Yount Oil Company was chartered on February 13, 1909, with a capital stock of $6,000. Peter Cannon was the president, but Yount ran the company as vice-president and manager. Phelan was the secretary and treasurer. The company came about as a result of a luncheon conversation between Yount and Phelan. The stockholders met every week in Sour Lake at Belle Knapp's boarding house or under a shade tree outside on the street. The occasions for the meetings were Phelan's regular weekly calls to the town. Phelan would bring his books, and the subjects discussed included drilling, leasing, buying, selling and dividends. There was never any way Yount could get his partners stirred to action, so the company was liquidated in 1910. But not before several significant things had happened.

The company's first well was sold to Lynn Gilbert, son of John Gilbert of the Higgins Oil Company. Yount tried to get his partners to buy a small tract at Sour Lake, but when Phelan and Cannon learned that the land was surrounded by Texas Company dry holes and that Yount was being influenced by a hunch, they turned him down. Yount said he did not believe the Texas Company wells were dry, but that he would later prove to his associates that the land would produce.

Then, the first Yount Oil Company led its manager to Spindletop. There he leased a single acre on the dome from a Negro former waiter who got it as a tip from a departing boomer who wanted some good to come out of his misspent efforts. Yount drilled two wells on the tract. The first one produced for a while, but the second was dry and consumed the company's assets. Before going completely bankrupt, the stockholders voted to liquidate.

Yount was happy to dissociate himself from his lukewarm, conservative partners. He left Beaumont and went to the Texas Panhandle where he spent a winter drilling a dry hole through hard rock on the banks of Bitter Creek. For the next two years he tried operating a Moon automobile agency, which failed because he could not sell, and a real-estate business, which was unsuccessful for the same reason.

One day in 1913 Frank Yount went to Harry Phelan's office in Beaumont with a story.

"Do you know what happened to that acre I wanted you to buy in Sour Lake?" Yount asked.

Phelan, who seldom paid much attention to the oil industry, said that he did not.

"Well, it produced oil and was sold out for $15,000 by a group of roustabouts and roughnecks who formed The Poor Boy Oil Company," Yount said, "and those Texas Company holes around there are now flowing oil. I'm going to form another oil company and I wish you would come in with me."

Phelan didn't say he would or would not. He had recently bought out the Heisig-Norvell wholesale grocery company and had extended his credit to swing the deal.

It was a month or so later that Yount again visited Phelan to solicit his aid in getting a lease on an acre he was positive would produce oil. The key to the lease was Joe Hebert, Phelan's friend and fellow churchman, and Yount said that Phelan could offer Hebert a chance to come into the company if he would help. Hebert got the lease for Yount but declined the opportunity to get into his company.

That lease was the foundation of the organization of the $4,500 Yount-Peveto Oil Company in 1914. Ras Peveto and others owned a half-interest. Yount had the other half, but he had made provision for Phelan.

It was sometime in January of 1915 that Yount again went to Phelan and asked for $750. Phelan, still financially cramped by his new company, was not only puzzled, but slightly embarrassed by the request. He asked what the money was to be used for.

"Why, Harry, it's for your stock in my company," Yount explained. "You see, I bought half of the stock myself and reserved a sixth for you and a third for myself. Now that we have hit oil on that lease you helped me get, I thought you would like to have your interest. Of course, I will have to have my $750 back," he smiled.

Phelan was barely able to get the money from his banker, but it was the last dollar he would ever have to pay for Yount stock.

Yount ran into his old trouble with his new partners when the Yount-Peveto Company was less than a year old. He wanted to buy a small tract in Sour Lake where his intuition led him to believe he would find oil. His partners, with the exception of Phelan, were unwilling.

An incident that had occurred only a few months before, however, enabled Yount to get the help he needed. Joe Cullinan had walked out of the Texas Company in protest over the stockholders' voting to move the company's headquarters to New York. As he left the eventful board meeting, he tapped Thomas P. Lee on the shoulder and told him he was going to form a new company and would welcome Lee into it.

Within a few weeks Lee and E. F. Woodward, the Texas Company's "formation man, joined Cullinan in the Farmers Oil Company, which would later become the producing unit of the American Republics Company, under the name of the Republic Oil Company.

When Tom Lee left, he expected his brother, William E. Lee, to take his place as head of Texas Company's Sour Lake production division. The fact that another man was put on the job indicated to the Lee brothers that the company resented Tom's leaving and that Bill could not expect much future advancement.

"Stay on the job and look for something of your own," Tom told Bill. "If you find it call me and I'll help you get away from the Texas Company."

When Yount's partners refused to back him in the Sour Lake lease he wanted, he approached Bill Lee on going in with him on it. Bill called his brother in Houston and Tom came to Sour Lake with Woodward to look into the matter. It was then that Yount talked Tom Lee into buying out his partners with the exception of Phelan. He said $25,000 would take out the partners and leave enough money for the lease and a well. Lee bought the half-interest. He offered Woodward part of that and Woodward said he would like to have it, but that he did not have the money at the moment. Lee agreed to take a block of Texas Company stock Woodward had as collateral for $12,500 for half-interest. Then, in order to get Bill away from the Texas Company, Tom Lee gave his brother a third of his own stock. The other third he gave to his daughter and son-in-law, Tal F. Rothwell, an oil-field worker who had started out as a mule skinner. The stock was put in Rothwell's name and the company changed its name to the Yount-Rothwell Company. Neither Tom Lee nor Woodward had much time to devote to the new Company, so Rothwell and Bill Lee assumed responsibility for their interests.

Yount bought his leases on the Lynn and Blaffer and Farish land and hit as he expected to. The first stock dividend from the leases paid for all stock Lee and Woodward purchased. Woodward was never required to put a cent of cash into the company. He redeemed his Texas Company stock from Tom Lee out of his first dividend check. For the next five years the company's success was far greater than any had anticipated, except Yount. In 1920 the company's capital stock was increased to $500,000 when a 900 per cent stock dividend was voted. At that time the name was changed for the last time. It became the Yount-Lee Oil Company.

On April 13, 1922, the Yount-Lee Oil Company hit the first great flank well on the Gulf Coast. It was located on the ten-acre Stengler tract in the Hull field. For months thereafter 5000-barrel wells were not unusual for Yount. As a 1922 Christmas present the company again paid a stock dividend, this time for 300 per cent, increasing the number of shares to

20,000 and the capital stock to $2,000,000 The amazing fact at that point was that the stock Phelan had borrowed the $750 to purchase was now valued at more than $330,000; and of course he had received dividends all along.

III

It was November 13, 1925. There was something about the 13th day of the month that seemed to bring significant events to Miles Frank Yount. He wasn't a superstitious man, although he did play hunches to the utmost and he staked oil locations with uncanny determination, always insisting that they not be moved an inch for any reason. Today Frank Yount had one of his strongest hunches. He had organized his company on February 13, 1909, and he had hit his first great producer at Hull on April 13, 1922. Maybe this November 13th would be his day of days.

He studied his morning report from Johnny Hatcher, his drilling superintendent. The McFaddin No. 2 was bottomed at 2,518 feet. Screen had been set in sixty-three feet of oil sand between 2,453 and 2,515 feet. If that evening's flow test was successful, he would have accomplished something that men had been trying to do for more than twenty-five years.

Harry Phelan, his right-hand man, who had now moved permanently into the company; Frank Thomas, who had joined him from a railway clerk job in Sour Lake in 1915; M. W. McClendon, his accountant, who had been with him for several years; judge Beaman Strong, former member of the state's commission of appeals, who had been lent two months before by T. P. Lee from the American Republics office; and Dad Kellam, Yount's oldest crony and field supervisor at Sour Lake, were all there to accept an invitation to the well that evening. Yount told them in his quietly optimistic manner that he believed they would enjoy the party.

Another man Yount invited out that night was Marrs McLean, the man who had made it possible for him to have all of the acreage he required to justify deep drilling. Marrs was there, quiet and grinning, as the test was made. He knew that this hill had the same kind of hold on Yount that it had on him. He recalled Yount's first try on the one-acre tract, his purchase of a 6.9-acre tract in 1917 that would soon become the center of one of the most celebrated legal battles in the history of Texas jurisprudence, his statement that someday he would find the oil on Spindletop's flanks, and, most of all, his satisfaction and relief when the leases were signed.

The test that evening was successful. It definitely confirmed everything both Yount and McLean had believed. Johnny Hatcher was ordered to put the well on production as soon as possible. Hatcher said he would have it flowing the next day unless trouble showed up. Gulf, Amerada and others had made such tests and it was believed advisable to have the oil flowing into the tanks before making an announcement. Yount was not worried. He knew that no others had ever before had the same showing he had in this well which was located a little more than a quarter of a mile southeast of the Lucas gusher site.

Still there was no great excitement around Beaumont. In fact, there was little information about the well among the local oil men. Here was an event that had been looked forward to for a quarter of a century, yet few Beaumonters knew or cared any more about Yount's well than the generation before had about Lucas' well until the day it came in. All day Yount's small office was the scene of activity. Everyone except Frank Yount was expectant and worried.

About eight o'clock that evening thousands of people at Beaumont's South Texas State Fair received an electrifying announcement over Magnolia Petroleum Company's new experimental radio station. "Spindletop has come back," John W. Newton, the announcer, said excitedly. "The Yount-Lee Oil Company's No. 2 McFaddin on the south flank of the dome came in not more than an hour ago flowing an estimated 5000 barrels of oil a day through a small choke."

There was a hush, and then a great shout went up from the crowd. Few recalled enough of the old field to realize the difference between Newton's words over the air waves and the wild ride of old Charley Ingals on January 10, 1901.

Back on the hill there was calm excitement. There was no duplication of the old rampant gusher. The McFaddin No. 2 had come in under perfect control. It was flowing into a wide burning pit and the flames lit the hillside like a great star shell. The well crew, the company officials, office workers, friends, hundreds of curious sightseers, oil scouts and newspaper reporters were there. It was the second most significant event in the history of Beaumont, and a landmark in the oil industry. What Hull, Sour Lake and other flank producers had failed to do, this colorful old hill would do. It would prove the importance of offside production on salt domes.

Frank Yount turned to Harry Phelan and said, "Harry, these flanks will produce another 60,000,000 barrels of oil."

IV

As soon as he had his flank discovery well under way, Frank Yount moved directly north of the dome on Gladys City property. He drilled two wells almost as far out as the old Kiser-Kelly dry hole and they both wound up in salt. In between the time he drilled his first and second Gladys City dusters, however, he had returned to the McFaddin-Kyle-Wiess lease and brought in the McFaddin No. 4 as an excellent producer. The well came in on January 13, 1926, making 5,000 barrels a day and again pointing up Yount's magic date. For the next few months his producers were troublesome and the smart operators returned to the thinking of the calumniators of 1901. They believed Yount had hit a small pocket of oil and that flank production would be short-lived, as it had been around other domes.

Even when he brought in the Gladys City No. 3, slightly more than a half mile due west of the Lucas, there was still no great consternation among the majors. But the day he brought in his Gladys City No. 4, on exactly the spot where Marrs McLean had staked the location for his first well before the materials were off-loaded in the wrong place, the lid was off. There was a mad scramble for every available acre around the dome. Acreage prices became almost as fantastic as they were on top of the old hill, in view of the fact that there wasn't more than twenty acres open in the oil play around the flanks.

As soon as Yount had proved there was oil on both sides of the Douthit Survey, Marrs McLean, who had a five-acre triangle between producing wells, moved in two rigs and started drilling. Before he could get down to the oil sand, Atlantic Oil and Refining Company offered to lease. McLean was not interested. He reasoned that it would be ridiculous to lease on land where it was almost certain he would find oil. He could now afford to drill at his own expense. Finally Atlantic made an offer he could not turn down. It was true that some wells were dry even when offsetting wells produced. Atlantic gave McLean a bonus of $50,000 whether the lease produced or not. If the lease proved productive, however, his total bonus would be $100,000, plus a 20 per cent royalty, and 50 per cent of the profits. The deal was a good one for Atlantic, because the company was in dire need of oil to meet certain markets, and the company's Neches River loading docks were not more than two miles from the lease. But it was also one of the most favorable leases a landowner ever made.

That was for five acres, but Gulf Oil Company paid $200,000, probably the highest price ever paid for a one-acre tract by a legitimate company in the history of the field. The ironic fact was that almost every acre in the play had been under Gulf control five years before, and then turned back to the owners. When Yount first hit oil on the flanks, B. E. Quinn, Marrs McLean's old hotel partner in High Island, leased the tract from Mrs. Daisy Roche and her sister, Mrs. F. C. Joesting, who had a fifth interest in it. Quinn paid $500 for a one-eighth lease because he was early. Later he sold the lease to H. E. Hines and his brother, coal-mine operators from West Virginia, for $6,000 and retained a one-thirty-second overriding royalty. Hines Brothers drilled one small well and then sold the lease to Gulf for $140,000 cash and $60,000 in oil. Six more wells produced 3,000,000 barrels of oil off the acre. Quinn's check for his one-thirty-second interest in the operators' seven-eighths amounted to $23,573.62 for the month of December, 1926, alone. Daisy Roche and her sister, for their one-eighth royalty, received several $100,000 monthly payments.

Quinn had one unfortunate experience. He leased the 6.9-acre tract 7 in the Douthit Survey to the Walker Oil Company, an independent, for $34,500 cash, $45,000 out of oil and a one-sixth royalty. The operator drilled a 700-barrel well, but was dissatisfied when he saw a Yount-Lee well producing ten times as much on the next location. He pulled the screen, drilled a little deeper, and never produced another barrel of oil. The well went completely dead, and others drilled on the same tract were dry.

Sun Oil Company had been haunted and annoyed by Marrs McLean's attempts to sell his leases before Yount bought them. Sun officials were spending some $2,500,000 at High Island on McLean's suggestion without getting enough oil to lubricate a watch and were, therefore, inclined to ignore McLean. When the field came in, McLean went to young geologist Phil Justice, with a high-priced, but relatively small, tract for lease. Justice recommended it to his superiors, but they were not particularly interested at the price. Finally, justice sold Joe Pew on the deal, but Pew took it only after warning Justice that if it did not pay off, he would find working conditions more pleasant elsewhere. The lease paid off with 3,000,000 barrels which was enough, in fact, to overcome Sun's losses at High Island.

Gulf Oil Company, hard pressed for production in an area it once controlled, paid a magnificent price for another tract of less than an acre on the Jeannette Mann lease. The lease produced almost a million barrels of oil during the first three years.

Outside of these companies and Magnolia and the Texas Company, both with infinitesimal parts in the play, no others participated in the second boom. There was no wild speculation, no mad scramble for hotel rooms in Beaumont, no excursions and no oil exchanges. W. P. H. McFaddin formed the Hyland Oil Company from a small tract he found open on his land, but its one test was dry. Mr. Yount was virtually the complete master of the mound this time. In spite of the fact that he had everything under control except scattered acres, he drilled wells practically as close together as they were drilled in the Hogg-Swayne, Yellowpine, or Keith-Ward tracts in the old field.

Yount believed it would take a lot of wells to get all of the oil. Furthermore, he believed that one tract might drain another, so he offset everything that threatened his production. The fact is that he found multiple producing sands in the field. One well might produce from 2,500 feet and the one next to it produce from 4,000 feet. He said that the sands were broken up and unrelated in most instances. He found more than a dozen good paying horizons of production in the field.

To prove his point and his theory he once compared a salt dome's flanks to a shattered glass. Pointing to the plate glass top of his great desk, Yount explained, "If I should hit that glass with a hammer hard enough to crack it all over, you would have my idea of what a dome's flank is like. The center, of course, would be the salt plug, and the cracks radiating out in all directions would represent the flank area. The strata of the surrounding area has been shattered by the rising of the salt. Anywhere, in any direction, oil might be located. The irregularity of the breakage accounts for oil being found in certain places, and being drained off under a tract a few feet away."

V

The result of the Yount discovery was one of the most prolific productions of oil in the country since the first Spindletop boom. Yount's company produced well over 50,000,000 barrels of oil in the first five years and others produced some 9,000,000 barrels. The ring of wells started on the south and swung west and then due north up the side of the railroad track. Within a few months the scenes of the old hill were almost duplicated as far as oil drilling activity was concerned. The men in the field were more mature about their work. Fighting was not engaged in merely as an outlet for surplus energies, and there were no saloons or ladies on horseback filling up date books. The men had grown up with the industry. Now Spindletop was again sparking the imagination of the wildcatters. Its example would soon result in greater discoveries.

There was never a gusher in the field. Wells came in under complete control, except on occasions when unavoidable accidents occurred. The one resemblance to the old hill days was the row of eating shacks and bunk houses. Steaming hot coffee and ice-cold drinks substituted for the more invigorating menu of the old Log Cabin saloon.

However, there was still hell on the hill. One morning about three o'clock a well blew out with a terrific roar in the Rio Bravo area thirty feet from the S.P. tracts. The well-head assembly was blown high over the crown block and a roaring column of gas immediately caught fire from a spark caused by a valve striking the steel derrick. The flames shot more than 300 feet and within a few minutes the entire hill was menaced. Soon every man in the field realized the seriousness of the situation, shut down the other rigs, and joined in fighting the fire. There was no time to call an expert fire fighter.

For fifteen hours men performed feats of heroism that are not uncommon in oil fields. Metal barricades were built behind which roustabouts and roughnecks took hoses and played water on the geyser of liquid fire while others sprayed the men with streams of water and mud from the slush pits. Their efforts were futile. Even the hosemen in the background occasionally ran screaming for mud and water holes with their oil-impregnated blue jeans and boots smoking.

The Southern Pacific sent a high-pressure Foamite car to the scene and was able to get it fairly close to the fire. Then hose lines were snaked into the area from eight sides, and eighty-two well boilers were tied into them. At the given signal of a whistle from the S.P. engine, all of the steam pressure in the field was turned into the open seven-inch tower of inferno. Simultaneously, the high-pressure car shot Foamite into the well. The great blast was sufficient. It completely snuffed out the blaze and the still blowing but unignited gas and oil was capped in a matter of minutes. When the fire, which could have destroyed the entire field, was extinguished, two giant steel derricks nearby were found to have been melted from the heat of the flames.

One afternoon the McFaddin 29 blew completely out of control. Three thousand feet of heavy steel pipe shot out over the top of the derrick. As fortune would have it, the first lifeline in the field had been put on this particular well. At the first rumble, the derrick man, Lewis Sanders, jumped from his perch one hundred feet above the ground and started sliding down. The derrick collapsed, however, before he made it, and he spent months in the hospital, fortunate to be alive. There were other casualties, but the only other serious one was Johnny Chance, one of Yount's drillers. Although he had taken cover in a tool house, a sudden change in the wind shifted a barrage of shale, in the form of large slabs of slate, in his direction. A large boulder smashed through the metal roof of the tool house and fractured his skull. In spite of his serious injury, however, he lived to drill many more wells for Yount, and became a successful operator on his own.

Probably one of the most unusual blowouts happened on the Gladys City No. 17 well, when disaster was narrowly averted by a most fortunate circumstance. The well was down 2,100 feet when it blew out suddenly and shot mud, shale and rock over the derrick. The light on the gin pole extending from the top of the derrick was broken by flying rock and burst into flames. The fire shot down the electric-light lines on all sides of the derrick. With two large tank batteries nearby, the danger was sensed immediately. A major explosion could not have been avoided had not a blast of mud from the hole sprayed the entire superstructure and extinguished the fire in less than a minute. Fortunately, the fire was out when the burst of gas came out seconds later. The terrific pressure caused the well to bridge over, and the blowout was killed. The force of the gas pressure, however, had driven large particles of shale into the metal sheaves in the crown block. Disaster drilled a duster in that blowout.

The flank wells were among the most incredible ever found in the oil industry. In some instances the oil sections were 1000 feet thick. Several wells logged as many as nineteen separate oil sands in a single hole. The McFaddin No. 63 ran so long with a remarkable 1,800-barrel flow through a quarter-inch choke that it wore out one side of a Christmas tree. The opposite side was opened and the outlet there was virtually gone before the well fell off in production. One gauger in the field estimated that old No. 63 flowed 3,000,000 barrels of oil in its lifetime.

Millionaire that he was already and getting richer by the hour, Frank Yount made his regular call at the field at eleven o'clock every morning in the first year or so of the new boom. The men would frequently see him, always in a white Panama hat in the summer, manning the chain tongs or helping on a derrick floor in some other way. He was a hero, a genius and a fabulous character to his men. He knew them all by name and spoke to as many of them as he could get around to every day. The day after the big fire on the Rio Bravo tract he had all of his field hands line up at the Wilson supply store for a pair of Witch Elk eighteen-inch boots, or a pair of dress boots of the finest quality, if they desired. No Yount man was ever without Witch Elk boots, the last word of roughneck sartorial perfection.

VI

Miles Frank Yount was a name that few knew in Beaumont before November 13, 1925. Two years later, however, it was a name that was on the lips of every man in the now prosperous city of 50,000. No man ever stood higher in any community than Yount. He was an example for all men of wealth. His faith and determination and struggle had given Spindletop the revival it required to keep the old champion again in the eyes of the industry it created.

Yount was a self-effacing man who seldom made public appearances, yet he and his company were represented in every civic enterprise and community charity in far greater measure than most others. No man ever left the Yount-Lee Oil Company of his own accord and few left at all. The company adopted a policy of paying the highest wages in the industry. Its veterans never retired. They simply had their heavy duties and responsibilities removed and they stayed on the payroll to work when and if they chose to do so. By 1928 the company was operating in a dozen different areas. By 1931 it was one of the largest operators in the giant East Texas field. Also, it had succeeded in solving the mystery of High Island after taking from Marrs McLean the leases that Sun had given up. Yount's success was so phenomenal there that McLean's royalty checks ran around $75,000 a month for several years. Hackberry, one of Pattillo Higgins' old prospects in Cameron Parish, and other Louisiana prospects were paying off big. Yount drilled two dozen expensive dry holes there and never gave up until he proved the field. He spent his money with faith and courage.

McLean had complained that Sun, when that company dropped his leases at High Island, was walking off from a prospect totally untested, but he had no such complaint against Yount. Frank Yount never entered a field he didn't intend to test and he never entered one where he didn't expect to find oil. He was, until Michel Halbouty came along, his own geological, geophysical and engineering department. And his uncanny success led some to believe that he was using some kind of "wiggle stick" or "doodlebug." He is the only operator oil men can recall who discovered oil in every single wildcat area he entered.

But in addition to being an oil man, Yount was a man of extraordinary culture and refinement. His free hours were spent in reading and study. He was a connoisseur of the arts and a collector of note. He loved and appreciated music, and he was an authority on literature. Yet his retiring nature kept him from making a display of his vast store of knowledge.

When Ignace Jan Paderewski, the great pianist, went to Beaumont, he told Yount he wanted to see one of his Spindletop gushers. Yount couldn't tell the old man that Spindletop now had great wells but no gushers. Instead he arranged with Johnny Hatcher for a gusher. A four-inch connection was rigged up on the well-head. Alton Prentiss, a Yount driller, was given his instructions. As the Yount car came into view a derrick man on the northmost outpost of the field relayed a signal to Prentiss. The "gusher" was turned on and Paderewski marveled.

"Frank," he said as he listened to the steady roar of the spouting oil, "I think this is the kind of music I like best."

Yount was a kindly, generous, useful man. His courtesy, even to the office workers, the building janitors and the Negro shoeshine and elevator boys was legendary. At Christmas time every Yount employee not only received a generous bonus and a tremendous basket of food, but every newsboy, messenger boy, telephone operator and others who serviced his company in any way were remembered. The men in the field all got Elk boots and Stetson hats in addition to their other gifts. One Christmas during the depression the city of Beaumont was unable to meet its payroll. Frank Yount met it that Christmas so that city workers could have a good holiday.

Yount's discovery brought Beaumont a new era of prosperity. There were more than 10,000 men directly employed in producing oil and thousands of others indirectly employed in allied pursuits, such as making tanks and supplying the needs of the oil-field workers.

His boom resulted in the construction of the twenty-one-story Edson Hotel, the slightly smaller LaSalle Hotel, the beautiful Goodhue Building, the new American National Bank skyscraper, and the remodeling of most of the old buildings. During the same time the city built an elaborate new city hall, and the old county courthouse was replaced by a new one that is virtually a replica of the Huey Long-built Louisiana state capitol building. A great high-school building, junior high schools, South Park junior College and the magnificent new Jefferson theater all resulted from the Yount boom.

When the depression came Yount helped his town by forming a real-estate company and buying property, not at distress prices, but at prices far above their depressed value.

His first building project was an elaborate apartment house and office building on the site of the famous old Oaks Hotel across from his beautiful mansion on Calder Avenue. He named it for his daughter, Mildred.

Yount built the greatest oil-tank farm in the world south of his fields and across the fresh-water canal he once worked on as a ditch digger. Work was started August 13, 1932. There were one hundred 55,000-barrel tanks and five 80,000-barrel all-steel tanks on the property. The order made Cullinan's Petroleum Iron Works plants in Beaumont and Sharon, Pennsylvania, hum through most of the depression. He built a pipeline to East Texas with Sun and filled the tanks to their 6,000,000-barrel capacity. It was an example of his daring and foresight that paid tremendous dividends. Oil was 10 cents in East Texas and 80 cents or more at tidewater. Yount preferred to purchase the oil of others at the surplus prices and retain his own production for a day when he could produce it at a profit and pay his royalty owners a good price. He paid royalty owners on a 25-cent basis even when his oil was worth only 10 cents.

As the years passed, his Yount-Lee family grew, but always the men who had helped him build his empire were closest to him. Harry Phelan was his constant adviser and balance wheel. W. E. Lee, though inactive, was a constant source of sound experience. Judge Strong was like a sturdy and dependable oak. Frank Thomas was Yount's alter ego. Next to the top man himself, the men in the field loved Frank Thomas. He was forthright and answered their questions and their problems straight from the shoulder. And there wasn't a man in the field too new or too insignificant to get an audience with Thomas any time he wanted one. Yount gave Thomas complete authority. The result was that when union organizers were working on every other oil company on the Gulf Coast, they steered clear of Yount's men. Neither Yount nor Thomas ever opposed unionization. It was simply that their men wanted no outsiders coming between them and the men upstairs in the San Jacinto Building.

On the eighth anniversary of Spindletop's second discovery, Frank Yount died suddenly of a heart attack in his fifty-third year, in apparently vigorous health. The master of the mound had performed his task well. He had done what he promised Harry Phelan he would do. Not only had the year 1927 seen the greatest record of Spindletop production since its discovery—21,000,000 barrels—but the flanks had produced more oil in eight years—to the day—than the caprock produced in its entire existence. Now production on the flanks was declining rapidly. Some other son of the hill would have to take over for its next phase.

It was November 13, 1933!

CHAPTER SIXTEEN

Accent on Success

FRANK YOUNT'S death was an unexpected, paralyzing and demoralizing blow to Beaumont and to his company. Miles Frank Yount was the Yount-Lee Oil Company. As able, as loyal and as cooperative as his lieutenants were, there was none who could step into his shoes.

Tal Rothwell, Lee's son-in-law, assumed the presidency, but he was a field-production man, not the master of an empire. Even in the field he had leaned on the genius of Yount. One of the Lees or Woodward might have qualified, but they were occupied with Cullinan. Phelan was no oil man, and without Yount he didn't feel at home in the business. Frank Thomas, Judge Beaman Strong and Max Schliecher were eminent in their particular fields, but there was no Frank Yount among them. A few months before his death, Yount said he would not sell his company for $100,000,000. The storage tanks, leases, reserves, equipment and organization were probably worth that much. With Yount at the management helm, the value was incalculable.

The Yount-Lee Oil Company, a successful operation before 1925, had become the most successful independent oil company in the world because of Spindletop. The company's first stage of existence in Sour Lake and Hull provided a stability gained through struggle. Its second stage at Spindletop gave it complete financial independence, leadership in its class and unparalleled prestige. Yount was ready to embark on the third stage, that of becoming a major integrated oil company, when he died. He had acquired reserves as a backlog, good leases for future development, a start in pipeline communications, a deep-water terminal and the largest tank farm in the world. Furthermore, the company had never lost a dime in its history, had never borrowed a single dollar, and had a tremendous cash reserve.

This third-stage plan was not mere speculation. Everyone sensed Yount's ambition. The people of Beaumont knew about it, and they felt certain Yount would keep his company at home instead of deserting the town as had the others after the 1901 boom. Yount was sounder than either the Texas Company or the Gulf had been in their early stages.

There was a feeling that when the Yount-Lee Company entered the major-company class, that would be the day Beaumont would take its long delayed step toward becoming the largest and most prosperous city in the South. Yount's death ended that dream. Slowly but completely, Beaumonters realized that Yount's great company, born of Spindletop Hill, had died with him.

For about a year the company moved forward on its founder's built-up momentum. Then the difference could be seen. The spirit was gone. Beaumont began to feel the depression after the years of Yount-Lee prosperity. Around the company's offices there was a void. Not only was Yount's presence missing, but his genius, daring, individuality, leadership and genuine desire for progress were gone. Those in the inner circles felt that the end of the company was near. In spite of that, however, the first rumor that the company might be sold came as a shock. Weeks passed and the word spread. There was nothing definite, but it was regarded as inevitable.

It was clear that the Yount-Lee situation was fraught with opportunity. The way, however, was blocked with obstacles that discouraged ordinary men. In the first place, the value of the Yount company, or its total stock, narrowed the field of potential buyers to a mere handful of major oil companies. Even among those it was doubtful that one would be willing to risk the Texas antitrust laws by purchasing the company outright. Any major company would consider the proposition long and seriously before purchasing Yount-Lee's pending lawsuits, unorthodox business methods, and other liabilities. Add to those obstacles the fact that the Yount-Lee stockholders had no reason to sacrifice their stock on the altar of excessive taxation, and it was easy to come up with a riddle that lacked a solution.

II

Wright Morrow, a young Houston lawyer, discussed the possible sale of the Yount-Lee company many times with his client, T. P. Lee. Lee was anxious to see the company sold because he knew that without Yount it was through. For more than a year there had been no dividends, and it was reasonable to expect that the company would never reach a higher value than at the present. Lee suggested that if Morrow could interest some buyer, he could make a good brokerage fee.

With Lee's consent, Morrow made a trip north to talk with his friend, Melvin A. Traylor, president of the First National Bank of Chicago. Traylor was close to the official family of

Standard Oil of Indiana, and the word was out in oil circles that the company was interested in building up production of crude oil for its refineries. If its principal drilling and producing subsidiary, Stanolind Oil and Gas Company, could purchase producing properties and good prospects to fill that need, it would obviate the necessity of relying heavily on outside sources. Traylor confirmed the report, but said that Standard would not purchase the Yount-Lee Company or its stock. It might, Traylor added, be interested in the purchase of the company's assets.

This threw a new light on the subject. Morrow saw that the possibility of a brokerage fee from either side of the deal was impractical. Then he came up with a daring, almost fantastic idea. Maybe, he thought, he could buy the company from the stockholders, liquidate it, and sell the assets to Stanolind. As he turned the idea over in his mind Morrow chuckled to himself. Here he was, thinking about buying the biggest independent oil company in the world when it was doubtful that his credit at any bank would exceed $10,000. Wright Morrow was a smart, struggling, young attorney. His prospects in his profession were good enough. But thinking in terms of borrowing millions of dollars seemed absurd.

It was absurd, but it haunted Morrow all the way back to Houston. He expected Tom Lee to laugh at him and he was reluctant to even mention it. Lee, however, didn't think it was ridiculous. All he said was that the idea could certainly be carried out—but a man would need guts to go through with it. Morrow went to work on the plan immediately.

First, he found out that the Yount-Lee stockholders individually would give him options on the condition that they get the benefit of capital gains, and that no share of stock would be sold unless all was sold. If the sale of the stock was by company action, the tax would have been some 70 per cent. In view of the fact that stockholders had owned their stock for twenty years, each was entitled to the 25 per cent capital-gains benefit as an individual. Morrow was authorized to negotiate a deal. It was decided that a fair price for the stock was $2,200 a share for the 21,540 shares. The total stock of the company that Yount had valued at $100,000,000 could be purchased for approximately $48,000,000.

Only $48,000,000! That's all Wright Morrow had to raise. And the deal had to be for cash. Staggering as it was, the figure did not deter Morrow. He informed Traylor that if Stanolind would valuate the properties, there was a chance the deal could be made. E. F. Bullard, vice-president and geologist of the company, and a staff of experts were sent to make the evaluation. After months of inspections of properties, investigations of books, and studies of undeveloped prospects, Stanolind told Morrow it was willing to pay $42,000,000 for the oil properties and operating equipment.

Now Morrow had a complicated decision to make. The $6,000,000 difference between the stock purchase price and the sale price for the oil producing assets was his problem. It was a tremendous speculative transaction in which only one man was to gamble millions he did not have. Miscalculation or bad management could mean disaster.

The Bureau of Internal Revenue was given the details of the proposal. If a deal could be made, the government stood to gain $12,000,000 in taxes. If not, there would be no government gain in those days when tax dollars were most acceptable to a treasury depleted by the ravages of depression. Harry Weeks, Fort Worth tax lawyer, and H. I. Wilhelm, tax accountant, had been engaged by Morrow to study and explain the details. Guy T. Helvering, tax commissioner, and Robert H. Jackson, assistant general counsel for the Bureau, heard the proposal. Morrow understood that it was necessary, to get the capital-gains benefit, that he neither act as agent of the stockholders in disposing of their property nor of the Stanolind in purchasing the company. Instead, he must be engaged in a speculative transaction of his own. A sale by company action would not entitle stockholders to capital gains benefit. Stockholders had to sell their shares individually. He explained that such was the case and that he was to pay more for the stock than he would receive from Stanolind. The complete deal was presented in writing. Shortly, he received an approval by opinion of the Internal Revenue Department, also in writing. So far, the going had been good, but expensive. Morrow had more than $40,000 of his own invested and it was $40,000 that he did not have in cash.

For his part, Morrow was to get all assets of the company that were not included in the oil properties and equipment. This, fortunately, included some $4,000,000 in cash and negotiable notes, valuable Beaumont and Lake Charles properties, certain oil and bank stocks, some business enterprises and other Yount holdings including undeveloped oil properties Stanolind was not interested in purchasing, and $1,700,000 in accounts receivable.

Now all he had to do was borrow the $48,000,000. He explained the situation to his young, brilliant banker, William A. Kirkland of Houston's First National Bank. The difference between the liquid assets Morrow would receive immediately and those he would have to wait for was $2,000,000. Kirkland agreed to take a close look at the deal and confer with the National City Bank of New York. He expressed hope.

On February 27, 1935, the Stanolind Company, yielding to the pressure of the Beaumont, Houston and Tulsa newspapers, admitted that negotiations were being carried on with a third party for the purchase of the Yount-Lee Company. The brief release, which was the first official news, dropped like a bombshell in Beaumont. It closed with the statement that negotiations were still far from a conclusion.

III

Far from a conclusion, Morrow thought as he read the release, was an understatement. Borrowing even $2,000,000 from financial institutions in the middle of the great depression wasn't easy. Morrow's friend Jesse Jones had placed a ban on Reconstruction Finance Corporation loans on oil deals.

From what Morrow knew of the Yount-Lee properties he stood a chance to make millions in the long run. His problem, however, was immediate. Within a few days Kirkland informed Morrow that the deal could be handled. He was over one of his biggest hurdles, but before him still were hundreds of smaller obstacles.

An injunction suit by W. D. Gordon to hold up any deal pending the final outcome of the Federal Crude Oil Company suit for some $15,000,000 was one such obstacle. When this impediment was finally removed, there still remained the hostility toward the sale on the part of almost everyone in Beaumont. Some of this proved difficult to overcome. Through the first half of 1935 Morrow wrestled with his problems. There were thousands of loose ends to gather up. He could not be certain that the deal would turn out right for him. There was risk and gamble at every turn. He had to assume all of the company's liabilities, including several important lawsuits and innumerable minor claims. The magnitude of his undertaking was brought home to him as he realized that his interest payments on $2,000,000 would amount to $300 a day and his taxes on the company's Beaumont holdings alone were $20,000 a year.

As weeks passed and details were ironed out, the day for the great transaction loomed. The stock in the company was still held in exactly the proportions as it had been held in 1914 when Harry Phelan gave Frank Yount $750 for a sixth interest, and by the same principals. Lee had divided his quarter interest with his daughter and son-in-law, Rothwell, and his brother, W. E. Lee; Phelan had made a division within his own immediate family; the Yount one-third interest was divided in his estate between his wife and daughter, but Woodward still held his quarter interest intact. For all practical purposes there had been no changes in the stock holdings, although some non-voting shares were held by Thomas, Strong and Schliecher. Morrow held the conditional options on all stock and the conditional agreement from Stanolind to purchase the oil properties and operating equipment.

July 31, 1935, was the date of the dramatic event. It was the date of the greatest financial transaction in the history of the oil industry. Papers were put in order, meetings were set, and details were lined up for a schedule of action. Pinpoint precision was absolutely necessary. Even a small hitch could throw the schedule off and mean delays that would cost Morrow, the only gambler in the picture, hundreds of thousands of dollars, possibly millions. Yount-Lee stockholders were assembled in one place and the Stanolind representatives, including A. W. Peake, chairman of the board, F. O. Prior, president, and Bullard, with a staff of assistants and experts, in another. Morrow stood by in immediate communication, by runner and telephone, with both parties. He was armed with the money to purchase the individual stock holdings and he had 10,000 personally signed deeds and other documents ready to turn over to Stanolind. The timing had to be perfect. As hours of the hectic day passed, every detail, minutely planned for weeks by Morrow and his staff, went off on schedule. The bankers, tax experts and others interested were at assigned places for immediate action. The day was tense, historic, and exciting. Morrow himself lived a lifetime in seventeen hours. His career and his future depended on the outcome.

When the day came to a close, the producing properties that Yount had built over the years were in the hands of Stanolind. The Yount-Lee Oil Company, still rich in other assets, was almost out of the oil business. Morrow was its new president, and Roger Guthrie, a Houston lawyer, was secretary, and Weeks and Wilhelm were directors. For the first time in its twenty-one-year history the company was in debt. Its new owner owed $2,000,000 and his troubles were just beginning.

The Stanolind Oil and Gas Company took possession of 358,120 acres of oil lands and leases, of which only 49,352 acres were proven. There were 2,000 acres of undeveloped land in the heart of the great East Texas oil field. Leases covered holdings around twenty piercement-type salt domes. The company's net daily production was 20,000 barrels and 5,000,000 barrels of oil were stored in Yount's great tank farm. Stanolind's need for production had been met.

Edward G. Suebert, president of Standard of Indiana, made the announcement in a release that covered barely more than one double-spaced typewritten page. Details came from the reporters assigned to cover the transaction. The newspapers and radio broadcasters sounded the end of the golden era of the company built by the master of the mound called Spindletop.

IV

At the 1940 Democratic National Convention, Wright Morrow, one of the most active party members in Texas, nominated John Nance Garner for the presidency as Texas' favorite son. His speech bristled with a denunciation of any intention of upsetting the tradition of two terms for the president. Steeped in constitutional traditions by a family background of distinguished jurists, including a famous father who served on the state supreme court, the idea of a third term was repugnant to Morrow, although he had been a Roosevelt stalwart. His speech was heard around the nation. Parts of it were used later by Willkie forces. It was almost as daring a move as his Yount-Lee deal had been, in a sense. But it was far from being as wise. New Deal forces were incensed.

At the time, the Bureau of Internal Revenue was taking another look at his Yount-Lee deal. He had explained the transaction in full before it was made and had followed with a complete report with exhibits after the deal was completed. In both instances the matter had been approved by opinion of the department. After the Democratic convention, Morrow's troubles with the income tax investigators seemed to mount. After almost five years of rigorous and costly investigation, which absorbed much of his time and money, his position was finally confirmed again.

Morrow and his associates fought out many of Yount's old lawsuits, resisted claims against themselves, and defended new lawsuits. For instance, among Morrow's assets was some $800,000 involved in litigation over oil produced from the right of way abutting Yount's fee tract in the Douthit Survey at Spindletop. The matter had been settled in a test case, but it was Rio Bravo Oil Company's right to delay settlement of the Yount-Lee claim by going to court. Morrow was anxious to retire his debt and reduce the interest as fast as possible. He settled with the defendant company without getting the full amount, but he gained by the action in interest savings. The settlement was a windfall to Rio Bravo. It was the only profit realized out of some 15,000,000 barrels of oil produced by the Rio Bravo. The receipts, less expenses, had been impounded during eight years of the lawsuit. It was almost ten years after Morrow closed the deal, however, before he actually knew exactly how he stood. The street gossip had him making a million dollars from each principal as brokerage fees. That, of course, was totally false. Morrow did find out, however, in 1944, that he was about a half-million dollars ahead despite hundreds of thousands of dollars of expenses that he had not anticipated. His gamble had paid off and it continued to do so for some years.

For their total investment of $25,000 some twenty years before the stockholders received almost $48,000,000. The Yount Estate received $15,000,000; Woodward, $11,500,000; the Lees each got $3,400,000; the Rothwells, $5,700,000, and the Phelan family $7,500,000. For their loyalty and good services Thomas Strong and Sechliecher each got about $300,000.

The deal ended the second glorious era of Spindletop.

CHAPTER SEVENTEEN

Suits and Countersuits

"IF THE court please, your honor, I should like to make a motion." Judge Campbell nodded his approval. "Your honor, since this cause was first instituted, one of the defendants, W. P. H. McFaddin, has had born to him a son. That son has grown up in our city, attended the grade schools and graduated from high school. He has since graduated from the university with a law degree, and has passed the state bar examination. That son has been admitted to the bar, entered the practice of law here in Beaumont, and is, even at this very moment, pleading before you in this case. Your honor, in view of these facts, plus the additional fact that the plaintiffs seem to want for prosecution, I move the dismissal of this case."

Caldwell McFaddin was the attorney addressing Judge Campbell and the judge knew that Caldwell McFaddin was the boy whose life had begun since the litigation over the Humphries survey started. He dismissed the case.

That was in 1926, when the cause of the Humphries heirs was twenty-five years old. In 1951, even after the federal courts had banned the suit, there were still four Humphries survey cases on the dockets in Jefferson County, two of them in federal court. The Humphries survey is the 3400 acres that were leased from McFaddin, Wiess and Kyle in 1900 by Lucas, and it is the land upon which discovery wells for both the 1901 and the 1925 Spindletop booms were located. It probably has the most fantastic legal history of any strip of land in the country. That, despite the fact that it apparently never has been in the slightest danger of being lost to its owners.

Legal controversy over the William Pelham Humphries survey has become an institution, like the hill itself. The original Humphries went to Texas in the early thirties of the last century as a colonist under the Republic of Mexico. He was granted a league of land in Jefferson County in 1835. That is all anyone seems to know for certain about the man. Even his name is in doubt. It has been established fairly well that Pelham was a nickname, but proof is not positive. Deed records show that the entire league was conveyed to William Inglish in 1836, that 500 acres were conveyed to John G. Love in 1840, both by William Humphries. The records further show that Pelham and William Humphries, as heirs and joint heirs of Pelham Humphries, deceased, conveyed the entire league to Stephen B. Dozier in 1859. None of these conveyances were filed with the county clerk, however, until 1860.

No one knows definitely where the original Humphries came from, whether he had any relatives or not, whether or not he left a will, or when or where he died. The three conveyances recorded in 1860, of course, led to conflict over ownership between the Humphries and the Inglishes. In the midst of the litigation between the two sets of heirs, the Beaumont Pasture Company, owned by the McFaddins, Wiesses, Kyles and others, stepped in and bought out the claims of litigants on both sides. The land was fenced that year and kept under fence until 1912. Under all statutes of limitations, laws of adverse possession and rules of tenancy, the land thereby became the property of McFaddin, Wiess and Kyle.

The Lucas gusher brought heirs out of every hill and valley in Tennessee from both the Humphries and the Inglish sides. That was the start of a march on the title of the survey, which the courts have consistently agreed was unquestionably owned by the McFaddins and their associates and heirs, that seems to grow with each new batch of heirs over the generations. The claims had reached an all-time high in 1951, with almost a billion dollars involved in the four cases on the docket. One was for $500,000,000 and another claimed $150,000,000. The defendants include practically every company that has ever gotten a drop of oil off the land, plus the Reconstruction Finance Corporation, which lent money to a company holding a right of way across the land.

There are thousands of alleged heirs involved. The half-billion-dollar case alone lists more than 1300 of them. In the early days there were cases where only ten or fifteen heirs were concerned, but the lines are both prolific, apparently, and the lists grow with each passing year. No one is able to estimate how much money has been spent on fees, court costs and incidentals over the years. It might have amounted to as much as the profits on all of the oil produced from the survey.

The fact that the Jefferson County clerk has been forced to mimeograph a form letter to answer inquiries from hopeful heirs indicates the volume of interest lawyers are able to stir up. The form letter even points out the numerous unsuccessful suits, all of which have failed to break the title, and the fact that a complete abstract costs more than $3000. These facts do not deter the heirs in their determination to share in the untold wealth that has bubbled out of the caprock over the years.

Although every acre of land on Spindletop dome and its flanks has been fought out in the courts in hundreds, even thousands, of lawsuits, the Humphries survey is the only land still under active attack. And that is in spite of the fact that its title is probably safer than any of the others.

Young Caldwell McFaddin is not young any more. His trim waistline has spread and his hair has long since vanished. Somehow, he doesn't seem to mind the cases brought against his father's estate. They never worry him because he knows that both the law and equity are on his side. In fact, it is a source of entertainment that he might miss if the matter were ever definitely settled. It is expensive entertainment, yet Caldwell, and his brother, Perry, believe they can afford the fun better than the myriad would-be heirs who come into court year after year with the twinkle of gold in their eyes.

II

The Lucas gusher brought forth the greatest assembly of lawyers and heirs that any event has ever attracted. Within a year after Spindletop came in, the people of Beaumont were probably better versed in conversational Latin than most Irish priests. The language of the day was sprinkled with *ipso facto, nunc pro tunc, ex parte, res adjudicata, mesne* and *laches.* On Beaumont's streets you could hear court authorities quoted with the same facility that an Apostolic preacher quotes scripture. Lawyers made as much profit out of oil as the operators, with half the work, none of the gamble and twice the social prestige. There was no known case of a Beaumont lawyer going broke, yet former oil men could be found digging ditches, washing dishes in second-rate chili houses and panhandling on corners.

Even before the calumniators had to take cover in late March of 1901, the Jefferson County court dockets were running over with suits by, against, and between Pattillo Higgins, Captain Lucas, George W. Carroll and others. Before the field was a year old not an acre within miles was uncontested. Lawyers outnumbered drillers, operators, landowners, confidence men and stock speculators. Also, lawyers could be found in all of these categories. Before long law took its place with geology, engineering and finance as one of the fine arts of petroleum.

The early days of Spindletop saw every company in the field, with few exceptions, either headed by lawyers or with lawyers on the board of directors. Some outfits, like the Hogg-Swayne Syndicate, were composed of nothing but lawyers. It was inevitable, therefore, that the gentlemen of the bar would head some of the largest companies, like Farish of Standard of Jersey, Beatty of the Texas Company, and the present day Baker of Humble.

Spindletop set a dizzy pattern for legal pyrotechnics. It is there that a specialized petroleo-legal branch of the bar was created. The need for land men came out of the old field and a new profession was born. Today no man drills a well without first determining beyond a doubt that all titles are cleared. That was not true in the days when leases and land sales were written out on napkins, wrapping paper, the backs of coffee coupons and the inner wrappers of Mail Pouch or Brown Mule tobacco, if they were written at all. Often deals were consummated without a scratch of the pen.

It wasn't long after the Lucas well came in that thousands of phony heirs and a handful of rightful ones were on the scene. They came from almost every state and many foreign countries. Many of the cases provided both fascinating and sensational newspaper stories. The history of Texas' colonization was reviewed from the days of the Spanish land grants, through the Republics of Mexico and Texas, and down to the carpetbag era when everything was thrown into confusion. The *Lake Charles American* commented that

> the next man who brings suit for Spindletop property will claim that it was the site of the Garden of Eden and that he is a direct descendant of the peaceable settlers who were ejected by force of arms and without due process of law. . . . Such a claim would doubtless be as lawful as many of those which have found their way into the courts since the great gusher started tinting the magnolias for miles around with oil spray.

With all of its chicanery, fraudulent claims and legitimate suits, Spindletop served to put emphasis on the rights of landowners and their heirs. The oil industry became acutely aware of the importance of those rights. Spindletop cases, in several instances, served as landmarks of jurisprudence.

Probably the most interesting of all legal land battles were those fought over the Veatch survey.

III

Dr. John Allen Veatch was an adventurer and a man of culture. He was a scholar, geologist, engineer, teacher and physician. In fact, he was once the surgeon general of Sam Houston's ragged army of the Texas Revolution. Like Humphries, he received a land grant from the Mexican government in 1835. He had his headright divided into three parcels and on each explorers have found great oil fields. One of these was at Spindletop, another at Sour Lake and a third at Orange. He selected high mounds in each case out of a knowledge of either real estate or geology.

With all of his education and experience, Dr. Veatch died in poverty, leaving only the "worthless" land in Jefferson County to his six children. One of these children, Andrew, himself an outstanding engineer, died and left his sixth of the life estate to his wife, Annie, and two children. In 1891 Captain George W. O'Brien purchased the rights of the Veatch heirs for $300, but through some error failed to obtain the eighteenth life interest of Allen Veatch's widow, Annie Snow, although he did deal with her two children. This was the land Captain O'Brien put into the Gladys City Company.

Spindletop hadn't been going for more than six months when the Snow case cast the first serious cloud on every oil well in the field except three. Her case was taken by W. D. Gordon, Amos L. Beaty and judge R. R. Hazlewood. Although the suit was bitterly contested, there seemed to be little doubt that Mrs. Snow was entitled to her claim. Her attorneys took the position that a life estate was entitled to inherit mineral as well as surface rights. This involved a principle that the courts of the land had never been required to decide on before. It was the first landmark case in Spindletop's legal history. Mrs. Snow's recovery entitled her to an eighteenth of every barrel of oil produced on the Veatch survey. Even with oil selling at 5 cents a barrel, it was estimated to have a value of more than $200,000. This she shared with her lawyers who took the case on a 50 per cent contingency.

Shortly after the suit was settled Judge Hazlewood purchased Mrs. Snow's interest for $10,000 for the Hogg-Swayne Syndicate. Gordon, one of Hazlewood's partners, was indignant over this action, and induced his father-in-law, Judge McLean, father of Marrs McLean, to bring suit against Hazlewood and the syndicate to recover the interest for Mrs. Snow. Judge McLean lost the suit in federal court and refused to appeal because his old domino-playing partner, Judge Bryant, had made the ruling. Gordon, however, overcame his personal objections to suing a partner and took the case to the New Orleans circuit court and won a clear-cut decision on the appeal. The Supreme Court refused to hear the case on a writ of error.

The Snow case, however, was only the opening gun in the barrage of litigation that involved the Veatch survey for the next few years. The fireworks started when claim was made for three-fourths interest in the survey in the name of George A. Howell of Kentucky, and others. The chain of title had been traced back by an entire army of energetic lawyers who came up with the allegation that John Allen Veatch had sold his Spindletop land to a Colonel James Morgan in 1841. This was a matter of record, but the record also showed that Morgan had sold the land back to Veatch a few years later. This latter sale, the Howell attorneys claimed, was a forgery. The Colonel had stopped paying taxes, they contended, because of a misunderstanding.

Regardless of what Colonel Morgan had believed, the record also showed that he sold the land to a man named Baker in 1865. But in 1847 Veatch had sold the property to J. H. Burton who, seven months later, had given a power of attorney to W. Goodwin, who in turn had sold the south 2000 acres to H. S. James. In 1871 James sold the land to Mark Wiess who sold it to Charles Cleveland in 1884.

About that time the thing was so embroiled that a lawsuit resulted. This caused Cleveland to settle for 500 acres which later became the location of a subdivision known as Spindletop Heights and from which the old hill got its name. This was the same Cleveland Heirs land that the Gladys City Company once authorized George O'Brien to purchase, but which he was unable to get before everyone lost interest in Pattillo Higgins' project.

Finally the various parties to the Morgan suit, including the attorneys for Annie Trench of England, started suing each other. There were prosecuted judgments, agreed judgments, settlements and other actions that finally resulted in some kind of order. The lawyers who had taken their cases on contingencies wound up with small tracts and little cash. Some of the prominent men of the bar included J. O. Davis, J. H. Trembley and T. C. Rowe. These names are on Spindletop leases today. But, as far as anyone knows, the legal controversy came to a happy ending with all concerned glad to get out of the legal firing range unscathed. No one knows for certain who is who in the picture yet, but a satisfactory settlement of all ownership was arrived at sufficiently in 1946 to allow the Texas Gulf Sulphur Company to satisfy itself with the situation.

The Veatch survey had more concentrated activity in the courts than the Humphries, but it is now virtually forgotten as a battleground for barristers. The Humphries, which has never had but one case get into the courts, is still the all-time champion of litigation on a longevity basis.

IV

As far as anyone recalls there was never much title trouble with the John Douthit Survey. In the first boom there is not even any record of a lawsuit involving tracts on the land. The legal star shells that illuminated the clouds over a few of its small tracts following the second discovery, however, made up for the survey's freedom from attack in the blustering days of the first boom.

The John Douthit is a long, narrow strip of land between the Humphries and Veatch surveys. The strip once extended all the way across the two large surveys. The north half, known as the Ingals Survey, was wiped out during the Annie Snow case.

The fifty-two acres on the northeast end of the Douthit Survey were owned jointly at one time by J. M. Hebert and the heirs of Jeff Chaison. The fifty-two acres were checkerboarded into eight lots, with Hebert owning all of those with even numbers and Charles J. Chaison, representing the Chaison heirs, owning the odd-numbered lots. Either before the Lucas gusher or shortly thereafter Hebert entered into a deal with Jim Weed whereby the two men shared the even-numbered lots, some divided and some undivided.

Three of the hundreds of companies formed in the first boom bought small tracts in the Douthit Survey and all of these companies were destined to have their names perpetuated in the annals of jurisprudence by future lawsuits.

One of these was the Federal Crude Oil Company, which purchased lots 5 and 7 from Chaison, who became vice-president of the company. The president was D. A. Duncan and the manager was H. L. Fagin. In 1901 the Federal Crude Oil Company missed immortality by about 300 feet when it stopped drilling an off-side well at a depth of 2400 feet. Had it gone the other 300 feet, twenty-four years of trouble and strife might have been avoided and the geological theory of salt-dome flanks might have been proved that much earlier. But the company, which was capitalized for $450,000, went broke, and the owners abandoned their land because it was "not worth postage stamps." Duncan and Fagin left the state and for all practical purposes, the Federal Crude Oil Company evaporated into thin air.

A second company to be remembered in later years was the Buffalo Oil Company, which bought a part of lot 6 from Jim Weed for $18,000. The company flourished for a while and then followed the pattern of the Federal Crude Oil. When the Buffalo Company went broke, however, it went into receivership. When a receiver was appointed, Jim Weed bought back his 2.45-acre tract of land for $65, some $17,935 less than he had sold it for a few months before.

The third significant company as far as the latter-day lawsuits were concerned was the $500,000 Cartwright Oil and Development Company. Matthew Cartwright was a successful businessman from Terrell, Texas. His father had once leased Spindletop property for oil development—the first oil lease in the history of Texas—in the 1860s. That might have been why Matthew Cartwright, the second, was lured to Spindletop. Cartwright's company was not a promotion. Most of the stockholders were members of his family. His company acquired relatively large tracts of land north of the hill. When the Kiser-Kelly well's failure forced everyone to the top of the dome, Cartwright even succeeded in getting one-sixteenth of an acre from the Hogg-Swayne Syndicate. There he could produce oil, but there was no way he could dispose of it. Cartwright purchased land for storage and trackage from Chaison in lots 1 and 3 of the Douthit Survey.

When the boom broke, Matthew Cartwright believed he had been a failure for the first time in his life with his oil company. He paid off his cash stockholders and formed the Oakwood Realty Company from the land holdings he and relatives had left. The new company was successful as conservative real-estate firms go, but Cartwright never got over his oil-business failure.

In several of the most famous cases in Texas land-law history, those three companies and the boom-time land they occupied became by-words in court circles.

V

The first Douthit Survey land to get entangled in legal controversy was that formerly owned by the Federal Crude Oil Company in lots 5 and 7. J. F. Guilmartin, a minority stockholder, went into district court in Jefferson County in 1907 and asked for an accounting of the company's property. Guilmartin sought receivership for the company since its charter had been forfeited the year before for failure to pay franchise taxes. The company had never been liquidated, so Guilmartin believed he was entitled to some action for his stock, however small the amount might be. The state had already sued to foreclose on a tax lien.

The district court appointed C. L. Rutt of Beaumont as receiver and ordered him to investigate. Rutt reported back that he could find no personal property but that the company still owned lots 5 and 7, which he had taken over as receiver. His report described the land as being of no present value and not liable to appreciable increase in value. He said that the state claimed $175 in taxes, but that the 13.8 acres were not worth it. Rutt said that Guilmartin, the stockholder, had offered $50 for the land and that he would recommend its sale for that price, provided Guilmartin would assume liability for taxes due. The court so ordered and Guilmartin took over the property. Almost immediately he sold lot 7 for $60 to R. W. Wilson. There was no protest and no one seemed worried over the case for some years. Chaison had refused to take part in the suit on the grounds that he had resigned as an officer in 1904.

In 1917 B. E. Quinn, McLean's old hotel partner, paid Wilson $700 for lot 7. That same year Frank Yount bought his first Spindletop property when he paid Guilmartin $600 for lot 5.

A slight oil flurry hit Spindletop in 1919 and for a few weeks it looked as if a new boom might develop. That was when one of the flank fluke wells flowed briefly. Suddenly, as if from out of a dim yesterday, came Duncan and Fagin, the two officers who had left the state in 1903. They were joined by Chaison and Peter Anderson, another former director, who sued Quinn for lot 7, a case which also placed Yount's lot 5 in jeopardy. W. D. Gordon, Annie Snow's attorney of old, brought the suit in Fagin's name for 50 per cent fee. The resourceful and able Gordon won his suit, but the case was appealed to a higher court. There, the decision was reversed and Quinn and Yount retained their property. By 1922 the oil scare had ended, land values dropped again and there was no further litigation.

That serenely peaceful situation prevailed until 1926 when Frank Yount started decorating lot 5 with 10,000-barrel oil wells. The case went into federal court and right up to the United States Supreme Court, where the decision was against Fagin and his associates in every instance.

In 1928, McLean, Chaison and a few others had a new idea. They purchased most of the Federal Crude Oil Company's old stock, paid all of the back taxes, and had the company's charter revived. By now Yount-Lee Oil Company had twenty-seven wells on the 6.9 acres of lot 5, and the prize was something akin to a boy's mental picture of the value of the pot of gold at the end of a rainbow.

Judge Beaman Strong, general counsel for Yount-Lee, and his first assistant, A. D. Moore, recognized not only the danger in the suit and the millions involved, but the fact that their other duties required most of their time and that some help would be necessary. Strong recommended that Will E. Orgain, probably one of the most brilliant land lawyers in Texas, be engaged to try the case. Shortly thereafter two former state supreme court justices, Judge R. L. Batts and Judge F. A. Williams, were added to the Yount-Lee legal battery. Not to be outdone completely by this array of legal talent and supreme-court prestige, Gordon enlisted the aid of another former supreme court justice, Judge Nelson Phillips, and C. W. Howth, one of the most colorful lawyers in Texas coast circles.

The history of the Federal Crude Oil Company, the receivership, the old cases and every available detail of the past were all rehashed. Distinguished and determined lawyers displayed talents that have seldom been equaled in the courts of the land. Gordon was the kind of lawyer against whom no opponent could let down his guard for a moment, and Orgain was a match for the old master.

For seven years the legal maneuvering went on. Orgain and the Yount-Lee Company won in every court, but knew they had a fight right down to the finish. Ownership under limitations was proved by the existence of an oil pick-up station on lot 5. Frank Yount did not live to see the outcome of the legal battle over his precious fee land, but his company was the ultimate winner.

VI

Even before the Federal Crude Oil case was finally adjudicated, Yount's fee land in lot 5 was under a new attack. The case was styled Ivy Wilkinson Counce et al. versus Yount-Lee Oil Company et al. Mrs. Counce was the daughter of G. B. Wilkinson, an old railroad man and teamster who had died before the great flank production was found on the side of the hill. The other plaintiffs in the case were Mrs. Counce's sister, Mrs. Stella Hart, and the husbands of the two women. They asked damages of $15,000,000 plus interest in the amount of another $5,000,000. The attorney for the plaintiffs was Oliver J. Todd, another most resourceful member of Beaumont's celebrated corps of lawyers. Todd took the case for a 50 per cent interest in whatever might be recovered from the claim. His idea for the suit might have come from testimony establishing limitations in the Federal Crude Oil suit. He took the novel position that he did not sue for possession of the tract. He admitted, apparently, that the Yount-Lee Company was entitled to it by adverse possession. Todd did contend, however, that his clients' father was entitled to the minerals produced during the tenancy of his period of prior adverse possession.

However, the plaintiffs had as their chief adversary the redoubtable Will Orgain, who had by then become the expert on the hill, as far as the land laws were concerned.

Todd's contention was that Wilkinson had occupied lot 5 since 1912 and had, therefore, come into complete possession of the tract by the ten-year statute of limitations in 1922. Orgain's job was to prove that Wilkinson never had exclusive possession of the land, and furthermore, that he had not occupied it in his own name for more than seven or eight years under any interpretation of ownership.

As the story unraveled in the courts it was revealed that Wilkinson himself never asserted ownership to the property as far as most witnesses, including his son, C. B. Wilkinson, knew. It had all started back in 1908 when Jim Nearen was appointed receiver by the district court for waste oil on the hill. The court was charged with the responsibility of preventing the oil from becoming a fire hazard. Many wells were flowing on the hill and pipelines and storage tanks were subject to leakage. The oil, as in the case of the first gusher, drained off to the southwest, across the flats, in the direction of Hillebrandt's Bayou.

Nearen selected a site in lot 6, alongside the road, and purchased an acre there for a very nominal price. He and Clint Chenault built an oil pit and pick-up station on the land. A year later, after Nearen had bought out his partner's interest, he died. He left the acre and the business to his wife, Jeannette. His brother, Bill Nearen, bought the business, but not the acre of land, from Mrs. Nearen.

Shortly thereafter a survey was made of the land and it was found that the Nearen oil pick-up station was not entirely on his acre in lot 6. Some of the tanks and pits slopped over onto Guilmartin's celebrated lot 5. Rather than move the equipment and dig new pits, he arranged to pay Guilmartin $20 a year for the right to use part of his land.

Later Nearen sold the station and within a year or so it changed hands again, finally falling into possession of Horace Blanchette, who had been appointed receiver. Blanchette was later appointed tax assessor for the city and was unable to continue to operate the station. Sometime in 1911 he made a deal with Wilkinson to operate the station, pay all expenses, and keep 75 per cent of the profits. Blanchette was to get 25 per cent of the profits.

The question upon which the case hinged was how long Wilkinson kept up this arrangement before taking the station over entirely. The plaintiffs contended that the change over was almost immediately, if, in fact, Blanchette ever had anything to do with Wilkinson's business. The defense contended that Blanchette was still the boss as late as 1918, when Frank Yount permitted him to continue using the land without cost.

Had Yount been a hardheaded businessman he could have taken the land over or insisted on payment, which would have precluded any possibility of claim by adverse possession. What he actually did, however, was merely tell Blanchette that when the land was needed he would give ample notice to move off. In fact, when Yount did move on the tract in 1926, he gave Wilkinson's son several weeks' notice and then generously purchased the old tanks for which he had no use, simply to help Wilkinson. Yount's big heart, however, must have cost him and his heirs and associates several hundred thousands of dollars in court expenses before the suit was settled.

The courts seemed to side with the Yount-Lee contention of when Wilkinson took the land over, plus the contention that the Counces had no right to a claim for damages under adverse possession. Todd admitted that Yount-Lee owned the property under the same ten-year law of limitations when the case came into court. Orgain had further proved that during the entire time that Nearen, Blanchette and Wilkinson had their station on the land the McFaddin-Weiss-Kyle canal had run across the property and had paid for the use of the land and had, therefore, used it. That ruled out any possibility of exclusive possession.

The trial was bitterly contested for several years and, on appeal, Yount's generosity again jeopardized the suit. Yount had insisted on paying the witnesses, who were mostly poor men and who had taken time out of their jobs to testify in his behalf, more than the $12.50 a day witness fee. He gave them from $250 to $1000 each over and above the necessary amount because his attorneys had insisted on their remaining in town during an entire trial period. On appeal Todd hinted that this might be evidence of intimidation and should disqualify their testimony. His plea, however, failed.

A most interesting sidelight on this case was the fact that the single acre that Jim Nearen bought and left to his wife, who became Jeannette Mann by a later marriage, produced almost a million barrels of $2 oil during the boom and has produced thousands of barrels since.

VII

Jim Weed watched as the Rio Bravo Oil Company, owned by the Southern Pacific, spudded a well on the railroad's right of way opposite his land on Spindletop's flanks one day in 1926, and came to the conclusion that there was a defect in the picture somewhere. Here, he reasoned, was a railroad way, granted for the purpose of easement for tracks, that was going to be used by the railroad company's subsidiary to drain oil from under the 2.45 acres which he had repurchased from the old Buffalo Oil Company for $65.

No one else seemed disturbed about the matter, not even the Gulf Oil Company, which had paid him $25,000 and a sixth royalty for the lease. But James F. Weed was a surveyor and a civil engineer. He had serviced Southern Pacific's right of way from the Sabine to the Rio Grande in 1889, and had later become chief engineer for the Gulf, Kansas City, and Beaumont Railroad. Not only that, but he was an oil man. The first boom had set him up in the business, and he had since discovered at least one field on his own.

Weed talked it over with Will Orgain, and Orgain agreed with him. He then went to Houston to discuss the matter with Gulf officials. The Gulf office did not follow his thinking. The tract the company leased from Weed had been described by metes and bounds that did not include the right-of-way strip. Jim Weed then asked the Gulf officials if, in view of their interpretation of the lease and the fact that they intended to take no action to stop Rio Bravo, they would grant him a release of any possible claim to the right of way abutting the lease. The request set the company men to thinking. They finally decided to explore Weed's idea further.

Orgain suggested a temporary injunction against Rio Bravo's drilling operation. This, he reasoned, should be filed before Rio Bravo hit oil, as a suit filed afterward would give the operating company an advantage in equity which might be difficult to overcome. All agreed with this and the injunction was requested and granted. Shortly thereafter, the Gulf attorney agreed with the Weed and Orgain argument and agreed to aid Weed in a suit against Rio Bravo. The company had more interest, of course, than Weed in his own tract. Gulf also had leases on the Oakwood Realty tract on the opposite side of the tracks with twice the right-of-way frontage of the Weed tract, as well as the Mann acre, north of the Weed tract.

The suit against Rio Bravo was styled James F. Weed versus Rio Bravo Oil Company. By agreement, Rio Bravo was permitted to continue drilling with the provision that the proceeds from oil produced on the right of way, less agreed expenses, would be impounded until the suit was settled.

Yount-Lee's highly controversial lot 5 came into the picture as it, too, bordered on the right of way. Yount's company, therefore, became an important party to the suit on the side of Gulf and Weed.

As the months passed Rio Bravo lined its 200-foot right of way with sensational producers. With each thousand barrels, and then each hundred thousand barrels, and finally with each million barrels of oil produced, the suit assumed greater and greater proportions in the courts.

The suit called for the clarification of an important principle of law. There was a definite establishment of metes and bounds to all tracts abutting the right of way, and those metes and bounds did not include the right of way. This, Rio Bravo contended, left the strip entirely in the possession of the railroad company, which had purchased it from Hebert and Chaison prior to the original Spindletop discovery. Before Weed got his idea, that was also the understanding of the property owners and their lessees.

The entire Rio Bravo suit revolved around the partitioning of the northeast fifty-two acres of the Douthit Survey. The partitioning had taken place before even the first boom and not one acre of the entire survey was productive in that boom. J. M. Hebert and the Chaison heirs had split the subdivision into eight lots, four of which contained 5.27 acres each and four containing 6.9 acres each.

Adding up the total of the lots partitioned, it was apparent that only 48.68 acres had been included in the partitioning of the fifty-two acres. The Southern Pacific right of way covered the other 3.32 acres of the subdivision. The entire contention, therefore, was over the 3.32 acres, and the fact is that Weed's claim was to only 45/100 of an acre occupied by the west side of the right of way abutting his 2.45-acre tract. The other abutting tracts, however, would be governed by whatever decision was made in the Weed case.

Hebert deeded the tract to Weed in April of 1901, before Weed had sold it to the Buffalo Oil Company. The deed carried conflicting descriptions. The first part described the lot as "The southeast one-half of lot 6 of the subdivision of a tract of fifty-two acres of land off the north end of the John Douthit survey, as shown by the plat attached to the deed of partition, etc." The second part described lot 6 by metes and bounds and excluded, thereby, the land occupied by the right of way.

Through all of the courts to the state supreme court it was the contention of Orgain and the Gulf attorneys that land fronting on a right of way for railroads, streets, highways and the like would include the fee to the center of the way, unless the deed contained some expression to the contrary. It was further contended that, in cases of conflict in description, a plat of a subdivision would prevail over a description by metes and bounds. The conflict certainly existed in the two descriptions. The plat favored Weed.

The case was brilliantly fought through the courts for almost ten years. Weed was the winner in each successive court. The case served as a precedent establishing the principle that a conveyance of land abutting a right of way, street, or highway passes title to minerals to the center of such right of way.

After the years of legal turmoil over the question, there was some $15,000,000 in the Rio Bravo kitty that had to be returned, less operating expenses, to the owners of the 3.32 acres. More than 3,000,000 barrels of oil had been produced from Weed's four-fifths of a half acre. The Cartwright company received more than $600,000 for its share, and several million dollars accrued to Yount-Lee Company, which owned its part of the right of way in fee. Matthew Cartwright died a few weeks before Yount's discovery. The oil on the old Cartwright land, plus that produced on the abutting right of way, proved his oil venture a success in the long run. His son, Lon Cartwright, had succeeded him as head of the Oakwood company.

CHAPTER EIGHTEEN

Commemoration

"WHERE was the Lucas gusher located?" Marion Brock naïvely put the question to a group of Spindletop operators whose conversation had centered on the impact of the great well. None could definitely answer the question. One man said it was in one place and another said it was a hundred feet or more away. But there was no conclusion. That was in 1920.

The incident haunted Brock, and he proposed that the site of the historical gusher be marked. Twenty years passed, however, and Beaumonters forgot. One day in the late '30s Brock, who had moved to Houston, wrote a letter to J. Cooke Wilson renewing his suggestion. Wilson was receptive and within a week he and Brock had formed a committee including Steve Pipkin, one of the original producers in the field, and Scott Myers, who was born at Spindletop.

They raised the money to purchase a handsome Texas pink granite monument, arrange for appropriate ceremonies, and mark the well site properly. Myers was the authority on the exact location. In October, 1941, the monument was unveiled. The *Enterprise* published a special Spindletop section reviewing the history of the field with biographies of Lucas and Higgins and other important men of the discovery. A paper by geologists J. Brian Eby and Michel T. Halbouty predicted a third phase with production possibilities on the north and east flanks. The importance of Spindletop oil to the development of the sulphur industry by providing the necessary fuel was reviewed. The fact came out that there were then forty-six oil fields within a hundred-mile radius of Beaumont with 2,440 producing wells. A picture of the plugged McFaddin No. 2, Yount's discovery, suggested to some the possibility of a second marker.

The ceremony was a success and a new generation of Beaumonters learned something of the old field.

Marion Brock and Scott Myers were not satisfied. They believed honor was due the Spindletop pioneers as well as the gusher. The war interfered, but by 1946 they were again working on a plan for a golden anniversary celebration. Their efforts aroused others, and by 1949 a charter was granted for the Spindletop Fiftieth Anniversary Commission, and Governor Shivers appointed John W. Newton, head of Beaumont's Magnolia refinery, as its chairman. Brock and Myers were members of the commission.

II

The date was January 10, 1951. The weather was cold and invigorating. There wasn't a cloud in the sky. It was the same kind of day it had been exactly fifty years ago.

Beaumont was a boom town again. Bands were playing and people were milling. Children galloped around the streets dressed in the fashion of 1900. There were promoters with tall silk hats, frock coats, shoestring ties and wide, black moustaches. In every store window there were displays depicting scenes of "then and now." Up and down the streets old-timers were greeting one another. Al Hamill, as spry as he was the day he unloaded the pipe for Captain Lucas, clambered over a perfect reproduction of the old gusher that was set up in Sunset Park, directly across the tracks from the site of the old S.P. station.

Pattillo Higgins, an honor guest of the day with Al Hamill and Anthony Fitzgerald Lucas, son of the Captain, watched the growing excitement of the early morning from his suite in Hotel Beaumont. His schedule for the day was a busy one. His official escort was J. W. Kinnear, himself a veteran of the hill, and George Carroll's son, Charley, was also with him. That morning they were to be present for the spudding of a 5,000-foot hole with a modem power rig on the opposite end of Sunset Park from the mock-up of the old derrick. With Al Hamill, he would go to the exhibit hall at the fair grounds, then to a gathering of old-timers in the Crosby lobby, a luncheon for the old-timers at noon, a talk by John D. Rockefeller's grandson, David Rockefeller, and a dedication ceremony at the Lucas monument. Higgins declined an invitation to the banquet that night because his eighty-nine years would not stand that much. But he would listen to the program on the radio.

Wherever Anthony Lucas went he was met with a standing ovation. The name had a magic appeal. Generations had forgotten Higgins and Hamill, but Anthony Lucas would never be forgotten. The gusher and the monument and even a Beaumont street kept the name of Lucas alive.

Beaumont responded enthusiastically to the celebration honoring its heroes of yesterday. The *Enterprise* that morning had a three-column reproduction of Trost's famous picture of the gusher. It covered the entire length of page one.

The *Journal's* streamer across the top of the front page was sketches of Higgins, Lucas and the old Crosby House.

At precisely ten-thirty, factory, refinery, switch-engine whistles, and automobile horns all over the city joined in a tumultuous din to salute the instant of time the geyser of oil spouted forth. At the same time a squadron of jet planes shot down from the north of the city over Pearl Street and out over the hill where they executed a spectacular circular formation. It was at that hour also that the old-timers assembled in the Crosby lobby to renew acquaintances and hash over the days of oildom's greatest glory.

All over the city there were club meetings and assemblies. Speakers included Wallace Pratt, retired vice-president of Standard of New Jersey, who was Humble's first geologist; Carl Coke Rister, one of the industry's important historians; Dr. E. L. DeGolyer, who conducted the first geophysical explorations in the world on Spindletop Hill and whose company then drilled three dry holes before the Yount discovery; John R. Suman, vice-president of Standard of New Jersey, and another graduate of the Humble company; Jack Pew, Beaumont-born son of J. Edgar Pew, of Sun, and Glenn McCarthy of Houston, another native of Spindletop Hill.

There was a press interview with Charles E. Wilson, president of General Motors; Walter S. Carpenter, Jr., chairman of the board of DuPont; and B. Brewster Jennings, president of Socony-Vacuum, parent company of Magnolia, at Hotel Beaumont. These three were the principal speakers at the Fiftieth Anniversary dinner that night. It was there that Hop Wright who, with Tom Fuller, had the leading café on the hill during the entire boom period, served a fabulous pheasant dinner.

In the afternoon there was a Parade of Progress that outdid anything Beaumont had ever experienced. Under the direction of Parade Marshal Louis R. Pietszch, descendant of George Carroll, the line of march was led by Higgins and

Hamill. Then came the great Texas Aggie band, dozens of floats, modern oilfield equipment mounted on trucks, old buggies and horses, a horse-drawn hearse, Mrs. Frank Keith riding her old electric runabout, the United States Army's 45th Infantry band and bands from every high school for miles around Beaumont. There were giant boilers, portable rigs and derricks, swamp buggies, model streamlined trains, a replica of young Tony Lucas' old schoolhouse at Spindletop and a caravan of veterans of the boom.

Thousands gathered for dedication ceremonies at the Lucas gusher monument in the afternoon and more thousands attended the great banquet. At the fair grounds there was a hall of exhibits that was one of the most complete displays of obsolete and modern oil equipment ever assembled. There were old pictures of the boom days, books of clippings, portraits of the men of distinction of the 1901 period, and demonstrations of drilling, refining, pipelining and other oil activities in miniature. The governor's commission had left no stone unturned.

The town was crowded with newspapermen from throughout Texas and the oil regions of the Southwest. Magazine writers and radio commentators were there, too. Celebrities such as Morton Downey, John Carroll, Theresa Wright, Robert Cummings, George Hicks and others mixed with the crowds and were roughnecks for the day. Hicks presented a commentary on his United States Steel hour, and DuPont's Cavalcade of America presented a play titled Spindletop. Gulf had Al Hamill on "We The People" to tell how the great gusher came in. Beaumont's own nationally famous Melody Maids presented a Spindletop song saga, and the women of Beaumont wore hairdos that featured derricks through which dark tresses spouted in the fashion of the famous gusher. An entire trainload of geologists came in from Houston and held an all-day meeting at the fair grounds with such noted scientists as Suman, Pratt, Alexander Duessen and Ira Cram as featured speakers. W. E. Wrather, chief of the United States Geological Survey, which had redeemed itself over the years for its former chief's error on the hill, was among the honored guests.

The day was one of the most magnificent in petroleum's history.

III

More than a hundred veterans of the hill's boom days sat around the Crosby lobby spinning tales. They knew that oil booms had come and gone and that none had come close to the days of Spindletop. Even those who had gone on to Sour Lake, Batson, Ranger, Burkburnett, Glenn Pool and East Texas could not compare those experiences with what they had been through in Beaumont.

In any corner of the lobby there was a fabulous story going. Slim Harrison, driller extraordinary, was happy to be there.

"I never got to the Crosby during the boom," he said. "Us field hands always ran into too many attractions on the way here."

But Slim could remember his early days with Ed Simms and how he got fired. Someone sent in a telegram of resignation and signed Slim's name to it. Howard Hughes hired him and it wasn't until later that Slim found out that it was Howard who sent the telegram. The Hughes will, however, left Harrison on Hughes's Tool Company's payroll for life.

Johnny Wynn, the best mechanic in the field and the driller on Higgins' first well, who lost a fortune in dry holes, was there. Johnny wasn't dressed in the finest clothes, and he didn't keep his present occupation of sharpening scissors and butcher knives for housewives a secret, but he was embraced and toasted by his more fortunate old buddies, some of whom were multimillionaires.

Carl Clemons recalled his days at the boom. He went to Beaumont to take a hotel clerking job and was hired by Ed

Boyington as a roustabout. He lived to become Gulf's production superintendent and one of his sons, Walter, who was now one of Gulf's attorneys, had been born in a covered wagon on the edge of Batson field on the fourth anniversary of the Lucas gusher. This was Walter's birthday.

J. W. Kinnear recalled the day when, right there in the Crosby lobby, a little squirt of a man inquired of a larger man whether or not he was a captain of a certain infantry outfit in Cuba during the Spanish-American War. Assured by the larger man that he was, the smaller gent produced a pistol and fired. He had been a private in the company and felt abused. The bullet went wild, tore through the ceiling and a bed on the second floor, igniting a boomer's pajamas, sending him scurrying down the stairs shouting "Fire!"

Cussing Mike Mitchell was busy denying the story that he had nailed a helper's Ingersoll watch to the derrick when he found it tied there. The story was that Mike had said, "That'll teach the bastard to hang his jewelry on my rig."

Al Hamill was wound up with one story after another of the old days, but he felt bad because Curt, who was seriously ill in San Antonio, couldn't be there.

The names of girls and saloons and gambling dives filled the air. And, they all agreed, there were no greenhorns on the hill except the "rope chokers" from Pennsylvania who could not make their cable tools work. The Easterners thought they knew what they were doing. The others had no such illusions. They talked of their problems of keeping the excursionists, especially the women and children, on the windward side of the gushers so they wouldn't be consumed by fire in the event of a conflagration. They all compared their progress in life since the great event. Some were retired executives, others, like Hamill and Higgins, were still operating, and still others, like Johnny Wynn, hadn't fared too well, but were rich in the experiences of their days in the field.

IV

All day and far into the night the big executives and the great scientists made speeches.

"The important product of Spindletop was men. Men to man the industry which gave birth to an age more glorious than man's mind had ever theretofore imagined."

"Lord Curzon said after the First World War that the Allies had 'floated to victory on a wave of oil,' and Nimitz credited victory in World War II to 'oil, bullets, and beans.'"

"Spindletop's discovery brought an end to the isolation, drudgery and loneliness of rural life, and it eliminated the long hours of toil in dingy workshops in cities choked with smoke and fumes."

"The *Literary Digest* can not be blamed for saying that the automobile would never be as popular as the bicycle any more than Edison can be censured for his statement that the airplane was a fad and would never be practical. No imagination was great enough to foresee the miracles that would come from Spindletop's bounty."

"The revolution wrought by this great economic epic has changed our way of life completely. At the end of 1901 there were 8,000 automobiles in America. Today there are 50 million. Moreover there are three million tractors, 35 million other farm vehicles, and eight million trucks. . . . There are 3,320,000 miles of highways and streets in this country over which vehicles annually consume 37 billion gallons of motor fuel. For this you can thank the diligence, labor and genius of the pioneers of Spindletop and their successors."

Pattillo Higgins sat on platforms, in expansive dining rooms, and before his radio in the hotel listening to all of these phrases and many more.

He heard a recitation of the volume of oil and gas and chemicals that had come from his hopes and plans and perseverance. He heard references to the billions of dollars in payrolls, profits and benefits to mankind, all from oil and its products.

"It isn't important," one speaker had said, "who made money or who has gone broke in oil. The balance is heavily in favor of the latter, of course. The important thing is what benefits it has brought to America and the human family as a whole. Those benefits are beyond calculation. The only problem we have today is how we will continue to provide the incentive for modern man in this practical age."

Higgins thought about this and the other things he heard. Then he turned to those around him and said, "If they only knew it, the surface hasn't been scratched. There are billions of barrels of oil right here on the Gulf Coast yet to be found."

Men once criticized Pattillo Higgins for saying things that were, in their day, far more fantastic. This time no one disagreed. His statement didn't seem plausible. But neither had it sounded plausible when the same man had said oil wells would produce thousands of barrels of oil a day on the hill and that he would make millionaires of all his friends.

V

Within a few weeks after Higgins and Hamill and the younger Lucas had departed, the Beaumont newspapers were headlining the story of Spindletop's impending third phase.

John Mecom, son of one of the field's pioneers, was punching holes deep into the south flank. As contrasted with the $5,000 wells of the boom days, however, he had spent almost a half-million dollars on only one of the new wildcats. Already young Mecom had brought into reality one of Higgins' prophesies. That was the one made to I. D. Polk about buying land across the river from the field, where there would someday be another great discovery. Mecom had brought in oil on the land adjacent to Polk's in Rose City.

Dr. C. B. Claypool, associated with Scott Myers, Earl Hankamer, and others under the name of Meredith, Clegg and

Hunt, had succeeded in bringing in a tremendous distillate well in the northern part of the Veatch survey, within the city limits of Beaumont. That was the story that captured the headlines. Claypool, like Mecom, a prophet of the third phase of the old field, had worked for four years promoting deeper flank production. Each day was bringing him closer to his projected goal. But the day of Spindletop's pioneers was not over, as he, Mecom and others were proving.

In even greater measure Yount-Lee's successor in Spindletop was proving a most worthy one. The Stanolind Oil and Gas Company was making notable finds on the north and east flanks, also within Beaumont's city limits. The company's program was a full one and promised results, although the tremendous investment of all of the deeper flank operators will require many years for a payout, even when the third bonanza is hit. The old hill was still feinting and challenging its sons.

Lucas had first gone to Spindletop in search of sulphur. Now, in 1951, the golden anniversary of the discovery, it seemed that the golden stone that burns would be found in abundance beneath the topographical high that was the hill known as Spindletop.

George Maercky, great genius of the sulphur industry, spent years dreaming of Spindletop's sulphur possibilities. In 1943 his Texas Gulf Sulphur Company took over the hill from the Jefferson Lake Sulphur Company which had already drilled a dozen or more exploratory wells. As Texas Gulf continued this exploratory program its agents spread to the four winds in search of answers to the jigsaw puzzle of land ownerships. Into every state in the union as well as into a half-dozen foreign countries they searched for owners and heirs.

They could not hope to develop sulphur without the dome's entire surface as a block. They found parcels of land as small as eight by nine feet in the old Hogg-Swayne tract. They found multiple ownerships and heirships of these minute parcels as well as the larger ones. In Beaumont and all over the country they found heirs who had no idea they were entitled to anything on Spindletop. Tireless land men and lawyers scoured the nation and, as the golden anniversary year was closing, they had virtually completed their task.

It was then that Maercky announced that his company would spend a minimum of $10,000,000 on the installation of a plant and other facilities, exclusive of the purchase of mineral and surface rights. Yet Maercky realized the gamble the hill required of him. When, in 1952, Texas Gulf's first tests for production started no one knew what the answer would be. The hill has been punched full of holes. The sulphur that explorations have proved is there might resist efforts to bring it to the surface. Even before the production efforts were attempted, the years of work required had forced Maercky into a premature retirement. Yet he can rest assured of achieving the goal of becoming one of Spindletop Hill's most intrepid sons.

Like Higgins and Lucas and Galey and the Hamills and the horde of others before him, he is gambling against tremendous odds to bring to the surface the bounty of nature that will make life everlastingly more abundant for mankind.

APPENDIX ONE

How Deep Is a Hill?

PATTILLO HIGGINS had a belief—a faith—that there was a producing "rock" at Spindletop. He felt that only hard rock could cause the slight uplift of the surface of the earth that formed the mound or hill, and therefore the rock must be somewhere below that mound. He also assumed that there would be oil under that rock because he calculated that if the surface was uplifted, the beds under the surface would also be arched. The oil, being lighter than water, would seek its own level, and would thus move through the water in the geological formations until caught in the arched beds. That was probably the extent of Pattillo Higgins' original knowledge of geology, but it was excellent thinking and was based on sound geological principles, even by today's standards.

Pattillo Higgins told everyone about his rock and that it would be found at shallow depths—at approximately 1000 feet. When Kennedy, the State University Geologist, visited Higgins and was told about the rock, he publicly refuted Higgins by stating that no such shallow subsurface rock existed in the vicinity of Beaumont and offered as proof a well located in the town of Beaumont which was drilled to 1400 feet for water, exceeding the depth of Higgins' theoretical rock layer. Even after the discovery of oil and the drilling of the first few tens of wells at Spindletop, no salt had been penetrated, and Higgins still believed in his theory of arched beds and his idea of oil being trapped therein—although Lucas had told Higgins that a salt dome was responsible for the uplift.

Higgins even expounded his ideas in a booklet, and he went to great lengths to explain his theories. The remarkable thing about Higgins' old writings is that they were phenomenally accurate according to present-day geological knowledge. He did not discuss salt or salt domes, as the drill had not yet penetrated salt, but his reasonings as to structure, oil accumulations, drilling and production were very good. Higgins could easily be called the first practical oil man the Gulf Coast produced. He was daring and outspoken, and an optimist, yet so practical that his knowledge borders on that of a scientist and engineer.

It was difficult for the layman in 1901 to comprehend the "why" of the existence of a salt dome—and it still is. Very little professional geology was being done in the Gulf Coast, and there was practically no petroleum geology being practiced anywhere else. The fact that oil would be found only in an area within the influence of the dome was recognized long after the Spindletop discovery. Even Lucas, who was the first to consider the salt-dome theory at Spindletop, leased land for miles from the center of the mound, which indicates that he did not really know what effect a dome would have on oil production.

Just what is a salt dome like Spindletop?

The Spindletop salt dome is actually a stalklike core of rock salt which has protruded up through the overlying beds of sands, shales and limestones, thus causing the pierced sedimentary beds to dip radially away from the salt core. The effect of the uplift of the salt on the dip of the overlying sediments can be illustrated by laying a flat, unwrinkled handkerchief on a table and gradually lifting the cloth with the fingers from the very center. This will show the radial effect of the plug forcing itself through the strata.

The Spindletop salt core is roughly circular in shape, about one mile in diameter. The uplift of the salt mass had an effect on the surface area overlying the dome, forming a mound or small hill, approximately the same diameter as the subsurface salt core, which is quite perceptible above the flat prairie lands of the Gulf Coast. This topographic feature is a characteristic surface expression of most of the piercement-type domes in the Gulf coastal plain. The mound at Spindletop rises barely fifteen feet above the general level of the plain, but this rise stands out against the very flat and gently sloping land.

After the discovery of oil at Spindletop this topographic feaure was one of the main "surface indications" that wildcatters looked for in their search of other oil fields. This led to the quick discovery of many domes a few months after Spindletop. Wildcatters did not know what was underneath those surface mounds to cause the accumulation of oil, but the one thing that they did understand was that a mound must first be found before plans were made to drill. This type of "surface" wildcatting resulted in the discovery of many domes in Texas and Louisiana. Pattillo Higgins was attracted to Spindletop not only because of the mound, but also by the gas seeps, paraffin dirt, and sour waters which existed in the vicinity of the mound. These surface indications led to the drilling of the first well at Spindletop and forever after all wildcatters, geologists, operators and oil men looked for the same indications.

The existence of a core of salt below the surface of the earth raises a number of questions in the layman's mind. The two big questions are, when was the salt deposited, and how did the domes rise through the vast thickness of formations to their present positions? These two questions have stumped geologists to this day, and many theories have been expounded, discussed and "cussed." The general idea accepted by most students of salt domes is that the mother salt beds were deposited millions and millions of years ago in the old coastal lagoons and embayments during Lower Jurassic or Upper Permian time, or after, and that as much as 5000 feet or more of salt might have been laid down before the first deposits of sediments were laid down over them.

Many salt domes like Spindletop are located in the Gulf coastal plains of the United States. The area representing the Gulf coastal plains was, throughout early geologic times, either a very shallow basin of water or dry land, and successive cycles of rising and ebbing of the old seas took place, depositing, eroding and redepositing sediments. The thick mother salt bed was deposited during a time when extreme and conditions prevailed in this part of the world. The climate was very hot, the land dry and the seas shallow. Very little rain fell in the area. The shallow seas became supersaturated with salt, so that salt dropped out of solution from the sea water and solidified on the bottom of the sea. Successive layers of salt thus deposited were packed into a bed of vast extent covering the entire Gulf coastal plain area. This great mother salt bed gave birth to the domes that lie beneath the landscape of the Gulf Coast and under the waters of the Gulf of Mexico.

The depth at which the mother salt bed might be expected to be encountered under the Spindletop area is estimated at more than 30,000 feet below the surface. This gives an idea of the thickness of sediments overlying the salt and the overall extent of the movement of the individual salt core through the younger beds. There are many ideas and theories as to the cause of the initial upward movement of the salt plugs from the mother bed. It is believed, however, that movement did not begin until sufficient sediments had been deposited over the salt bed to cause an appreciable static weight on top of the salt.

The weight of the sediments above the salt is a most important factor in the upward movement of the salt. The salt has a specific gravity of 2.19, whereas the average specific gravity of the sediments is approximately 2.7 at great depths. This difference in the specific gravity of the two is likened to that of oil and water. Oil being lighter than water, the forces of buoyancy cause oil to rise through water. This same principle is applied to the salt and overlying sediments. Because the salt is much lighter than the sediments, it rises in a sort of plastic state through the sediments.

The force of buoyancy is one of the factors that causes the salt to move through layers of sediments of higher specific gravity as oil moves through water, not necessarily with the same ease, but by the same principles of the laws of physics. There are other factors that contribute to the movement of the salt mass, such as tectonic forces (internal earth movements) which might have caused the buckling of the mother salt bed, cracking and distorting the salt, as well as the overlying sediments. In turn these movements created lines of weakness in the sediments adjacent to the salt bed which permitted the initial movement of salt through them. Once the movement of salt begins, the forces of buoyancy are constantly at work, depending on the static weight of the sediments above the salt and on the flanks of the salt core. The main *motive* force of the uplift of the salt through the sediments is the static weight of these sediments, *principally* on the flanks of the salt core. The salt stock moves in stages through geologic time, depending on the thickness and the weight of the sediments above and around the salt mass. The sediments at very shallow depths, from the surface down several thousand feet, are less dense than those at greater depths and also less dense than the salt, and afford no contrast therefore to cause the salt to move appreciably. For that reason the upward movement of the salt core gradually slows down, but does not necessarily stop altogether as it approaches the surface. Generally, when such an equilibrium of density is approximated between the sediments and the salt, a stage of semi-dormancy prevails. During this time more sediments are deposited over the salt-core area, which gradually raises the static weight, and increases by compression the density of the beds being buried. This in turn causes an increased compressive action on the peripheral flanks of the dome which, with the forces of buoyancy of the salt thereby revived, causes the accelerated upward movement of the salt stock to begin all over again.

Cycle after cycle of this procedure took place until the domes gradually pierced their way through the overlying beds to their present position under the surface of the earth. It must be emphasized, however, that it appears that there was variation in the rate of the upward rise of the original salt stocks. Some of these moved upward rather slowly, so that they could not keep pace with the rapid deposition of sediments and eventually became buried beneath many thousands of feet of overburden. These domes are referred to as "deep-seated," and gas and oil production is generally found in the arched, but unpierced, formations lying over the super-dome area. Other salt stocks, including this one at Spindletop, seem to have developed under conditions that resulted in the salt stocks remaining near the surface throughout their growth history. These are commonly referred to as the "piercement-type" domes, because the salt pierced the overlying sediments with growth and remained, therefore, only a few thousand feet below the surface. Gas and oil production at these domes is therefore likely to be important in the pierced formations which butt against the sides of the salt mass. It was one of these salt cores that finally settled under an area that is known as Spindletop.

In order to show clearly the steps involved in the birth and growth of a salt dome like Spindletop several illustrations have been prepared. These illustrations are wholly schematic, in that considerable detail has been omitted. In studying these drawings it must be remembered that oil is now thought to be the remains of the abundant microscopic life such as plankton, accumulated through many millions of years in the shallow seas of the early geological periods, and trapped and compressed through later periods by successive layers of sediments.

Figure No. 1 shows the thick layer of salt deposited in late Paleozoic and/or early Mesozoic time. The geologic timetable is shown on the left of the illustrations to indicate the growth

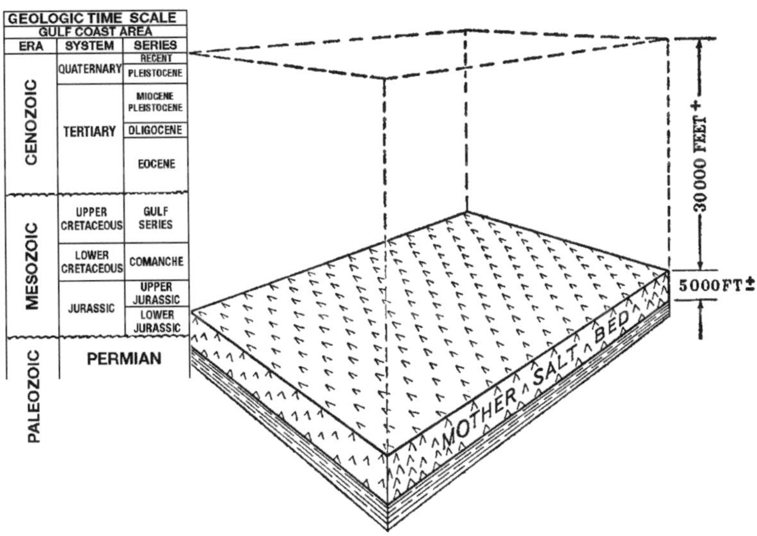

Figure 1

of the dome through the appropriate geologic ages. To accumulate and concentrate such a thick body of salt required the evaporation of much sea water, which is a slow process even in dry climates. Similar processes are taking place today in such bodies of water as the Great Salt Lake of Utah.

Figure No. 2 illustrates the effect the initial upward movement of the salt had on the overburden. It is logical to assume that once the movement of salt began upward, the overlying sediments were fractured, due to the piercement of the salt through them. If one would take several layers of paper and force a pencil from underneath, a general idea of the fractured effect of a dome on the sediments would be obtained.

Figure No. 3 is a cross-section of Figure 2 to show the extent of growth of the dome through the overburden. Erosion predominates over the high areas and deposition predominates in the low areas. Since the individual dome is strictly a local geologic feature, the forces of erosion act on the mound which is created by the uplift, and the debris from the erosion

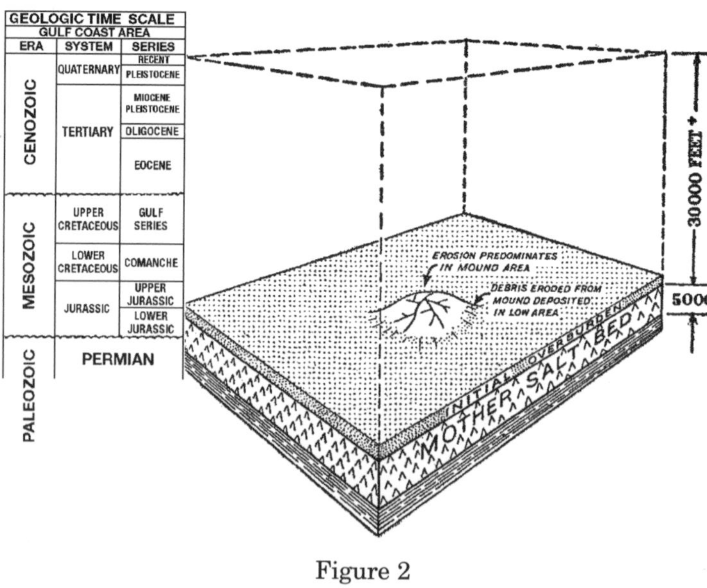

Figure 2

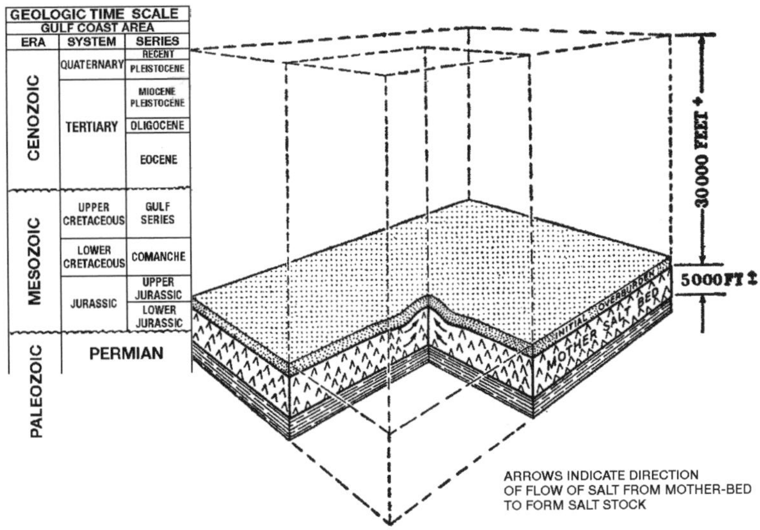

Figure 3

is deposited in the low peripheral areas of the dome. Therefore, the load on top of the super-dome area is lessened, whereas the load or weight on the flanks of the dome area is increased. This static weight on the flanks of the dome is really the motive force behind the upward movement of the dome. Therefore, the dome gradually moves upward through cycle after cycle of overburden, erosion, and deposition.

Figure No. 4 shows further growth of the dome based on principles outlined above. Successive layers of sediments through the Mesozoic Era added weight on the salt area. Each formation was first deposited over the dome, then later pierced by the salt as the stock moved upwards. The layers varied in texture, composition and strength. There were layers of sands, shales, sandstones, limestones and a combination of all, and, consequently, each stratum resisted the upward movement of the dome according to its physical characteristics. The sandstones and limestones were more difficult to penetrate than the softer layers, and the rate of upward movement of the salt varied accordingly.

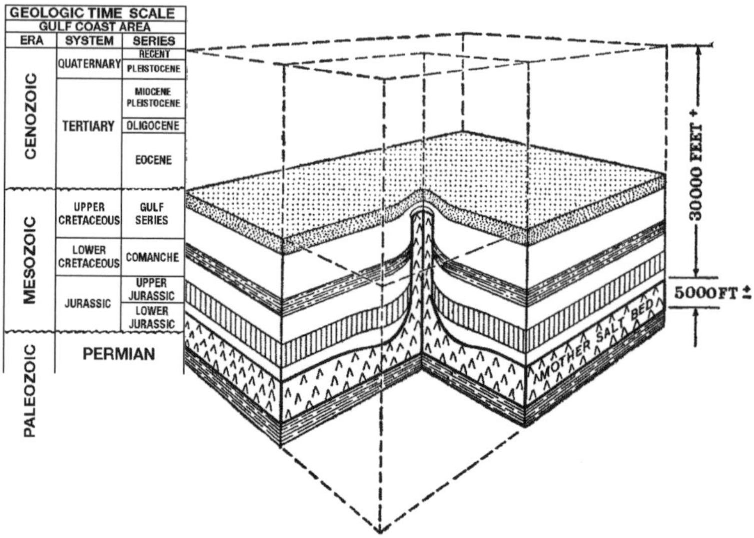

Figure 4

Some domes are mushroomed-shaped, that is, the upper portion of the salt mass is greater in circumference than the salt stock or stem which extends downward. This feature is not shown in any of the drawings, but certainly warrants explanation. This mushrooming is probably attributable to the abutment of the top of the salt stock against a resistant layer of sediments during upward movements, which caused the salt to flow horizontally for a short distance before penetration was effected. The horizontal and vertical extent of the overhang depends on the number of such occurrences during dome growth. Another explanation of mushrooming is based on the probability that the salt mass occasionally grew so fast that the salt actually pushed up on the surface from time to time, causing the lateral expansion of the salt in flowing out on the old surfaces, thus forming the overhang.

In all of the piercement-type domes drilled in the Gulf coastal plains of Texas and Louisiana, a rock layer is found only above the very cap of the salt. Such a layer is never found on the steep flanks. This layer of rock is appropriately called the "caprock" and is made up principally of anhydrite, which is a form of calcium sulphate, and which is present in the salt mass in small percentages. Generally, there are two possible origins of the formation of the anhydrite caprock. One is referred to as the residual-surface theory and the other as the residual-sub-surface theory. The first theory assumes that the salt rose to the surface and that it was readily dissolved with rainwater. The admixed anbydrite in the salt was not dissolved as easily as the salt and it was left on the surface above the undissolved salt plug to be later pressed into a rock layer as the salt plug moved upward after the top of the residual anhydrite and dome were buried again. The second theory assumes that the salt plug did not reach the surface and that the anhydrite caprock was slowly formed below the surface. Actually, the principle underlying the deposition of the anhydrite is the same except that instead of surface rainwater dissolving the salt, it was dissolved by circulating subterranean waters.

Geological evidence indicates that the anhydrite caprock, once formed, becomes subject to alterations as the dome grows. Underground waters attack the rock, causing the leaching out of the more soluble portions. These waters deposit lime in the form of calcite in those places made porous by subterranean waters. Portions of the anhydrite are also altered into gypsum. Eventually, the rock becomes an admixture of anhydrite, gypsum and calcite. The texture of the rock becomes a honeycomb of cavities. Into these cavities oil sometimes migrates from the off side sands, as it did at Spindletop and elsewhere. Chemical processes made possible by the subterranean water and heat break down the composition of the anhydrite and gypsum, extracting sulphur therefrom and redepositing it as free sulphur in the cavities or in veins of the caprock.

It was in such a caprock that oil was discovered 1020 feet below the surface at Spindletop.

A depression on the flanks of the salt dome is caused by the horizontal displacement from a large area of the mother bed of the salt which is necessary to make up a sufficient mass for the dome stock. Sediments which are deposited in this depression assume the configuration of it; that is, they are lower there than away from the dome or against the side of the dome. This area is often referred to as the "rim syncline" of the dome, and the feature is shown in stages of its growth in the cross-sections.

Figure 5 illustrates the growth of the dome to the end of Middle Tertiary times. Tertiary formations are thick in the Gulf Coast area and it is likely that the domes began to grow upward more rapidly during this than during any other earlier geologic time.

Migration of oil into the dome area occurred during the uplift of the dome. For example, after the dome pierced the Eocene series, oil that was formed in the muds of the basal

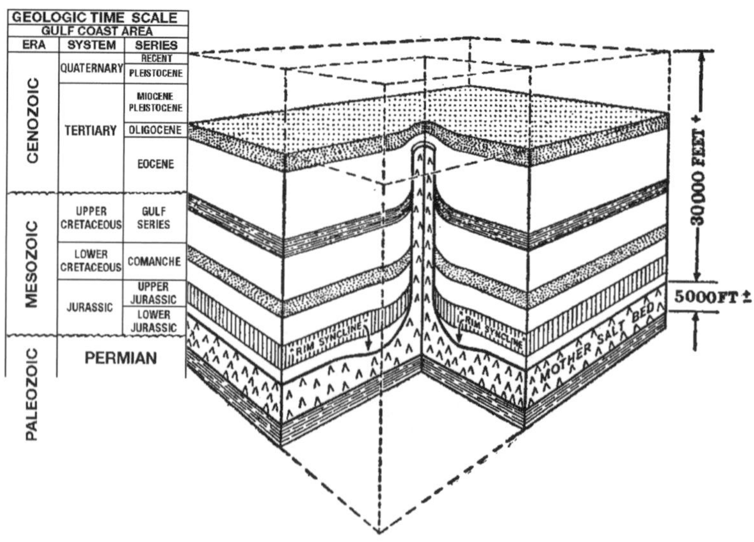

Figure 5

Eocene seas was squeezed out of them by compaction, migrated through porous media to the dome, and was then trapped in the uplifted reservoirs. Since shales, which are the hardened and compacted muds of the old sea bottoms, like those of the Eocene, were deposited at various geologic times, each group of formations, within a series with such shale deposits, could have its own source for oil and its own oil-producing zones. Such a multiplicity of different oil formations on the flanks of salt domes, as at Spindletop, is the one big factor responsible for their importance as oil fields.

Figure 6 illustrates the final uplift of the dome as we know it today. By correlation with other strata in the Gulf coastal province and other oil-producing provinces, oil-bearing formations have been proved to exist from the Pleistocene Series down to the mother salt bed, but production has not been proved to extend to the salt bed on a single salt dome in the Gulf Coast. Exploration on domes in the Gulf Coast of Texas and Louisiana have been no deeper than the Eocene Series and most of them not even that deep. There is every reason to

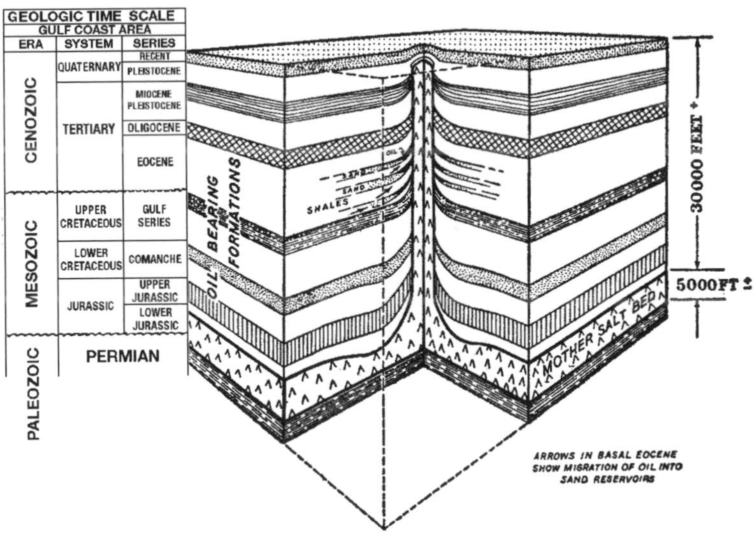

Figure 6

believe that when and if the lower formations on these domes are penetrated, gas and oil will also be found in them.

Figure 7 shows the effect of the salt on the producing horizons and the manner in which the sands dip away from the dome. Some of the zones butt against the salt mass, which is the result of the piercement of the salt through the formations, whereas other zones are shown to be uplifted, yet a distance away from the salt mass. The latter zones consist mainly of sands laid down during uplift of the dome, and thereby were not deposited over the super-dome area. In other words, these sands were "pinched-out" during deposition in the flank area of the uplift.

One must bear in mind that the uplift of the dome fractured and distorted the sediments as they were pierced, and sometimes the fractured planes opened avenues for the movement of oil from the lower formations into the upper strata. Many faults are associated with a fractured zone. The geologic definition of a fault is a dislocation, or displacement,

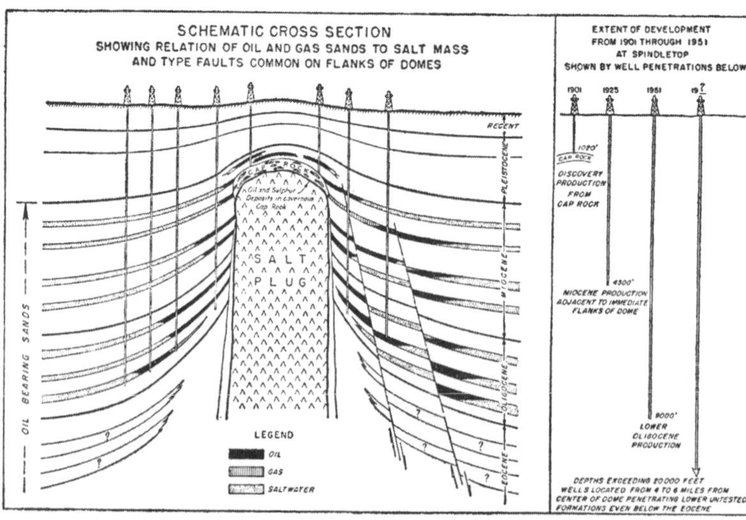

Figure 7

caused by a slipping of strata along a plane of fracture which is commonly referred to as the fault plane, and the result of this movement is referred to as a fault; the displacement of the beds varies from a few feet to many hundreds of feet. Faults have an effect on the accumulation of oil. Some fault blocks are very prolific, whereas adjacent blocks are dry. Because of the fractures and faults which accompany these zones, the oil is usually present in most important quantities close to them and sometimes only on one side. To develop production, therefore, it is necessary not only to know the location of the flanks of the dome, but also of these fractures and faults and of the relation of the oil accumulation to them. On domes like Spindletop, where faults control the position of the oil, it has been established that there will be great differences in drilling and production between wells close together, but which are located on opposite sides of a fault. Faults separate the oil and prevent the migration from one fault block to another, and many dry holes are drilled only tens of feet from oil wells. Wells have been abandoned without oil on a flank of a dome, which, to the so-called practical oil man, condemned the acreage, only to have a later wildcatter drill a test between dry holes and open up prolific production.

As previously stated, faults play an important role in the accumulation of oil. In Figure 7 the center fault block has oil in only a few sands, whereas the sands in the inside and outside blocks are more saturated with oil. There are many examples where the fault plane acts as a barrier and prevents the movement of oil to adjoining blocks, thereby causing a restricted movement and accumulation of the oil into a small area. A good example of this is the old Yount-Lee Oil Company's Guilmartin Fee 6.9-acre tract at Spindletop, which produced more than a million barrels of oil to the acre, whereas adjacent leases produced far less from the same sands but in different fault blocks. The Guilmartin tract happened to be located above a well-saturated fault block, which contained many sands carrying oil, whereas adjacent tracts were located over fault blocks which had most of the same sands carrying water.

It is for such reasons that operators consider that every well drilled on the side of a dome is a wildcat irrespective of its proximity to existing producers. Yet it can be safely stated that, regardless of the hazards and risks involved in the drilling and development of production on domes, the productive tracts on them, on a per-acre basis, are by far more prolific than from any other geologic feature in the world.

APPENDIX TWO

A New Day on the Hill

THE most amazing geological negligence in the history of the Gulf Coast oil development was the "big forget" for nearly a quarter of a century of the importance of salt domes in the search for new oil reserves. Exploration on the piercement-type domes was shoved in the background in favor of the use of geophysics to locate deeply buried structures. Geophysics played an extremely important part in the discovery of new fields in the Gulf coastal oil province. Operators as far back as 1922 conceded that no new domes could be found by surface indications, and that some other means had to be employed to find new structures. In this respect geophysics was very successful. In turn, the old piercement-type salt domes were forgotten and very little drilling activity was conducted on them during the time when attention was focused largely on geophysics.

Geologically, there are three basic factors necessary to the discovery of oil; first, there is structure, then, good sand or reservoir conditions, and finally, evidence of oil accumulation or source beds of oil in the area. All three are important, but the most important is structure. Without structure, or a trap enabling the oil to accumulate, the other two factors are insignificant. Therefore, when geophysics made its advent in the Gulf Coast the result was the mapping of deepseated structures with many hundreds of feet of closure above regional normal. A closure is the vertical uplift of a stratum above its original (regional) position. For example, if a stratum is arched in the shape of a hill, the elevation measured from the base of the hill to its top is the structural closure of the stratum.

Most of the structures which were first found by geophysical instruments were the deep-seated domes with closures approximating 1000 feet, like the one which is responsible for the existence of the fabulous Hastings oil field, twentyfive miles south of Houston. Later, structures with 300 feet of closure were considered excellent, and after all of these were mapped in the province, operators were glad to find areas with one hundred feet and then fifty feet of closure. Today any minute geophysical curvature or wiggle of a few feet of relief is given the stamp of approval. Millions of dollars have been spent in the last few years in the drilling of deep, low-relief structures. Often this resulted in finding only hard and practically impervious thin, oil or gas sands. Payout on this kind of drilling and development is usually in the negative and not more than a dollar-for-dollar trade.

Compare these meager geophysical prospects now available in the Gulf Coast with the actual *known* geologic conditions prevailing on or around piercement-type domes. The structural closure of these domes, measured only from the depths penetrated, is from 2000–6000 feet above regional normal. Multiple, thick, very porous and permeable sands exist in the stratigraphic column governed by the structural influence of the dome. Accumulation of oil has already been established by early drilling and it simply remains for a new program of exploration to find new reserves. The per-acre recovery from tracts on a piercement-type dome is much greater than from any other type of structure.

So, in the last few years when operators became desperate again to find new oil reserves to supplant the small, unprofitable production found in fields of low closures, they looked around and realized that under their very office windows were the most prolific producing structures in the province practically untouched for twenty-five years. A development program is now in effect that will once more bring these domes to the forefront.

Such a revived interest in the domes is understandable, since so many of the requisites for finding oil exist on and around them. These structures, irrespective of their past production or lack of it, still remain as major sources of the oil reserves yet to be discovered and produced. It is anticipated that every salt dome in the province will eventually produce oil if properly tested, and those which have already produced will again yield additional reserves from down-structure, away from the old production, just like Spindletop which will continue to produce new oil as long as wildcatters have the courage and incentive to drill deeper, and farther away from the center of the dome. And this can be said for all of the other domes. The salt domes are still the most important geologic features in the coastal plains and they will surely be explored deeper and deeper, each additional foot probing into a vast unknown, eventually through the entire group of sediments, 30,000 feet or more, to the mother salt bed.

How many millions of barrels of oil or trillions of cubic feet of gas are hidden in the lower depths is a question that can be answered only by the drill.

The answer will be supplied by the imagination, inventiveness, courage and determination of the successors of Higgins, Lucas, Galey, the Hamills, Sharp, Hughes and the others who immortalized Spindletop. It will require geological, mechanical and operational daring. It will require great risks and great losses, bolstered by tremendous financing and continued incentive for the wildcatters without whom nothing has been nor will be accomplished toward bringing greater abundance and prosperity to the nation and the world. There will be greater prosperity in terms of sources of new energy and chemical advancements. These in turn provide individual comfort and convenience and national power and security. Oil will be found wherever and whenever these forces are combined. For Spindletop, and domes like it, there will undoubtedly be, before many years have passed, a new day on the hill.

INDEX

I

J

K

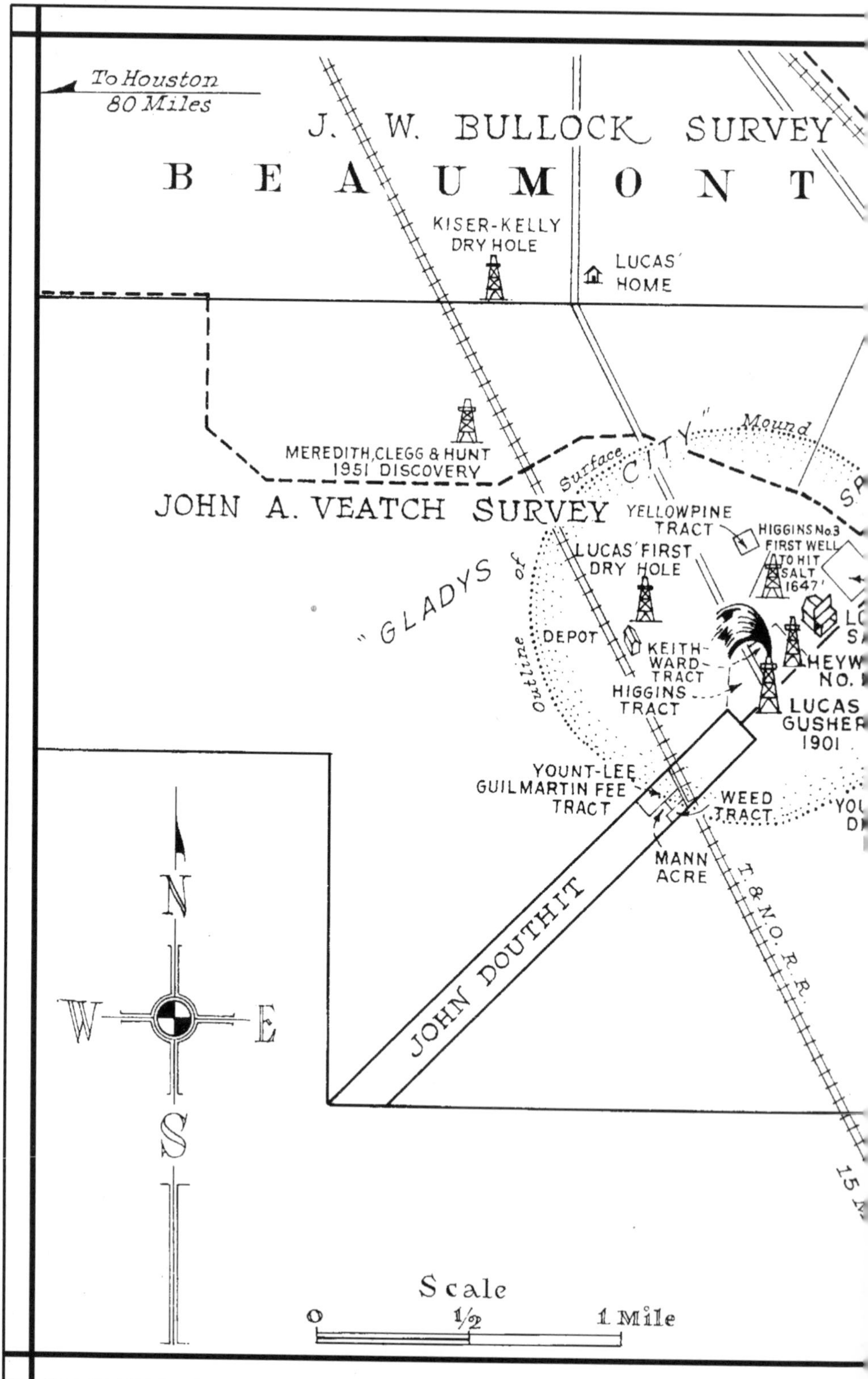

To Houston
80 Miles
J. W. BULLOCK SURVEY
B E A U M O N T
KISER-KELLY
DRY HOLE
LUCAS'
HOME
MEREDITH, CLEGG & HUNT
1951 DISCOVERY
Surface "CITY" Mound
JOHN A. VEATCH SURVEY
YELLOWPINE
TRACT
HIGGINS No.3
FIRST WELL
TO HIT
SALT
1647'
LUCAS' FIRST
DRY HOLE
"GLADYS of
Outline
DEPOT
KEITH-
WARD-
TRACT
HIGGINS
TRACT
LUCAS
GUSHER
1901
YOUNT-LEE
GUILMARTIN FEE
TRACT
WEED
TRACT
MANN
ACRE
JOHN DOUTHIT
T. & N.O. R.R.
N
W
E
S
Scale
0
½
1 Mile